Concise Guide to Jazz

Third Edition

Mark C. Gridley

Heidelberg College
Tiffin, Ohio 44883

Prentice Hall
Upper Saddle River, New Jersey 07458

Library of Congress Catalog-in-Publication Data
Gridley, Mark C., 1947–
    Concise guide to jazz   Mark C. Gridley. -- 3rd ed.
        p. cm.
    Includes bibliographical references and index.
    ISBN 0-13-088682-3
    1. Jazz--History and criticism.   I. Title.

ML3506.G736 2001
781.65--dc21   99-089416

Acquisitions editor: Christopher Johnson
Editorial/production supervision: Harriet Tellem
Prepress and manufacturing buyer: Benjamin Smith
Cover design: Jim Schafer
Cover art: "Bow Tie and the Horns" by John Russ
Typesetting: Albert Kishman and LaDua, Inc.

Portions of the Louis Armstrong coverage in chapter 4 originally appeared in *Jazz Educators Journal*, Vol. XIV (1984), No. 3, pp. 71–72 as "Why Is Louis Armstrong So Important?" and are reproduced by permission of the editors. Portions of the section designated "The Popularity of Bebop" in chapter 6 originally appeared in *Popular Music and Society*, Vol. IX (1984), No. 4, pp. 41–45 as "Why Have Modern Jazz Combos Been Less Popular Than Swing Big Bands?" and are reproduced by permission of the editors. Portions of the first ten paragraphs of chapter 10 originally appeared in *Popular Music and Society*, Vol. IX (1983), No. 2, pp. 27–34 as "Clarifying Labels: Jazz, Rock, Funk, and Jazz-Rock" and appear here by permission of the editors. The first six paragraphs of chapter 8 are adapted from "Clarifying Labels: Cool Jazz, West Coast, and Hard Bop" in *Tracking: Popular Music Studies*, Vol. 2 (1990), No. 2, pp. 8–16, and are used by permission of the editors.

©2001, 1998, 1992 by Mark C. Gridley
Published by Prentice-Hall, Inc.
A Unit of Pearson Education
Upper Saddle River, New Jersey 07458

Printed in the United States of America

10 9 8 7 6 5 4 3 2 1

ISBN 0-13-088682-3 book alone
ISBN 0-13-088981-4 book with demo CD and classics CD package
ISBN 0-13-088979-2 book with demo CD package
ISBN 0-13-088970-9 book with classics CD package
ISBN 0-13-088792-7 classics CD
ISBN 0-13-088694-7 demo CD

Pearson Education (UK) Limited, *London*
Prentice-Hall of Australia Pty. Limited, *Sydney*
Prentice-Hall Canada Inc., *Toronto*
Prentice-Hall Hispanoamericana, S.A., *Mexico*
Prentice-Hall of India Private Limited, *New Delhi*
Prentice-Hall of Japan, Inc., *Tokyo*
Prentice-Hall of Southeast Asia Pte. Ltd., *Singapore*
Editora Prentice-Hall do Brasil, Ltda., *Rio de Janeiro*

CONTENTS

ILLUSTRATIONS

LINE DRAWINGS AND INSTRUMENT PHOTOS

MUSICIAN PHOTOS

LISTENING GUIDES

PREFACE

This book is intended as a brief introduction to jazz. It outlines the ways jazz is made and the major jazz styles that have evolved during the twentieth century. It tells why the big names are important and how their styles differ. The *Demonstration CD* provides examples of the instrument sounds and explains the methods and terminology of jazz. The Elements of Music Appendix explains the basic terms that are used to describe music. Listening guides are provided to accompany selections on the *Concise Guide Jazz Classics Cassette/CD*, and they give the reader more information about techniques of making jazz by applying the terms learned in the *Demo CD* and the Elements of Music Appendix. This helps listeners to detect more in each repeated hearing. Chapters end with lists of recordings and books to supplement the information that is introduced in the chapter. Most of the selections on the *Concise Guide Jazz Classics Cassette/ CD* complement those on the *Jazz Classics Cassette/ CD* for the *Jazz Styles: History and Analysis* textbook by Mark C. Gridley and the *Smithsonian Collection of Classic Jazz* rather than duplicating them. They were chosen so that each of the three sources would begin filling the historic and stylistic gaps within each other.

This book originated because professors and students asked for an introduction to jazz that was as clear and accurate as *Jazz Styles* but without as much detail. (*Jazz Styles* profiles 148 musicians and mentions about 1200 others.) Many professors also said they wanted a book that was easy to complete in a ten-week college

quarter. Some said the ideal introductory text would focus on only about ten major figures. Reducing jazz history to a maximum of ten musicians was not feasible, however, because few authorities agree on which ten to discuss. But by increasing the minimum number of musicians to 40, we were able to accommodate the combined preferences from most authorities' "top ten" lists and still not overload students. Though this approach neglects some of the richness of jazz history, it also makes conveniently comprehensible a diversity of styles in a way that provides a basis for further explorations. If students or professors want to begin fleshing out the basic skeleton of styles treated in the present book, they can start with two resources that are already available in most colleges: *Jazz Styles: History and Analysis* and its *Jazz Classics CD* and the recordings in the *Smithsonian Collection of Classic Jazz*. If your school does not have these resources, contact Prentice Hall (College Marketing, Prentice Hall, Inc., 1 Lake Street, Upper Saddle River, NJ 07458; 800-526-0485) and Smithsonian Press. For more resources, see the Album Buying Strategies and A Small Basic Collection of Jazz Videos, in this book's appendix. Your first purchase might be *Listening to Jazz*, a one-hour video version of the *Demonstration CD* of instruments and methods for making jazz, prepared by Steve Gryb. It can be ordered by phoning 800-947-7700 and asking for ISBN 0-13-532862-4.

The first two editions of this book have been used successfully at more than one hundred different high schools and colleges in courses about jazz history and appreciation for non-musicians. No technical knowledge of music is required to understand its contents. The optional listening guides are most useful, however, if students first familiarize themselves with instrument sounds on the *Demo CD* and the terms explained in the Elements of Music Appendix. Students appreciate live demonstrations and instructor assistance with this, also. Repeated listening is the key to familiarizing yourself with the sounds and their names. Appreciation increases with each rehearing of the selections on the *Jazz Classsics CD*. It is not realistic to expect to grasp the subtleties immediately. In fact, for most selections, it is not even realistic to expect to follow all the notes until at least the fourth or fifth hearing. For this reason, most instructors devote the first few weeks of their course to the Elements of Music Appendix and Chapter 2: How to Listen to Jazz, with their accompanying illustrations on the *Demo CD* and the *Listening to Jazz* video by Steve Gryb. Many instructors base quizzes and exams on the contents of the *Demo CD*, instrument sounds, blues form, and A-A-B-A form. Some instructors devote the first third of the course to developing these basic listening skills before moving on to comparing different jazz styles. In other words, learning listening skills is essential before learning the style differences that make jazz history interesting. In fact, some students report that without adequate instruction in such skills, they are often clueless when they try to appreciate modern jazz selections.

In designing a semester-long or quarter-long course in jazz appreciation, instructors need to tally their own priorities, not necessarily the same topics that appear in this book. Topics, musicians, and entire chapters can be skipped without doing serious damage to a brief Introduction to Jazz or Understanding Jazz course. For example, if emphasis is placed on in-depth appreciation of particular recordings and the musicians on them, an entire class period can be devoted to each one. Dissecting a given selection, chorus by chorus, phrase by phrase, and then replaying it five times is not excessive if students are led to focus on a different aspect each time. Therefore, a respectable course could be constructed around only eight to ten major figures, perhaps just Louis Armstrong, Lester Young, Duke Ellington, Charlie Parker, Dizzy Gillespie, Miles Davis, Ornette Coleman, and John Coltrane, and in-depth appreciation of just ten to fifteen selections from the *Jazz Classics Cassette/CD*. Alternate ways for organizing jazz survey and jazz history courses are outlined within sample course syllabi in *Instructor's Resource Manual for Concise Guide to Jazz* (available from Prentice-Hall sales representatives as well as from Prentice-Hall faculty services; phone 800-526-0485). Sample items for listening exams are available in *How to Teach Jazz History*, a teacher's manual published by the International Association of Jazz Educators (P.O. Box 724, Manhattan, Kansas 66502; phone 785-776-8744; email info@IAJE.org). Both books outline pitfalls to avoid in teaching jazz history, jazz survey, and jazz appreciation courses. They also offer many lecture-demonstration strategies and teaching tips for first-time instructors.

Instructors may wish to substitute or supplement some of the text coverage and classics recordings with lectures and recordings representing such topics as Latin jazz (Tito Puente, Eddie Palmieri, Cal Tjader, Mongo Santamaria, et al.), the Chicago Avant-Garde of the 1960s and 70s (Sun Ra, The Art Ensemble of Chicago, Anthony Braxton, et al.), the New York Avant-Garde of the 1980s and 90s (John Zorn, Bill Frisell, Don Byron, et al.), the Dixieland revival of the 1940s and 50s (Turk Murphy, Dukes of Dixieland, et al.), the hard bop revival of the 1980s and 90s (neoclassicists such as Wynton Marsalis, Roy Hargrove, Benny Green, Cyrus Chestnut, Joey Defrancesco, et al.), the 1980s–90s revivalists of the mid-1960s Miles Davis style (Wynton Marsalis, Wallace Roney, et al.), lightweight jazz of the 1980s and 90s (Yellow Jackets, Al Jarreau, Spyro Gyra, The Crusaders, Kenny G, Najee, et al.), or regional jazz orchestras (Gerald Wilson, Thad Jones-Mel Lewis, Maria Schneider, et al.).

ACKNOWLEDGEMENTS

Since this book is basically an abridged version of *Jazz Styles: History and Analysis*, all the people who helped put together the first seven editions of *Jazz Styles* deserve thanks for working on this book as well. Their names are found in the acknowledgements sections of those volumes. I am especially grateful to the hundreds of students who spoke with me, wrote critiques, and corresponded with me about the best ways to approach the preparation of this book. Their names are too numerous to mention since this has been a continual process since 1973.

A few individuals who are mentioned in the acknowledgements sections of *Jazz Styles* must be singled out for their hefty contributions to this volume. The biggest influence on the thinking and organization in this material is Harvey Pekar, who has contributed almost continuously to my work since 1971. His original ideas and penetrating observations can be found in every chapter. Much of the research for these books was made possible by Pekar's generosity in giving me unlimited access to his collection of over 14,000 albums and his intimate knowledge of jazz history. He always shared his latest research with me and continued to keep me abreast of changing currents in jazz. Chuck Braman served as a technical consultant and a copy editor on five editions of *Jazz Styles* as well as a copy editor and prime figure in the conceptualization for the first edition of the *Concise Guide to Jazz*. He was additionally helpful in choosing photos. As in the past editions of *Jazz Styles*, Bill Anderson has continued to provide indispensable suggestions and updating regarding discography, bibliography, and overall organization.

Joel Simpson began supplying suggestions in 1985 that were incorporated into the 1988 and 1991 editions of *Jazz Styles*. He rewrote portions of the manuscript for this present book as well and contributed concepts of writing and organization that helped give it a somewhat different tone from its parent text.

Karl Koenig and Lawrence Gushee generously shared the results of their research on the origins of jazz and allowed it to be used in *Jazz Styles* and the *Concise Guide to Jazz*. Carl Woideck performed a similar function with respect to Charlie Parker and John Coltrane, as well as contributing a considerable amount of proofreading and fact checking. Woideck also worked on the test banks. Listening guides were prepared with the help of Anita Clark, Bart Polot, Dave Berger, David Such, Carl Woideck, Karl Koenig, Kean Sakata, Bob Belden, Wayne Shorter, Joe Zawinul, Jerry Sheer, and Pat McCarty. If I have omitted the names of any other contributors, I apologize.

The first two editions of the *Concise Guide to Jazz* have been required in more than 100 different high schools and colleges for their courses in jazz history and appreciation. I am thankful for all the comments conveyed to me by students and instructors, but I cannot remember the names of all sources of feedback, and I apologize for any omissions. Recent feedback on how well the second edition worked for their jazz appreciation and jazz history classes was contributed by Paul Ferguson, Jeff Halsey, Lee Heritage, Tom Horning, Alan Kaplan, John Richmond, and Howie Smith.

For the new coverage of singers, the following people shared their observations and allowed me to use them: Iris Sharp, Fred Sharp, Gary Pildner, Bob Fraser, Nan O'Malley, George Gridley, Chad Gearig, Grant Cook, and Tom Inck.

Consultants in the preparation of the coverage on acid jazz and smooth jazz include David Miyares, Rob Hoff, Dan Polletta, Chris Hovan, Bob Belden, Wayne "DJ Smash" Hunter, Gilles Peterson, Chris Bangs, Randy Norfus, Carlo Wolff, Harvey Pekar, and Ed Stephens.

I remain deeply grateful to Al Kishman, Jim Schafer, Ed Harrington, Kathryn Penn, and Ryan Upton for their patience, generosity, and resourcefulness in helping me convert my work into the electronic form required by my publisher.

The accuracy of coverage in this textbook is due in part to the cooperation of many musicians whose music is discussed on its pages. Unfortunately several of them passed away before seeing the finished product. The following players helped by means of conversations, proofreading, and/or correspondence with the author: Benny Goodman, Stan Kenton, Bill Evans, Wayne Shorter, Joe Zawinul, Eric Gravatt, Herbie Hancock, Tony Williams, Joe Venuti, Al McKibbon, Dizzy Gillespie, Paul Smith, Richard Davis, Bob Curnow, Jimmy Heath, Jaco Pastorius, Red Rodney, and others who are mentioned in the acknowledgements sections of the first six editions of *Jazz Styles*.

CHANGES IN THIS THIRD EDITION

For the convenience of the many professors who have geared their assignments, syllabi, and exams to the second edition of *Concise Guide to Jazz*, we have retained the organization and facts from it for this new edition. At the request of professors and students, we have also

1. added coverage of Billie Holiday, Ella Fitzgerald, and Sarah Vaughan
2. expanded discussion of acid jazz and smooth jazz
3. updated all references to books and recordings
4. added 13 new photos of musicians
5. added a "For Musicians" Appendix of basic musical foundations of jazz, such as modes, comping, and chord progressions for the 12-bar blues
6. increased the numbering and italicizing of main points within paragraphs

CHAPTER 1

WHAT IS JAZZ?

Photo by Herman Leonard

The world of jazz includes many different kinds of music. Some is light and happy. Some is heavy and serious. Some makes you want to dance. Some makes you think. Some is filled with surprises. Some is smooth and easy. Some is fast and complicated. Some is slow and mellow. Jazz is played by big bands and small groups. It has been played on almost every musical instrument. It comes in varieties called Dixieland and swing, bebop and cool, hard bop and fusion. But most jazz has no style designation. We refer to the sounds just by naming the musicians, for instance, Duke Ellington, Miles Davis, or John Coltrane.

Jazz is heard in numerous settings. Many bands present it as serious music in concert halls. Some jazz is played in ballrooms for dancers. There is jazz in background music on the radio. A lot of jazz is offered in night clubs where people gather to hear music while they drink and talk with their friends.

Jazz has an impressive reputation. It is so interesting that it is played and analyzed in hundreds of colleges. Almost every high school and college has at least one jazz band. Though it originated in America, jazz is so compelling that musicians on every continent have played it, and today there is no city without it. The sounds of jazz have influenced the development of new styles in popular music and the work of symphonic composers. Jazz is so sturdy that the old styles are still being played, and new styles are always being developed. In fact, jazz is regarded as a fine art, not just a passing fad.

DEFINING JAZZ

The term "jazz" has a variety of meanings because it has been used to describe so many kinds of music. And the term has different meanings according to who is using it. Different people use different ways to decide whether a given performance is "jazz." Some consider only how it makes them feel. Some rely on what it reminds them of. Some people decide it must be jazz if the performers have a reputation for jazz. Others consider how the music is made. They look at what techniques are being used. But despite these different attitudes toward defining jazz, there are two aspects that almost all jazz styles have in common—improvisation and swing feeling.

Improvisation

To improvise is to compose and perform at the same time. Instead of saying "improvise," many people say "ad lib" or "jam." This means that *jazz musicians make up their music as they go along. Much of their music is spontaneous. It is not written down or rehearsed beforehand.* This is like the impromptu speaking all of us do every day when we talk "off the cuff." We use the same words and phrases that we have used before. But now we improvise by using them in new ways and new orders that have not been rehearsed. A lot of originality can result. This is significant because being original is very important to jazz musicians. They try to be as spontaneous as possible. In fact, they try never to improvise the same way twice. Several versions of a tune made during the same recording session may be entirely different from each other because of this.

Improvisation is essential to jazz. If you are not very familiar with jazz, however, you might not be able to tell what has been written or memorized beforehand from what is being improvised. One clue is that if part of a performance sounds improvised, it quite often is. Improvised parts sometimes sound less organized than the written or memorized parts.

Another clue comes from knowing about a routine that most jazz musicians use. The players begin with a tune they all know. First they play it once all the way through. The melody is played by the horns. The accompaniment is played by the piano and bass. Then the piano and bass keep doing what they did before. But this time the horns make up and play new melodies of their own. *They improvise their own melodies to the tune's accompaniment chords.* The way the chords progress in that accompaniment guides the notes they choose to play for their new melodies, which we call improvisations. In other words, when the melody of the piece itself ends, what follows is improvised. Then it is all improvised until that same melody begins again. This kind of improvisation distinguishes the practices of jazz musicians from most pop musicians, who merely decorate a tune by changing some of its rhythms or adding notes to it.

Even though improvisation is the big emphasis in jazz, not everything is spontaneous. Most jazz bands use arrangements of some sort. In the case of large jazz bands where the players are seated with written arrangements in front of them, a player is usually improvising when he stands up alone and takes a solo. Otherwise the music is coming from the written parts. In the next chapter, we will examine more practices that can help us know what parts in a jazz performance are worked out in advance.

Charles Mingus, jazz bassist known for his composing and improvising. He is important for getting his musicians to improvise their own parts to fit with his prewritten music in colorful and provocative ways.

Photo by Bob Parent, courtesy of Don Parent

Swing Feeling

Next we are going to consider the way that jazz makes people feel. This has been called "jazz swing feeling." To begin, let's discuss a few elements which contribute to swing feeling in all music, not just jazz. If music makes you want to dance, clap your hands, or tap your feet, it has the effect we call "swinging." This effect can be created by almost any kind of music that keeps a steady beat and is performed with great spirit. In that sense, many non-jazz performances can be swinging. But to specify the unique ways a jazz performance swings, let's first discuss the general characteristics of swinging. Then we can discuss the characteristics that are specific to jazz swing feeling.

Chick Corea (electric piano), Dave Holland (bass), Jack DeJohnette (drums), Wayne Shorter (tenor saxophone), leading musicians in jazz of the 1960s and 70s.

Photo by Ray Avery

One of the clearest causes of swing feeling is a steady beat. This helps us distinguish it from the kinds of symphonic music where conductors are free to vary the tempo while playing a piece. A steady beat is nearly always kept in jazz pieces. Constant tempo brings a certain kind of momentum that is essential to swing feeling. Much of the excitement in jazz comes from musicians in the band tugging against this very solid foundation by playing notes slightly before or after the beat.

Dizzy Gillespie, modern jazz trumpeter who devised a highly syncopated style of improvising. He specialized in rhythmic surprises.

Photo by William Gottlieb

To call music "swinging" also means that the performance conveys a lilting feeling. This property is also sometimes referred to as a "groove." In fact, verbs derived from the nouns "swing" and "groove" are commonly applied to the sound of jazz: "The band is swinging tonight." "That pianist is really grooving." For many listeners, swinging simply means pleasure. A swinging performance is like a swinging party. Both are very enjoyable. Jazz has a reputation for being highly spirited music. In fact, the word "jazzy" is sometimes used instead of the word "spirited." To "jazz up" and to "liven up" are often used interchangeably, and some people call clothes "jazzy" if they are gaudy or extraverted.

Music that swings, then, has constant tempo and is performed with lilt and spirit. But for music to swing in the way peculiar to jazz, more conditions have to be met. One is an abundance of syncopated rhythms. "Syncopating" means accenting just before or just after a beat. You might think of syncopation as off-beat accenting, or the occurrence of stress where it is least expected. Jazz swing feeling requires certain combinations of these off-beat accents. The tension generated by members of a band accenting opposite sides of the beat is essential to jazz swing feeling.

One more component of jazz swing feeling is not actually a rhythmic element. It is the continuous rising and falling motion in a melody line. This pattern makes you alternately tense and relaxed, tense and relaxed, over and over again.

We must keep in mind that listeners disagree about whether a given performance swings, and, if so, how much. So, just as we often hear that "beauty is in the eye of the beholder," it is also true that swing is in the ear of the listener. In other words, *swinging is an opinion, not a fact about the music.* Ultimately this becomes another reason that it is difficult to reach a workable definition for jazz. We find that the same music one listener calls jazz will not necessarily be what another calls jazz because the listeners disagree about whether it swings.

STUDYING DIFFERENT JAZZ STYLES HISTORICALLY

Jazz comes in many varieties. The easiest way to introduce a lot of these varieties is to group them into categories called styles. Every jazz musician has a personal style of playing. But this can be a confusing way to use the word "style" because we also use it to designate a larger category of ways musicians like to play. These larger categories have names such as bebop and Dixieland. Each of these styles includes particular ways the musicians like to improvise and the types of accompaniment harmonies and rhythms they prefer. Throughout this book we will be examining the particular styles of famous jazz musicians. But we also have to categorize them within the larger styles, such as Dixieland and bebop, so that we can divide the book into chapters. Grouping the players in these ways is not always fair because styles vary considerably, and some players from the same era don't play at all like each other. But because some musicians' approaches have more in common than other musicians', we rely on the common aspects to help us decide which musicians to discuss in each chapter.

As we study styles in a chronological order it is important to keep in mind several considerations. First, the musicians discussed in this book did not create their styles entirely by themselves. Their work reflects the influence of other players in addition to their own original ideas. Second, jazz history is not a single stream of styles that developed smoothly from Dixieland to swing to bebop and so forth. Several streams exist at the same time, and streams overlap, merge, and influence each other all the time. Third, each new style does not render the previous ones obsolete. Many different styles of jazz exist at the same time, though some are more popular during one era than another. Fourth, jazz history is not merely a series of reactions in which one style made musicians angry and so they invented another to oppose it. However, many journalists and historians believe this because they look for conflict, and they attach great drama to the development of new styles. The truth is that most musicians find their own favorite ways of playing. Often it is an existing style they like. Sometimes they choose one traditional approach and modify it to suit their tastes and capabilities; sometimes they combine different approaches to make a mixture they like. Many players stick with that style for good; some change their styles

Clarinetist Benny Goodman, the most prominent of all improvisers in the 1930s and 40s.

Photo courtesy of Cleveland Press Collection/Cleveland State University Archives

whenever they become bored with what they are doing or whenever they hear something new that they like more.

A fifth consideration is also important to keep in mind. Many people tend to think that jazz is just the music that they first heard termed "jazz." They are not aware of the diversity of styles that have been tagged "jazz." On the other hand, some people who are aware of numerous styles prefer that certain styles not be included in the jazz category. For instance, during the 1970s and 80s many people felt that jazz-rock fusion should not be called "jazz." Granted, different jazz styles do convey different rhythmic feelings, and some even use different instruments and differing amounts of improvisation. But classical music fans and popular music fans find jazz styles more distinguishable from classical music and popular music than from each other. No matter how sticky these controversies get, though, remember that learning how to label the styles is just a handy way to keep track of what you want to hear. The most important goal is to increase your enjoyment of jazz.

CHAPTER SUMMARY

1. Defining jazz is difficult because there are so many varieties.

2. The most common elements that appear in definitions of jazz are improvisation and swing feeling.

3. Improvisation means making it up as you go along, as with impromptu speaking.

4. Jazz musicians usually begin by playing a tune they all know. After that, they make up their own music and guide their improvisations by the accompaniment chords that came with the original tune.

5. Swing feeling is the rhythmic property perceived by listeners who enjoy a particular performance.

6. Jazz swing feeling seems to be perceived in listeners when music has a certain combination of
   a. steady tempo
   b. a certain kind of off-beat accenting
   c. a continuous rising and falling of the melodic line

7. Listeners do not always agree that a given performance is jazz. One reason is that jazz swing feeling is an opinion about how the music feels, not a fact.

8. Jazz style designations are often more expedient than accurate. Style designations are made in this book to present a variety of musicians in the smallest number of chapters.

SUPPLEMENTARY LISTENING

What Is Jazz? by Leonard Bernstein (originally Columbia CL 919, LP, reissued many times under different numbers, SMK 60566, CD). The best introduction to jazz, explains swing feeling, improvisation, the blues, A-A-B-A song form, Dixieland, swing, bebop; has Louis Armstrong, Bessie Smith, Miles Davis, John Coltrane, and other musicians to illustrate Bernstein's narration. (Alternate versions are in *Concise Guide Demo CD*.)

SUPPLEMENTARY READING

"Three Approaches to Defining Jazz" by Mark Gridley, Robert Maxham, and Robert Hoff (*Musical Quarterly*, 1989, Vol. 73, No. 4, pages 513–531)

Anatomy of Jazz by Leroy Ostransky (University of Washington Press, 1960; reprinted by Greenwood)

The Book of Jazz by Leonard Feather (Horizon-Dell, 1957, 1965, 1976)

CHAPTER 2

HOW TO LISTEN TO JAZZ

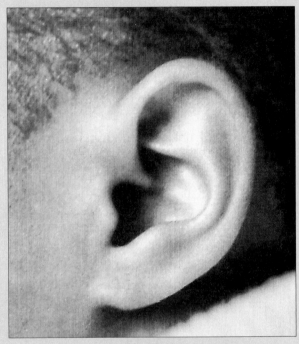

Photo by Nancy Ann Lee

Much pleasure can be derived from listening to jazz improvisation. But many people say that they cannot enjoy it because they do not understand it. If you are one of those people, this chapter will be quite helpful. Remember that with knowledge and practice, listening to jazz becomes easier, and it becomes more and more fun.

Hearing the improvised lines of a jazz soloist as melodies in themselves should help you enjoy much of jazz. Experienced listeners get as much pleasure from hearing their favorite improvisations as most people get from hearing their favorite songs. It might help to keep in mind that *some jazz improvisers strive to invent lines that are as catchy as the melodies in pop tunes and classical pieces.* On the other hand, many improvisers tend toward more elaborate lines. Some passages in their improvisations are more melody-like than others. For this reason many listeners pay close attention as the improvisations are unfolding. They want to notice when the line becomes particularly melodic. (Listen to *Demo CD* Track 32.) Then they can have the pleasure of hearing a new song being composed. There are gems of inspired melody hidden in many improvisations just waiting to be discovered by attentive listeners. We need to remember, however, that melody is more important in some styles than others. For instance, in some avant-garde and jazz-rock fusion performances the music focuses instead on variations in mood, sound qualities, and rhythms. Sometimes the mood alone may be the most prominent aspect instead of only part of the effect.

One way a lot of jazz fans listen is to **imagine layers of sound, one on top of another, all moving forward in time. Each layer can represent the sound of a different instrument.** Once you become skilled in visualizing separate sounds, you will begin to notice relationships between the sounds. **Try to imagine a graph of the solo line**. The horizontal side of the graph represents time passing. The vertical dimension represents highness and lowness of pitch. Your graph can be embellished by colored shapes and textures representing the accompanying sounds of piano chords, drums, cymbals, bass, and so on.

Some people hum the original tune to themselves while listening to the improvisations which are guided by its chord

Tenor saxophonist Lester Young (soloist) and drummer Jo Jones (accompanist). Both men contributed to the smoothly swinging music of Count Basie's band in the 1930s.

Courtesy Robert Asen—Metronome Collection

changes. Try to synchronize the beginning of your humming with the beginning of a solo improvisation, and then keep the same tempo as the performer. (Listen to *Demo CD* Track 33, and you will begin to hear the chords in the accompaniment more clearly.) You will become aware of two compositions based on the same chord changes: the original tune and the improvised melody. As you become more aware of how they go together, your appreciation of jazz will deepen considerably.

To help follow the music in a jazz performance, you might **try to divide the sounds into the functions they serve**. For instance, there are two kinds of roles that instruments have in a jazz combo: the **soloist role** and the **accompanist role**. Jazz fans think of accompanists as members of a **rhythm section.** The standard instruments in rhythm sections are bass, drums, and a chording instrument such as piano, organ, or guitar. The soloist role can be assumed by any melody instrument, though saxophones and trumpets are the most common. (Listen to *Demo CD* Track 32.)

How Do Musicians Keep Their Place While Improvising?

To improvise is to compose and perform at the same time. Jazz musicians make up their music as they go along. Most jazz is guided by the musicians agreeing beforehand to maintain a given (1) tempo, (2) key, and (3) progression of accompaniment chords. They then invent and play their own melodies and accompaniments in a way that is compatible with those chords. Frequently, the agreed-upon harmonies are borrowed from a familiar melody, and the melody itself is played before and after the improvisations. This is easy because jazz musicians tend to know many of the same tunes in the same keys.

Jazz musicians often keep the original melody in mind while they improvise. This helps them keep their place in the progression of accompaniment chords that guides them. Despite this, *the improvised lines are not usually variations on the original melody. They are entirely different melodies. The improvised melodies and the original melody have only a progression of accompaniment chords in common.* To understand what goes into creating jazz, try learning the melody of a piece. Then try to keep your place in the improvised section of a jazz performance of that piece by listening for patterns that you remember hearing under the melody.

Another help in following a jazz improvisation is the form of the piece being played. For instance, when a jazz group plays a blues, the melody of the piece is usually played twice by everyone. (See page 206 and *Demo CD* Track 19.) Then the soloists improvise over the progression of chords in its accompaniment. **One complete progression of accompaniment chords is called a chorus**. Each soloist ordinarily improvises for several choruses. When one soloist ends an improvisation, another soloist takes over. The chords continue to progress in a cycle that never varies. In that way, the whole group stays together. That particular progression of chords and its tempo are the glue that holds the music together. After all the solos are taken, the group concludes by playing the melody to the piece twice more.

Jazz musicians often improvise over tunes written in the form of four sections. The most common arrangement for such pieces has one section called the A section and another called the B section or bridge. The A section is played two times in a row. Then the B section is inserted, followed by the A section again. The sequence is **A-A-B-A**, and thousands of tunes composed from the 1920s through the 50s were organized in such a format. You might recall the format if you hum the melody to the Christmas carol "Deck the Halls." The same format is used for "(Meet the) Flintstones." When jazz musicians play an A-A-B-A tune, they usually play its melody once before and once after the solo improvisations. Each solo fits the tune's chord progression so that the A-A-B-A chorus structure is repeated over and over again. The cycle continues A-A-B-A-A-A-B-A-A-A-B-A, and so forth. (See page 207 and *Demo CD* Track 33.)

INSTRUMENT ROLES

When you listen to a jazz performance, the large number of different sounds might be overwhelming to focus on. If this happens to you, try focusing only on one instrument's role at a time. Then after you become a more skilled listener, you will be able to identify combinations of instruments. You will also be able to move your focus of attention quickly from one activity to another.

One of the easiest parts to follow is the bass line. In jazz styles that were common from the 1930s through the 1960s, the bassist plucked a string once per beat. This (1) kept time for the band and (2) gave the group's sound a buoyancy. This style of playing is called **walking bass**. The notes played by the bassist are chosen from important notes in the accompaniment chords that are guiding the solo improvisation. (Listen to *Demo CD* Track 23.)

Also try to follow the sounds of the accompaniment pianist. Find a recording in which a trumpet or saxophone soloist is accompanied by piano, bass, and drums. When you listen, ignore the horns, bass, and drums. Listen only to how the pianist plays chords which support the soloist. Notice how the piano supplies a syncopated commentary on the solo. The pianist provides both harmonies and rhythms. The pianist uses both hands at the same time to play chorded rhythms behind a soloist. What the pianist is doing is called **comping.** This term is short for the word accompanying. (Listen to *Demo CD* Track 20.)

A particularly interesting role to follow is the drummer's. In styles rooted in jazz of the 1930s to the 1960s, the drummer uses his right hand to play rhythms which provide both (1) regular pulse and (2) swing feeling. The drummer plays these rhythms on the **ride cymbal** suspended over the drum set. *(Demo CD* Track 3) These rhythms are

Bass viol, also called
acoustic bass,
upright bass, bull fiddle,
bass fiddle, string bass
(shown here with
Ray Brown).

Photo by Anika Simpson

called **ride rhythms**. Occasionally they consist of one stroke per beat and they sound like "ting, ting, ting, ting." Usually they are more complicated, sounding like "ting tick a ting tick a ting tick a ting" or "ting ting ting tick a ting" or "ting tick a ting tick a ting tick a tick a ting." The drummer may play ride rhythms on other drums and cymbals, too.

The drummer's left hand is free to decorate the group sound by striking the *snare drum* that sits on a stand close to his lap. The snare drum has a crisp, crackling sound (*Demo CD* Track 5). The combinations of sounds made by striking the snare drum are often called "**fills**" because they fill in a musical gap left by the soloist. The snare drum can also be played to provide an undercurrrent of activity that seems to be "**chattering**" while the band is playing.

A drummer often interrupts the series of ride rhythms to strike a *crash cymbal*. (Listen to *Demo CD* Track 4.) This particular cymbal is chosen for its splashy sound quality and the quickness with which its sound disappears. This contrasts with the *ride cymbal* which is chosen for the quality of its "ting" and the fact that its sound generally sustains longer than that of a crash cymbal. (*Demo CD* Track 3)

The drummer reinforces every other beat by pressing his left foot on a pedal which closes two cymbals together, making a "chick" sound. This apparatus is called a **high-hat**. It will produce a "chick" sound if the pedal is depressed and very briefly held in closed

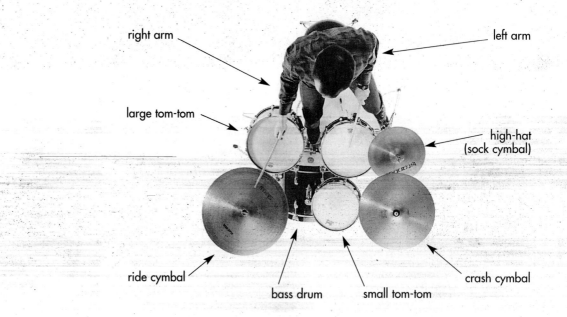

right arm

left arm

large tom-tom

high-hat
(sock cymbal)

ride cymbal

crash cymbal

bass drum   small tom-tom

position. It can then be opened and closed again for another "chick." Sounds can also be extracted from the high-hat if it is struck with a drum stick or a wire brush. (Listen to *Demo CD* Track 2.)

The drummer uses his right foot to press a pedal which, in turn, causes a mallet to strike the *bass drum*. The drummer sometimes plays the bass drum lightly on every beat. It can also be used to provide accents and "bombs." (Listen to *Demo CD* Track 1.)

The public often considers drummers merely to be timekeepers for a band. Though this is true in some bands, throughout jazz history drummers have also added sounds and rhythms that make music more colorful and exciting. Many of these colorful sounds do show where the beat is. However, much jazz percussion work does more than keep time. It dramatizes. In other words, **the drummer acts as a colorist in addition to acting as a timekeeper**. In fact, some bands have employed drummers exclusively for coloristic playing instead of timekeeping. Instead of "drummer," we say "percussionist" to describe that role.

The drummer not only (1) keeps time and (2) decorates the group sound, but also (3) **kicks and prods the soloist.** Drummers also (4) underscore the playing of the other band members by playing the same rhythm that the others have arranged for a particular moment in the piece. These tendencies expanded after the 1930s. By the mid-1960s jazz drumming had changed so much that the sounds made by drummers were often in the forefront of the band. They were as obvious as melody instruments. During this period of change in jazz styles, the amount of interplay between drummers and other group members also increased. Also keep in mind that a drummer's playing can control (1) the loudness level, (2) sound texture, and (3) mood of a combo's performance, much as a conductor does with a symphony orchestra. (Listen to *Demo CD* Tracks 8, 31, and 32.)

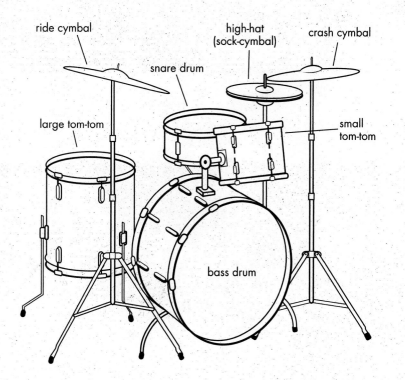

ride cymbal   snare drum   high-hat (sock-cymbal)   crash cymbal   large tom-tom   small tom-tom   bass drum

Audience view of drum set.

ARE SOLO IMPROVISATIONS COMPLETELY ORIGINAL?

Though we have said that jazz musicians make up their music as they go along, an improviser's lines are not totally original in each and every performance. There are themes in the improvisations that the musician has used before. In fact, these themes combine with the player's own unique tone qualities and rhythmic tendencies to help us identify the player's improvising style. Using such themes is an accepted practice. Beginners are advised to collect favorite "licks," those very themes which we later hear in their music. Most improvisers tend to play bits and pieces of lines they have played before. They also play melodic figures they have practiced and pet phrases of other improvisers. An improviser may actually play portions of a solo he remembers from another musician's recording. Sometimes an improviser will quote snatches of a pop tune or a classical piece. The separate parts of an improvised solo may not themselves be original, but the way in which they are combined usually is. However, there are a few extraordinarily gifted and disciplined improvisers, including Jim Hall and Wayne Shorter, who manage to devise lines that are largely free of familiar patterns.

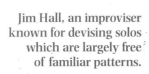

Jim Hall, an improviser known for devising solos which are largely free of familiar patterns.

Courtesy of Robert Asen, Metronome Collection

SUPPLEMENTARY LISTENING

Concise Guide Demo Cassette/CD that accompanies this book contains audio demonstrations for most of the concepts and techniques discussed in this chapter.

Listening to Jazz (video by Steve Gryb) ISBN 0-13-532862-4 (phone 800-947-7700) demonstrates instruments and their roles.

What Is Jazz? by Leonard Bernstein (originally Columbia CL 919, LP, reissued many times with different catalog numbers SMK 60566, CD; available in some libraries) contains demonstrations and explanations for many of the concepts and techniques discussed in this chapter.

J.J. Johnson, a trombonist whose solo improvisations are so logical that they are always easy to follow.

Photo by Chuck Stewart

CHAPTER SUMMARY

1. Unwritten rules are followed that enable jazz improvisers to piece together performances without rehearsal.

2. Musicians know many of the same tunes, and they follow common practices when performing tunes having 12-bar blues and A-A-B-A construction.

3. Jazz musicians play the melody before and after they play improvisations. Both the melody and the improvisations are guided by the same cycle of chord patterns in the accompaniment.

4. Walking bass style involves playing notes that keep time for the band as well as outlining the chord progression for the improvisers.

5. The jazz drummer uses bass drum, ride cymbal, and high-hat cymbals to keep time for the band and crash cymbal and snare drum to kick and prod soloists and dramatize their ideas.

6. Comping is the accompaniment style in which the pianist feeds chords to the improvising soloist in a flexible and syncopated way.

7. People can listen to jazz by
   a. humming the original tune to themselves while listening to the improvisations that are guided by the same progression of accompaniment chords
   b. imagining a graph of the solo line
   c. imagining layers of sound moving forward in time
   d. hearing the improvised lines of a soloist as melodies in themselves
   e. listening for variations in mood, tone qualities, and rhythms

8. Jazz musicians improvise by reorganizing phrases they have played before. However, some of the best manage to devise lines off the cuff that are largely free of familiar patterns: Jim Hall and Wayne Shorter, for instance.

CHAPTER 3

THE ORIGINS OF JAZZ

Superior Orchestra   Courtesy of William Ransom Hogan Jazz Archive, Tulane University

Jazz originated in blends of folk music, popular music, and light classical music. It developed from the kinds of music that people heard near the beginning of the twentieth century, especially in New Orleans. Several different trends led to the birth of jazz: (1) the practice of taking liberties with the melodies of tunes, which led to what we today call improvisation; (2) African Americans creating new kinds of music such as (a) ragtime and (b) blues; (3) taking liberties with tone qualities. For instance, musicians cultivated rough and raspy sounds to add to their collection of smooth tone qualities.

A glance back at the experiences of Africans in America will help us understand how these different kinds of music came together. When African slaves were brought to the United States, they were not allowed to bring musical instruments. But they did bring their own musical tastes and ways of performing. This is why European musical material often sounded different when played in the New World by musicians of African ancestry. *African Americans modified European church hymns, folk songs, and dance music to fit their own tastes and traditions.* Their children followed suit, and musical practices were thereby passed down from generation to generation.

NEW ORLEANS

Let's first examine the setting in which jazz was born. We will begin with the history of different groups of people who settled in New Orleans, paraphrased here from *The Creoles of Color of New Orleans* by James Haskins (Crowell, 1975). France began building New Orleans in 1718, and 147 black slaves were brought there in 1719. There were free blacks there as early as 1722. In 1763 France gave the territory of Louisiana to Spain. Despite Spanish rule, the language and customs there remained primarily French. In 1801, Spain gave Louisiana back to France. But Spain still continued to rule the territory until the United States bought it in 1803.

Significant social patterns can be traced back to that period of Spanish rule. At that time, marriage between the different ethnic groups in Louisiana occurred frequently. Furthermore, the Spanish freed many slaves. This increased the number of free blacks—there were 1,147 by 1789. Under Spanish rule, **free people of color began to be regarded as a class that was separate from the whites and the slaves. Their status was closer to that of whites.** Many light-skinned women of color became mistresses to white men and were set up as second families to the men in separate houses. The children from some of these unions were called *Creoles of Color.* Their ancestry was part African and part French. This distinguished them from the white Creoles, whose background was Spanish and French. Creoles of Color were never referred to as Negro. The term Negro was reserved for blacks who had little or no white ancestry.

By 1810, the number of free people of color living in New Orleans had increased to 5,000. As these population changes occurred and people of African or part-African ancestry became the largest ethnic group, the small white (non-Creole) population reacted to their own minority status with fear. The whites captured business and governmental power in New Orleans. With that power they made laws which took status away from the Creoles of Color and eventually placed them in the same position as Negroes.

A sharp separation existed between the two groups of New Orleans residents who had African ancestry. Negroes lived in a racially mixed neighborhood, a large portion of which was uptown. They worked primarily as house servants and unskilled laborers. Most of the white Creoles and the Creoles of Color lived downtown in the area of New Orleans known today as the French Quarter. Creoles of Color were mostly well-educated, successful people—businessmen, doctors, landowners, and skilled craftsmen. They spoke French. Many owned slaves, and often required their slaves to speak French, too. Children in Creole of Color families often received high-quality musical training, some even traveling to Paris for study at a conservatory. (See photo on page 28.) The Creoles of Color maintained a resident symphony orchestra and supported an opera house. This reinforced the intensely musical orientation of New Orleans, a city that had three opera houses, far more than any other American city of comparable size. By comparison with residents in other regions, they took the pleasures of music and dance more seriously.

Creoles of Color, like the white Creoles, wholeheartedly favored European music. European concert traditions were maintained by Creole music. Meanwhile, some music played by Negroes retained aspects of African musical practices. Though many Negro musicians received formal training, their music was generally less refined than that of the Creoles. It may have included improvisation. Moreover, it is significant to understand that the vocal music of the uptown blacks in New Orleans contained new blends of European and African vocal traditions.

The social history outlined here pertains to jazz for two reasons. First, it helps us appreciate how exceptionally musical New Orleans was. Second, it gets us thinking about how people of African and European-African descent combined their own traditional tastes to create a new form of music in their new American home.

Guitar and banjo, instruments used in African American music that led to jazz. The banjo was invented in the New World by African slaves. The guitar was brought to America from Europe. The guitar was an important instrument for accompanying blues singing. The banjo was common in minstrel bands and ragtime music.

THE BLUES

The term "blues" refers to several different kinds of music. The first kind was a black folk music that began developing long before outside observers noticed and took it seriously enough to describe. This was long before the invention of the recording machine in 1877. So we really don't know for certain how all its roots and developmental stages sounded. We do know, however, that it didn't come from Africa. It was developed in America by African slaves and their descendants. Researchers believe the blues originated from other vocal idioms such as (1) field hollers, which slaves devised from highly varied pitches and rhythms for the purpose of communicating among themselves while working in fields; (2) ballads, which come partly from European traditions for songs that tell stories; and (3) music devised for dances, such as the ring shout.

Performing the blues involves some of the same techniques that are used by singers and musicians who play stringed instruments in Senegal and Gambia, the northern parts of West Africa. For example, the earliest recorded blues have enormous variety in the ways notes are sung. In particular, what might sound like moans and wails may be merely the vocabulary of drops and scoops of pitch in vocal music of the parent culture. Or what may sound to us like odd starting and stopping points in the phrases probably reflects the rich variation of rhythms common to the music that influenced the blues. Creatively toying with the rhythms and pitches in the melody notes was commonplace. The effect of these manipulations became known as "bluesy" or "soulful." Twentieth-century recordings of Son House, Charley Patton, and Robert Johnson indicate how the earliest forms of blues probably sounded.

In the beginning, blues was a form of unaccompanied solo singing. After blues began to develop, singers began to accompany themselves on the guitar or banjo. The earliest accompaniments did not necessarily use chords or chord progressions. Their accompaniments often had only one note at a time or two notes played together. Eventually the singers began to use chords. But, at first, they used only whatever chords they already knew. They didn't necessarily go and learn a set of harmonies that would, in turn, dictate the notes they were allowed to use in the melody, as jazz musicians later did. Usually only a few chords were employed. There was much repetition, not only in the accompaniment but also in the lyrics. Then, as the blues evolved, a certain pattern of accompaniment chords became customary. It was similar to the pattern used in church hymns. (See Elements of Music Appendix pages 202-207 and *Demo CD* Track 19 for full explanation and illustration.)

As the blues developed, the pattern of words and the rhythms of words in the lyrics began to become more and more standardized. It had become fairly well developed by 1910. Eventually a rhyme scheme was adopted that had its own rhythm. (See the example of paired couplets in iambic pentameter, "Fine and Mellow," on page

209 of Elements of Music Appendix. Listen to Bessie Smith sing "Sobbin' Hearted Blues" on the *Jazz Classics CD*.) *Underneath that rhyme scheme, a given progression of accompaniment chords became standardized.* This pattern of chords, in turn, set the pace for the twentieth-century tradition of blues performances that had no singing. (Listen to the trumpet, trombone, and piano solos on "West End Blues" in the *Jazz Classics CD*.) *Instrumental blues, as it has been called, evolved as its own idiom.* By the 1930s, many chord changes were being made by jazz bands when playing the blues. By the mid-1950s, quite challenging harmonies had been explored within the blues form. (Listen to the saxophone solo improvisations on "Two Bass Hit" in the *Jazz Classics CD*. See page 236 for chord progressions.)

When trumpeters, clarinetists, saxophonists, and trombonists began playing jazz, they sometimes imitated the scoops and drops of pitch that blues singers used. They also decorated their songs with odd rhythms and tone qualities that had been demonstrated by blues singers. These nuances of rhythm and inflections of pitch allowed instrumentalists to spice up bland melodies by making their rhythms less predictable and the tone qualities and pitches of melody notes more flexible. Occasionally instrumentalists also picked tunes that had been first introduced by blues singers. So you see that *the blues tradition contributed to jazz in at least three important respects:* (1) modelling novel sounds, (2) offering a standard set of accompaniment harmonies, and (3) furnishing part of the jazz repertory.

After jazz and blues had both become recognizable forms, blues continued to change over the years, parallel to but usually separate from the course of development that jazz followed. Its progress occasionally overlapped with jazz, however. For instance, many blues singers hired jazz musicians to accompany them. And many jazz bands routinely featured a blues singer. Eventually blues became a major part of popular music in America and provided one of the roots for rock and roll. Jazz, on the other hand, became more complicated, less popular, and some of it was considered art music, instead of popular music.

BRASS BANDS

Historian-musicologist Karl Koenig has come up with a way to help us appreciate the musical setting that gave birth to jazz. He encourages us to imagine life at the beginning of the twentieth century. Consider for instance that there were no electronic devices. Trying to have fun on a night in New Orleans would be very different than it is now. You could not listen to any radio or television programs, CDs, or tapes. You could not call anyone on the telephone or visit movie theaters or video arcades. Candlelight would be needed for reading. However, you could go to the town square, which would be lit by gas lamps. There you could buy flavored ices from a vendor, exchange pleasantries with your neighbors, and take a walk in the moonlight. You could also listen and dance to the local band. In other words, there

A black military brass band of the Civil War period.

almost had to be *live* music. A town without a band was a very dull place to be. The social and fraternal organizations knew this, as did the newspapers and businesses. Therefore sponsorship was provided for most of the local bands by churches, social and benevolent clubs, fraternal clubs, fire departments, townships, undertakers, and plantation owners.

A band was present at almost every social activity, most of which took place outdoors: picnics, sporting events, political speeches, or dramatic presentations at the town hall, and dances in the open-air pavilions. The band played before the event and for the dance that followed. Dancing was the main social activity of the nineteenth century. A large brass band was used so that the music could be heard in outdoor settings. Note that in the narrowest sense, a "brass band" has only brass instruments, bass drum, cymbal, and snare drum. But the early Louisiana bands also included a clarinet and later a saxophone. When the social activity was held indoors, a large band was not needed. There the smaller "string band" was suitable. It was usually comprised of cornet, violin, guitar, bass, and piano or some combination of those instruments. (See photo on page 19.)

There had been bands in the New Orleans area long before the Civil War. Then, during the war, occupation by Union troops had exposed the city to many more. About thirty different regimental bands of the occupying forces were stationed in and around New Orleans. They were very conspicuous. They played for the many military ceremonies and for concerts of patriotic and popular music. Their presence was an additional stimulus for the band tradition in New Orleans.

RAGTIME

Another trend was important to the birth of jazz. By the end of the 1800s, ragtime was very popular in New Orleans. The word "rag" refers to a kind of music that was put together like a military march and had rhythms borrowed from African American banjo music. You could tell ragtime music because many of the loud accents fell in between the beats. This is called syncopation. Musicians would use syncopation on all kinds of different tunes and say they were "ragging" those tunes. So the term "to rag" came to mean giving the rhythms in a piece of music a distinctly syncopated feeling.

"Ragtime" ordinarily refers to a kind of written piano music that first appeared in the 1890s. The most famous composer of this style was Scott Joplin (1868–1917). The term has also been used to identify an entire era of music, not exclusively written piano music. For example, between the 1890s and the 1920s there were also ragtime bands, ragtime singers, ragtime banjo players, etc.

Many of the musicians we classify today as "jazz" musicians called themselves "ragtime" musicians back then. Because of this, some scholars consider ragtime to have been the first jazz style. However, ragtime does not qualify as a jazz style by the strictest definition of jazz because it lacked what today is called jazz swing feeling. Instead we can say that (1) ragtime was a forerunner of jazz and (2) contributed tunes to jazz repertory. (3) It popularized using accents before and after the beat instead of always directly on it. This was its syncopation, which gave ragtime its distinct character and charm. Today jazz musicians play "around" the beat partly because ragtime made the practice popular.

Scott Joplin,
the most important
ragtime composer.

Photo courtesy of New York Public Library

COMBINING INFLUENCES

During the 1890s, there were bands in almost every small town and settlement in southern Louisiana. Their music reflected several influences. It combined march music and ragtime. Moreover, these two styles were interrelated. John Philip Sousa, the famous bandleader, had included ragtime pieces in his band concerts. Ragtime pianists often performed Sousa marches in a ragtime style. Another significant force in New Orleans culture of that time was music of the Mexican bands that visited the city. Musicians from these bands settled in and around New Orleans, and some became music teachers. Their music was respected and enjoyed so much that it influenced the styles of New Orleans trumpeters.

Band music directly influenced jazz for several reasons. By the beginning of the twentieth century, New Orleanians were accustomed to hearing brass bands such as Sousa's, having already heard many military bands of the Gulf Coast Command. Dances held in the middle 1800s were often provided with music by the military band that was stationed in the region. In fact, the march form was sometimes modified and used as dance music. Later a popular dance called the "two-step" was done to march-like music. Moreover, the way that passages were organized in a ragtime piece followed the pattern found in marches. Eventually roles of various instruments were transferred from marching band to jazz band. For instance, flute and piccolo parts in marches were imitated by jazz clarinetists, and drum parts for marches developed into styles for playing drums in jazz.

THE PARTY ATMOSPHERE

Other factors besides the brass band movement made New Orleans an ideal setting for the birth of jazz. New Orleans was a center for commerce because of its nearness to the mouth of the Mississippi River, a flourishing trade route for America, the Caribbean, and Europe. Because the city was a seaport, it catered to travelers from all over the world, and New Orleans maintained a party atmosphere. There were numerous taverns and dance halls. One aspect of the entertainment it provided was a famous prostitution district known as Storyville. **The reason the party atmosphere of New Orleans is important to the beginning of jazz is that it generated so much work for musicians. There was so much demand for live music that there was a constant need for fresh material. This caused musicians to stretch styles. They blended, salvaged, and continuously revised odd assortments of approaches and material. This ultimately became jazz.**

Early jazz musicians have said that their repertory was constructed primarily to accompany dances such as the mazurka, schottische, quadrille, and one-step. These musicians were not hired specifically to play jazz. At the beginning of the twentieth century,

New Orleans parade bands (photo on page 29) and dance bands shared the same musicians and much of the same repertory. It was almost as though the musicians walked directly from the street parade into the dance hall, often putting down a brass instrument and picking up a violin. The performing groups that accompanied dances were termed "string bands" or "orchestras"—violin, guitar, bass viol, and one or two wind instruments, played by the same musicians who had paraded with trumpet and trombone. (See photo on page 19.) To satisfy the demands of dancers, these musicians often combined music from different sources. Sometimes they ended up creating new sounds that were very compelling rhythmically, such as "ragging" march music to make it more jumpy.

These approaches became the core of jazz style, and their manner of playing led to the idea that jazz is not *what* you play, but *how* you play it. In other words, **jazz was an outgrowth of treatments for many kinds of music being played on the demand of dancers.** Today we call these same musicians "jazz musicians," and their music "New Orleans jazz" or "Dixieland."

Another trend also led to jazz style. In parades as well as dance halls, small bands were trying to perform music originally written for large bands. This led to what became standard Dixieland style. In trying to fill out the sound, more activity was required of each player, so musicians improvised parts to order. They got in the habit of improvising, and as jazz evolved, this habit changed from being a necessity to being a choice. In essence, the musicians in New Orleans were combining diverse materials to please people who had a taste for special kinds of musical excitement.

Ory's Woodland Band, an early New Orleans "string band," posing during an outdoor picnic gig.

Courtesy of William Ransom Hogan Jazz Archive, Tulane University

CHAPTER SUMMARY

1. Jazz originated in New Orleans around the beginning of the twentieth century.

2. New Orleans was the ideal site for the birth of jazz because it was an intensely musical city with a history of rich ethnic diversity, especially French and African.

3. African American forms of music such as the blues and ragtime blended with European dance music and church music.

4. Jazz emerged when brass bands were at a height of popularity.

5. Ragtime was in such high demand that brass bands and string bands were improvising rag-like syncopations into their pieces to please dancers.

6. New Orleans musicians combined diverse materials to please people who had a taste for special kinds of musical excitement.

7. Jazz came out of the combination of instruments, repertory, and musical practices used by brass bands and string bands in New Orleans before the 1920s.

8. Improvisation became common as small bands attempted to perform music originally intended for large bands. Musicians improvised parts to order.

New Orleans Creole clarinetist Sidney Bechet, one of the first great solo improvisers in early jazz.

Courtesy of William Ransom Hogan Jazz Archive, Tulane University

SOURCES FOR LISTENING TO THE ROOTS OF JAZZ

Early Band Ragtime (Folkways RBF 38)

Jazz, Vol. 1: The South (Folkways 2801)

Jazz, Vol. 2: The Blues (Folkways 2802)

Riverside History of Classic Jazz (Riverside/Fantasy 3 RBCD-005-2)

That's My Rabbit, My Dog Caught It: Traditional Southern Instrumental Styles (New World 226)

Come and Trip It: Instrumental Dance Music 1780s–1920s (New World 293)

The Sousa and Pryor Bands: Original Recordings 1901–1926 (New World 282)

Steppin' On the Gas: From Rags to Jazz 1913–1927 (New World 269)

Jazz: Some Beginnings 1913–1926 (Folkways RF 31)

Street Cries and Creole Songs of New Orleans (Folkways FA 2202)

Roots of the Blues (New World 252)

African Journey: A Search for the Roots of the Blues (Vanguard SRV 73014/5)

Early Band Ragtime (Folkways RBF 38)

Note: New World records are in many libraries. For further information, write the company (701 Seventh Ave., NY, NY 10036). Folkways records are in many libraries. Many of its holdings also have been made available on audio cassette through Smithsonian/Folkways Recordings, 414 Hungerford Drive; Suite 444, Rockville, MD 20850.

Eureka Brass Band, a New Orleans brass band playing in a funeral procession.

Photo by Bill Russell, courtesy of William Ransom Hogan Jazz Archive, Tulane University

SUPPLEMENTARY READING

An in-depth summary of what is African and what is European about jazz can be found on pages 40–51 of *Jazz Styles: History and Analysis, Seventh Edition* by Mark C. Gridley (Prentice-Hall, 2000).

The Music of Africa by J. H. Kwabena Nketia (Norton, 1974)

African Music: A People's Art by Francis Bebey (Lawrence Hill, 1975 translation)

Roots of Black Music: The Vocal, Instrumental, and Dance Heritage of Africa and Black America by Ashenafi Kebede (Prentice-Hall, 1982)

Black Music of Two Worlds by John Storm Roberts (Praeger, 1972), with 3-LP set of records available as Ethnic Folkways FE 4602

Savannah Syncopators by Paul Oliver (Stein and Day, 1970), with a 2-LP set of records available as *Savannah Syncopators* from CBS (England) 52799

In Search of Buddy Bolden: First Man of Jazz by Donald M. Marquis (Louisiana State University, 1978; DaCapo reprint)

Ragtime: A Musical and Cultural History by Edward A. Berlin (University of California, 1980)

Scott Joplin: The Man Who Made Ragtime by James Haskins (Doubleday, 1983)

Ragtime: Its History, Composers and Music by John Hasse (Ed.) (University of California, 1980)

Scott Joplin: King of Ragtime by Edward A. Berlin (Oxford, 1994)

Brass Bands and New Orleans Jazz by William J. Schafer (Louisiana State University, 1977)

The Creoles of Color of New Orleans by James Haskins (Crowell, 1975)

Big Road Blues: Tradition and Creativity in the Folk Blues by David Evans (University of California, 1982)

Jazz in Print (1859–1929): An Anthology of Early Source Readings in Jazz History by Karl Koenig (Pendragon, 1999)

CHAPTER 4

EARLY JAZZ

Ma Rainey and her Georgia Jazz Band   Courtesy of Frank Driggs

Early jazz musicians often began improvising by embellishing the melodies of pop tunes. As jazz evolved across the 1920s, the embellishments sometimes became more important to a performance than the tunes themselves. In some performances of the 1930s, all that remained was the original tune's spirit and chord progressions. What is today called improvising was sometimes referred to by early jazz musicians as embellishing, "jassing," or "jazzing up."

Early jazz differs from its ragtime, blues, and brass band roots in several important respects:

1. Much of each performance was improvised.
2. Rhythmic feeling was looser and more relaxed, thus anticipating jazz swing feeling.
3. It generated much of its own repertory of compositions.
4. Collective improvisation created a more complex musical product than was typical in ragtime, blues, or marching band music.

Joe "King" Oliver's Creole Jazz Band of 1923. This group of New Orleans musicians performed steady engagements in Chicago. It was to join this group that Louis Armstrong (seated in center) left New Orleans. The playing style of Oliver (standing in back with cornet) was an important influence on Armstrong's solo approach. Pianist Lil Hardin was the band's only non-New Orleanian, and she married Armstrong.

Photo courtesy of Cleveland Press Collection
Cleveland State University Archives

Combo jazz began in New Orleans, and that city contributed several very important musicians. The best known were trumpeter Louis Armstrong and composer-arranger Jelly Roll Morton.

It was in Chicago that many black New Orleans musicians were first recorded in the early 1920s. Black New Orleans style jazz as played between 1900 and 1922 in New Orleans was not recorded. We can't say we know exactly what it sounded like. All we have is the music recorded by New Orleans musicians in Chicago during the 1920s. According to interviews and a few early records, the earliest forms of jazz featured collective improvisation, with all group members playing at the same time. This took place when every player created phrases which complemented every other player. This is a very exciting effect, and it captivated many listeners.

In the collective improvisation of early jazz, instruments tended to fulfill set musical roles similar to those established in brass bands. The trumpet often played the melody. The clarinet played busy figures with many notes. The clarinet part decorated the melody played by trumpet. The trombone would play simpler figures. The trombone's music outlined the chord notes and filled in low-pitched harmony notes. The trombone created motion in a pitch range that was lower than that of clarinet and trumpet.

New Orleans jazz was first recorded in Chicago and New York, not in New Orleans. **The Original Dixieland Jazz Band** made the first recordings. This was a collection of white New Orleans musicians who organized a band in Chicago during 1916 and played in New York in 1917. They used cornet, clarinet, trombone, piano, and drums. Under the leadership of cornetist Nick LaRocca (1889–1961), the band recorded its first 78 r.p.m. record in 1917. They played "Livery Stable Blues" on one side and "Dixie Jazz Band One-Step" on the other. It sold very well and was widely imitated. Even during the 1990s, musicians were forming Dixieland jazz bands in the style of this group.

LISTENING GUIDE

"Dixie Jazz Band One-Step"

Recorded February 26, 1917 by Nick LaRocca (cornet), Larry Shields (clarinet), Eddie Edwards (trombone), Henry Ragas (piano), and Tony Spargo (drums).

This record was made in New York by a group of white New Orleans musicians who had come together in Chicago the preceding year. They called themselves the Original Dixieland Jass Band (ODJB). "Dixie Jazz Band One-Step" (also known as "Original Dixieland One-Step") was on the reverse side of "Livery Stable Blues," one of the most popular discs in the first decade of recorded jazz. Worldwide sales of the record are said to have reached about a million copies by the late 1930s.

This is the first instrumental jazz recording ever released, and music by the ODJB has continued to influence musicians, partly because this band made the first jazz records. The roles that the different instruments assume on this recording were associated with what is known today as New Orleans, Chicago, or Dixieland style jazz. We can consider this record to be an example of music that was popular in New Orleans during this period because most of the fashions heard here were already common in New Orleans ragtime bands by 1917. So even though it was the first to be recorded, the ODJB was not necessarily the first or the "Original" band of its kind, as its name implies.

Of the five instruments playing here, the clarinet is the most evident, and the piano is least evident. The cornet and trombone sounds frequently blend so closely that you may have difficulty distinguishing them, though many trombone smears are conspicuous. As was typical for New Orleans drummers of the period, Spargo frequently switches instruments. At various moments he can be heard playing snare drum, wood block, and cowbell. He uses the cymbal sparingly, and a cymbal crash usually signifies a climactic moment in the music.

Many of the different sounds heard here are so close in pitch and rhythm that they blend together in your ear and disguise each other. But the more often you listen, the more distinct they will become. Can you remember peering at a trick sketch on a comic book, trying to recognize a tiger hidden in jungle ferns where overlapping lines camouflaged its contours? Your search for separate instruments here might resemble the experience you had with the trick sketch.

The ODJB's roots in the brass band tradition are reflected in this piece's opening. The rhythm of the first four-measure sequence is called a "roll-off," a device usually played by a parade band's drummer to prepare the musicians to march. By listening closely, you can hear the drummer playing the roll-off pattern underneath the horns. His rhythm is the same as theirs. The trombone smear in the third group of four beats coincides with a drum roll. Like other march-style popular music of this period, the "Dixie Jazz Band One-Step" was used to accompany a dance called the "one-step."

The first two themes in this piece were written by the band members. The third theme was composed by Joe Jordan. To guide you through the events in this recording, we will break the music into beats and groups of four beats, each of which is called a "measure." At the beginning we will identify what happens on each beat. This will clarify the drum roll model the ODJB used for playing their parts. After that, we will refer to each section of the piece in terms of what happens for each group of measures.

CD Track	Elapsed Time				
1	0' 00"	**First Theme**			
		First Measure:	*bang*	*bang*	*silence*	*silence*
		(numbered beats):	*1*	*2*	*3*	*4*
		Second Measure:	*bang*	*bang*	*silence*	*silence*
		(numbered beats):	*1*	*2*	*3*	*4*
		Third Measure:	*trombone smear*			
		(numbered beats):	*1*	*2*	*3*	*4*
		Fourth Measure:	*smear end*	*silence*	*crash*	
		(numbered beats):	*1*	*2*	*3*	*4*
	0' 03"	*Fifth, Sixth, Seventh, and Eighth Measures:*			
		Band plays a new theme, with clarinet playing around the cornet and trombone parts. The drummer plays a military snare drum rhythm as a counteractivity to the rhythms of the horn lines.			
2	0' 07"	**Repeat of the First Theme, but with different ending**			
3	0' 15"	**Second Theme**			
	0' 23"	**Repeat of the Second Theme, but with different ending**			
	0' 30"	**Repeat of First and Second Themes in above order**			
4	1' 00"	**Third Theme** ("That Teasin' Rag" by Joe Jordan)			
		Trombone exchanges with clarinet in a call-and-response fashion, playfully trading descending smears; "clickety-clacking" of the drummer's sticks sound military rhythms on the wood block for the first eight measures, then alternately striking wood block and cowbell.			

CD Track	Elapsed Time	

Trombone plays descending smears in unison with piano, as a "call." Cornet and clarinet harmonize a bobbing little figure as a "response." This section ends with the horn parts going in different directions. A robust trombone part emerges with a repeating figure near the end. Intensity builds and then culminates with a high-pitched descending clarinet smear.

1' 16"   Third Theme, with different ending

First beat is played by the drummer striking his cymbal for a crash. Then he plays wood block and cowbell. The trombone then briefly carries a melody of its own, using a style similar to the tuba parts of march arrangements. Near the end, the cornet chimes in with a sustained tone on an offbeat.

1' 32"   Third Theme

Drummer begins this section by emphasizing his cowbell and he uses wood block less than before. Notice the descending trombone smears. A quick, high-pitched clarinet smear ends the section.

1' 48"   Repeat of Third Theme, with different ending

Drummer begins with a cymbal crash, then plays patterns on wood block. He interrupts his pattern during the middle of this section and strikes the bass drum twice in succession.

2' 03"   Third Theme

If you listen closely during the last half of this section, you will hear the piano pounding out bass patterns. This section ends with a descending clarinet smear.

2' 18"   Third Theme, with different ending

Original Dixieland Jass Band (also called Original Dixieland Jazz Band), 1916. Left to right: Tony Spargo [Sbarbaro, Sparbaro] (drums), Eddie Edwards (trombone), Nick La Rocca (cornet), Alcide Nunez (clarinet), Henry Ragas (piano), the first jazz group to make records.

Photo courtesy of Duncan Schiedt

Chicago was the center for a very active jazz scene during the 1920s. Musicians there can be described in terms of three main categories: (1) The transplanted New Orleans African American musicians, (2) their white New Orleans counterparts, and (3) young white Chicagoans who imitated the older players. That third category is today called "The Chicago School" or the "Chicagoans." Eventually the Chicago musicians and the transplanted New Orleans musicians mixed with New York musicians. By the late 1920s, a strong jazz scene had also developed in New York.

Jazz piano styles were evolving in places other than New Orleans prior to 1920. In fact, many outstanding jazz pianists of the 1920s were from the East Coast. Many of them played unaccompanied. Early jazz piano styles evolved from ragtime. Playing ragtime did not always necessitate reading or memorizing written music. Once the style had been absorbed, skilled pianists appeared who could improvise original rags as well as embellish written ones. One jazz piano style with roots in ragtime is known as stride style. This uses percussive, fast-moving, left-hand figures in which low bass notes alternate with mid-range chords, while the right hand plays melodies and embellishments in a very energetic fashion. This is a difficult style to play. The best players kept a perfect stride going continuously.

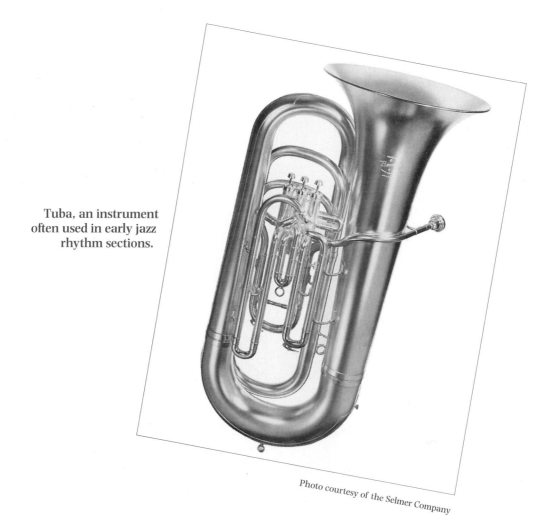

Tuba, an instrument often used in early jazz rhythm sections.

Photo courtesy of the Selmer Company

INSTRUMENTS IN EARLY JAZZ BANDS

The front line of most early jazz combos included trumpet, clarinet, trombone, and occasionally, saxophone. The rhythm section was made up of several instruments which might include guitar, banjo, tuba, bass saxophone, string bass, piano, and drums. No bands had all these instruments playing at the same time, but most drew some combination from that collection. It was not unusual for early jazz combos to be without string bass, and many early jazz recordings were made without drums. Some groups substituted tuba for string bass.

Clarinet and soprano sax.

Photo courtesy of the Selmer Company

DRUMMERS IN EARLY JAZZ

Early jazz drummers are poorly heard on records because early studio equipment was not well-suited to recording drums. At that time, records were made by playing into acoustic recording horns (see page 54). The small end of the horn was connected to a cutting needle which made grooves in a cylinder or a disc. Any loud sound, especially a blow to the bass drum, could knock the needle off the cutting surface. Many recordings during this period consequently represent working bands minus their drummers. Many of the recordings that do employ drummers either omit most drum equipment entirely or muffle it so much that, when combined with low recording quality, drum sounds are almost inaudible. We are often left with little more than the clickety clicking sound of drum sticks striking a small block of wood that has been hollowed out to increase resonance. (*Demo CD* Track 10) This was one of the only sounds drummers were allowed to produce when engineers were hesitant to attempt recording loud sounds.

Though the drumming sound described above was particularly convenient in adapting to the restrictions imposed by early recording situations, it represents only one sample in a range of sounds commonly generated by the earliest jazz drummers. Light, staccato sounds were also produced by striking a cowbell or the shell or rim of the bass drum, rather than the drum head that usually receives the blow. These sounds were also employed in some early recording sessions. A large cymbal or gong was sometimes used to signal a dramatic height in the music. When playing on the light-sounding instruments, many of the earliest drummers chose patterns from military and ragtime drumming.

JELLY ROLL MORTON

Jelly Roll Morton (1890–1941) was a pianist, composer-arranger, and bandleader from New Orleans. He was one of the first jazz pianists as well as the first jazz composer. Morton performed in both the ragtime style and the jazz style. He developed rhythmic techniques to make his lines swing. By doing this and reducing adornment, Morton played with a lighter and more swinging feeling than was typical of ragtime. It was the first style of piano playing that warrants the label of "jazz."

Morton's piano style was quite complex. He often played two or three melodic lines at a time, like a band. It was as though trumpet parts, clarinet parts, and trombone parts were all being heard coming from a piano! Morton put a variety of themes and dramatic devices within a single piece. Morton mixed ragtime with less formal, more blues-oriented New Orleans styles.

Morton's best known bands were a series of recording groups in Chicago called the Red Hot Peppers. Morton's compositions and arrangements on those recordings are still respected by jazz composers and scholars. Morton employed many of the same New Orleans-born musicians shared by other black Chicago groups. Under Morton's leadership, the resulting sounds were equally high-spirited but better organized. In summary, Jelly Roll Morton is historically notable because:

1. He was the first important jazz composer, and several of his pieces became well known in rearranged form when played by other bands.
2. He was one of the first jazz musicians to balance composition with improvisation while retaining the excitement of collectively improvised jazz.

Jelly Roll Morton (pianist) and his Red Hot Peppers. In this 1926 studio recording band, Morton combined the free-wheeling spirit of New Orleans jazz with a more highly arranged format. Morton was the first important jazz composer.

Photo courtesy of Duncan Schiedt

3. He recorded piano solos that were well-organized, forcefully executed musical statements with horn-like lines.

4. He bridged the gap between the piano styles of ragtime and jazz by loosening ragtime's rhythmic feeling and decreasing its embellishments.

JAMES P. JOHNSON

James P. Johnson (1894–1955) was born in New Jersey. He was part of the East Coast jazz piano tradition that was developing at about the same time as combo jazz was developing in New Orleans. Like Morton, his work smoothed the transition from ragtime to jazz. One of the first jazz musicians to broadcast on the radio, Johnson was already a prominent figure by the time jazz began to be recorded. He wrote his famous "Carolina Shout" in 1914 and recorded it in 1921. Johnson is considered "the father of stride piano." This is a style in which the pianist uses fingers on his left hand to play a bass note the first and third of every four beats and a mid-range chord on the second and fourth beats. These sounds are made very percussively. The right hand then plays melodies very energetically. The left hand motion resembles a striding kind of leg motion made by a person walking, hence the name. The technique is extremely demanding. Johnson's title of "father" was earned because his own brand of stride did the most to spread this style and because he was the best of the earliest stride masters.

Johnson's playing tended to be lighter, faster, and less bluesy than Morton's. He relied less on dramatic devices and more on a breathtaking flow, demonstrating great virtuosity. Like Morton, he perfected an orchestral approach to jazz piano playing, as though he were a one-man band. Many musicians feel that he was never surpassed in this style. At a time when informal competitions among solo pianists were common in New York, Johnson is said to have won more contests than anyone else. His speed, precision, dexterity, and imagination amazed musicians. The force and swing of his pianistic feats are legendary. Johnson influenced most pianists who emerged during the 1920s, including Fats Waller and Duke Ellington.

James P. Johnson, the greatest of all stride-style pianists.

Photo courtesy of Frank Driggs

Fats Waller, the most
popular jazz pianist-
composer of the
1920s and 30s.

Photo courtesy of Frank Driggs

FATS WALLER

Fats Waller (1904–1943) was one of the most popular figures in jazz history. Six of his recordings hit number one position on the sales charts, and many more rose into the top ten. Some were million-sellers. He was almost equally well known for three different talents: song writing, piano playing, and entertaining. From 1922 he was making records, and from 1923 he was broadcasting regularly on the radio. He collaborated in writing music for several Broadway shows. Some of his tunes remain among the most enduring in American music. "Ain't Misbehavin'," "Honeysuckle Rose," and "Jitterbug Waltz" are the best known. Waller was capable of bringing a tremendous sense of fun to almost any endeavor. Anyone who ever heard his music or saw him in movies could not help but smile. Much of his material was novelty songs, some of which he composed.

While accompanying himself on the piano, he cleverly half talked, half sang the lyrics. He often added witty remarks that he improvised during the performance. In these ways he was an important entertainer and a major figure in popular music as a whole, not just in jazz.

Waller was most important to jazz as an improvising pianist. He was probably the most gracefully swinging of all the stride-style pianists during the 1920s and 30s. He was the first to conquer the difficult style so well that it came out light and springy. He managed to extract a full, pretty tone quality from the piano, no matter how hard he was swinging nor how fast he was playing. His sense of rhythm was near perfect. His melodic ideas seemed to flow from a boundless imagination.

Some listeners have trouble deciding upon Waller's stature in jazz history. They overlook the extent of Waller's achievement for two reasons. First, he made his work sound so easy because he was such a good pianist and improviser. His skill combined with the lively, happy character of his music to make his playing sound so casual that it is hard to take seriously. The second reason is that piano listeners can get distracted by his vocals and clowning remarks. Yet his improvisations had real substance, and they often contained imaginative twists of harmony and rhythm that were quite subtle. In fact, many pianists were so impressed that they chose to imitate Waller's playing while developing their own styles. Art Tatum, Count Basie, and Dave Brubeck are just a few of the better known pianists who did this.

EARL HINES

Earl Hines (1903–1983) was an early jazz pianist who significantly influenced piano playing styles of the 1930s and 40s. Born in Pittsburgh, Hines moved to Chicago in 1924. He brought with him an assortment of different jazz techniques, all combined in the form of one catchy style. His playing began its enormous influence during the late 1920s when he recorded with trumpeter Louis Armstrong and made a series of important records of his own. This impact extended during the 1930s by way of radio broadcasts and tours with the big band he led at the Grand Terrace Ballroom from 1928 to 1939. Musicians as far away as Kansas and Texas heard his broadcasts. His style had a clear impact on Teddy Wilson, Nat Cole, Art Tatum, and Count Basie. Hines had an influence on modern jazz because these players, in turn, influenced the development of modern styles.

Much of the piano music made by Hines can be called "brassy." This is partly because of the great physical force Hines used to strike the piano keys. Even when Hines played in a flowery way, a roughness remained in his sound. Rarely was anything sustained, and nearly everything had a punching quality. These properties combined with his method of phrasing to lend that brassy quality to the sound of the piano. Because his right-hand lines sometimes sounded like jazz trumpet playing, the Hines approach earned the title of

trumpet style or **horn-like**. (*Classics CD* Track 9) His piano lines even seemed to breathe at the moments a trumpeter would breathe. Additionally they contained phrases and rhythms preferred by trumpeters rather than pianists. This manner stems partly from Hines having originally begun his musical training with the goal of becoming a trumpeter instead of a pianist, and it also came from what Hines did to be heard over loud band instruments. We must remember that he was playing long before electronic amplification came to the aid of pianists. To manage the task of cutting through, he played very hard, phrased like a trumpeter, and doubled his right-hand melody lines in octaves. (*Demo CD* Track 41)

Hines' "trumpet-style" approach is historically significant because, by playing more as a horn and less in the standard piano styles, Hines paved the way for modern jazz pianists who solo with essentially the same conception that is used by jazz trumpeters and saxophonists. It is less flowery and more direct. It is less classically pianistic and more swinging. Additionally, it is important to realize that the Hines approach is more flexible than the ragtime and stride approaches.

Earl Hines, the pianist known for his trumpet-style approach to improvising. His style spanned early jazz and swing to influence modern styles. Hines' big bands were heard by radio broadcasts from Chicago during the 1930s. This photo was taken in 1928, the year Hines recorded "West End Blues" with Louis Armstrong.

Photo courtesy of Frank Driggs

LISTENING GUIDE

"West End Blues" featuring Louis Armstrong and Earl Hines

Composed by Joe Oliver; recorded June 6, 1928 in Chicago by Louis Armstrong (trumpet and vocal), Jimmy Strong (clarinet), Fred Robinson (trombone), Earl Hines (piano), Mancy Cara (banjo), and Zutty Singleton (drums); on CD as *Volume IV: Louis Armstrong and Earl Hines*, Columbia CK 45142; also on CD in the Revised SCCJ.

CD Track	Elapsed Time	
5	0' 00"	**Introduction**

The opening phrases in this piece are among the most famous in jazz history. Note the drama as Armstrong reaches up to his highest note, the one he sustains. Then listen to the manner in which he gradually descends to finish with a note that makes you eager to hear what follows. Notice his warm, brassy tone and his sure-footed manner. This introduction is a masterpiece that you might want to hear several times before listening to the rest of the performance.

The idea of a bravura solo style, particularly an unaccompanied solo passage like this, was common in light classical music that was popular in America around 1900. Virtuoso cornet soloists were frequently featured in band concerts at that time. In addition, the trumpet sounds of Mexican bands that visited New Orleans had impressed musicians there. When Louis Armstrong devised this stirring opening, he was drawing, either consciously or unconsciously, from that tradition in light classical music, and he was establishing a tradition in jazz.

	0' 13"	Full band plays a chord
6	0' 16"	**First Chorus** (a 12-bar blues played slowly)

Melody Played by Armstrong on Trumpet

Notice Armstrong's firm, deliberate manner and quick vibrato.

Accompaniment includes:

soft, sustained trombone notes (often preceded by a smear of pitch that begins well below the ultimate note);

sustained tones of clarinet, sometimes paralleling the motion of the trumpet line (listen for the clarinet's edgy timbre and fast vibrato);

trombone and clarinet notes together indicating the chords changing underneath the trumpet;

piano chords sounded in unison along with banjo chords played staccato on each beat ("chomp chomp chomp chomp...")

7	0' 50"	**Second Chorus**

Trombone Solo

The trombonist uses the high register and many smears of pitch.

CD Track	Elapsed Time	

Accompaniment includes:

staccato chording from banjo;

tremolo chords from piano;

slow ride rhythm played by drummer on a hand-held "Bock-a-da-Bock" apparatus that brings together two cymbals that are each about three inches wide, played by drummer cupping the apparatus in his hand as in playing spoons.

8   1' 25"

Third Chorus

Improvised Duet Between Clarinet and Armstrong's Vocal

This chorus employs a call-and-response format, with the vocal supplying the responses. It is an early example of "scat" singing. Piano and banjo are chording in a staccato manner on each beat. The duet's last phrase is done in harmony. No percussion instruments are used here or in the next chorus.

9   2' 00"

Fourth Chorus

Unaccompanied Piano Improvisation by Earl Hines

First Four Measures

Pianist's left hand is contributing legato chording in stride style while right hand improvises flowery figures.

2' 10"

Second Four Measures

Style of playing by right hand switches to brash character and pounds out a double-time figure voiced in octaves. This is the famous "trumpet-style" piano playing of Earl Hines.

2' 20"

Third Four Measures

Style returns to flowery character.

10   2' 32"

Fifth Chorus

Trumpet Solo

First Four Measures

Sustained high note from trumpet for 16 beats. Accompaniment includes staccato chords from piano on each beat, and sustained trombone notes, and sustained clarinet notes.

2' 45"

Second Four Measures

Trumpet line features double-timing.

2' 55"

Third Four Measures

Horns stop playing for 12 beats while piano plays a descending sequence of chords, striking each in bell-like fashion, linking them with a glissando. Piano sustains a chord. Armstrong returns with a long, drawn-out bluesy figure played in a markedly slowed pace. It is accompanied by long tones harmonized by trombone, clarinet, and piano to form three different chords that conclude the piece.

Louis Armstrong, the most widely imitated trumpeter in the first twenty years of jazz. His improvised ideas were so well formed and swinging that he influenced pianists, saxophonists, and trombonists, not just trumpeters. Pictured here in 1927, near the time he made his most stirring recordings.

Photo courtesy of Frank Driggs

LOUIS ARMSTRONG

Trumpeter Louis Armstrong (1901–1971) is often called the "father of jazz." In fact, musicians often refer to him as "Pops." No list of jazz greats omits him, and most start with him. Born in New Orleans, he left in 1922 to join Joe Oliver's New Orleans style band in Chicago. The band's best known piece, "Dippermouth Blues," takes its title from another Armstrong nickname, a reference to his mouth being as large as a dipper. A third nickname, Satchmo, is a variation on the same idea: Satchel Mouth.

Armstrong's earliest appearances on record are in collective improvisations, with everyone playing together. But his most significant recordings were made in 1927 and 1928 with him presenting a dramatic solo style. The music that he played in those recordings became a model for the swing era that followed.

Louis Armstrong appeared in about fifty movies and sang in most of his post-1930 performances. During 1964, his vocal on "Hello, Dolly" was #1 for one week on the popularity charts. This put him ahead of the phenomenally popular Beatles. With the success of the 1988 revival of his "What a Wonderful World" (in the movie *Good Morning Vietnam*), Armstrong chalked up the longest career on the national singles charts, even outdistancing singers Bing Crosby and Frank Sinatra. Understandably then, the post-1930s public knows Armstrong more as an entertainer than as an innovative jazz improviser. Even though they have heard his name, most people are not aware of Armstrong's monumental contributions to the history of jazz.

Armstrong was the most widely imitated jazz improviser prior to the appearance of modern saxophonist Charlie Parker in the 1940s. Armstrong's style is especially easy to detect in the most prominent trumpeters of the 1930s and 40s. His influence extended not only to trumpeters, but to saxophonists, pianists, guitarists, and trombonists, too. Swing era players almost always cite Armstrong's influence. Moreover, pieces of his tunes and improvisations continued to be found in the work of post-swing era innovators

Let's examine a few aspects of Armstrong's work that musicians appreciated so much:

1. Armstrong showed that the New Orleans technique of collective simultaneous improvisation was not the only approach to jazz horn work. Intelligently developed solos could be effectively improvised apart from the lines of other band members. In other words, **Armstrong was one of the first great soloists in jazz history**. Partly because of him, post-Armstrong styles usually stressed solo improvisation instead of group improvisation.

2. Armstrong was one of the first jazz musicians to refine a rhythmic conception that
   a. abandoned the stiffness of ragtime
   b. employed swing eighth-note patterns
   c. gracefully syncopated selected rhythmic figures. Sometimes he staggered the placement of an entire phrase, as though he were playing behind the beat. This projected a more relaxed feeling than ragtime and exhibited more variety in the ways that notes seemed to tug at opposite sides of the beat.

   These rhythmic elements combined to produce one of the first jazz styles with what is today called "jazz swing feeling."

3. Despite the excellent players who came after Armstrong, few equal him as musical architects. Few had his degree of control over the overall form of a solo. He calmly forged

sensible lines that had both the flow of spontaneity and the stamp of finality. His improvisations are well-paced, economical statements. The organization of Armstrong's phrases suggests that he was thinking ahead, yet the phrases manage to sound spontaneous, rather than calculated.

4. He brought a superb sense of drama to jazz solo conception. His pacing was careful, allowing a solo to build tension. His double-time solo breaks were constructed to achieve maximum excitement. His high-note endings ensured a properly timed peak of intensity and resolution of tension.

5. At that time most improvisers were satisfied simply to embellish or paraphrase a tune's melody. Armstrong himself was a master at both, but he did much more. He frequently broke away from the melody, and improvised original, melody-like lines that were compatible with the tune's chord progressions. This became the main approach for improvisation in the next fifty years of jazz history.

6. Armstrong's command of the trumpet was possibly greater than that of any jazz trumpeter before him. It became a model to which others aspired. He had an enormous, brassy tone, and remarkable range. Altogether with his rhythmic and dramatic sense, he conveyed a certainty and surging power. Even during the final decades of his career, Armstrong maintained a tone quality that was unusual for its weight, breadth, and richness.

7. Armstrong popularized the musical vocabulary of New Orleans trumpet style and then extended it.

8. Armstrong's tremendously fertile melodic imagination provided jazz with a repertory of phrases and ways of going about constructing improvisations. In other words, he extended the vocabulary for the jazz soloist.

These next two contributions are less central to his reputation among jazz musicians, but they remain significant in the broadest sense of jazz history.

9. The Armstrong singing style influenced many popular singers, including Louis Prima, Billie Holiday, and Bing Crosby. In this way, he affected American music beyond the boundaries of jazz. Armstrong's influence was so pervasive that Leslie Gourse titled a book about American jazz singers *Louis' Children.*

10. Armstrong popularized scat singing, a vocal technique in which lyrics are not used. (*Classics CD* Track 8) The voice improvises in the manner of a jazz trumpeter or saxophonist. Recent examples of the technique can be found in the work of George Benson, Al Jarreau, and Bobby McFerrin.

BIX BEIDERBECKE

Bix Beiderbecke (1903–1931) was the most influential trumpeter of the 1920s, aside from Louis Armstrong. Even in the 1990s, jazz musicians were still studying his recordings. Beiderbecke offered listeners an approach that contrasted with Armstrong's. Whereas Armstrong was usually hot, Beiderbecke was usually cool. Whereas Armstrong liked to play loudly and feature high notes, Beiderbecke often played in a more subdued manner. Like Armstrong, Beiderbecke put solos together quite intelligently. But, unlike Armstrong, he played their rhythms with considerable restraint.

Beiderbecke was particularly interested in stringing together unusual note choices. He is widely admired for the modern tendencies in his improvisations. Similarly, he is known for rich harmonies in his compositions. Like the French composers Claude Debussy and Maurice Ravel, whom he favored, Beiderbecke composed piano pieces that combined twentieth-century harmonies with ragtime rhythms. His "In a Mist" is one example, and it was recorded in 1927 with Beiderbecke himself playing piano.

Bix Beiderbecke, the first "cool jazz" musician.

Photo courtesy of Frank Driggs

LISTENING GUIDE

"Sobbin' Hearted Blues" featuring Bessie Smith and Louis Armstrong

Composed by Perry Bradford; recorded January 14, 1925 by singer Bessie Smith, trumpeter Louis Armstrong, and pianist Fred Longshaw.

Vocal blues has always been important in some segments of jazz. Even during the 1990s a vocalist singing a blues was common in concerts of jazz bands. Vocal blues belonged to a stream of styles that were somewhat separate from ragtime-derived styles. Much popular music, especially rock and roll, drew upon traditions in vocal blues from the 1920s. Vocal blues were also significant because many hornmen imitated the ornaments of pitch and tone quality that were used by singers. Hornmen often decorated their melody lines in the manner of blues singers.

Listening to "Sobbin' Hearted Blues" we have a double advantage because we hear the most famous blues singer—Bessie Smith, and the most famous early jazz hornman—Louis Armstrong. Smith had enormous talent and influenced generations of singers, both inside and outside the field of jazz. Known as "The Empress of the Blues," Smith's voice was so powerful that she could be heard over the sound of a band, even without using a microphone. Her songs were quite simple, and most were similar. But her impact did not depend upon anything fancy. It relied on soulful emotions that appealed to millions of listeners. The lyrics she chose were often about disappointment and sorrow in love affairs. Most people could easily identify with these topics. Smith usually surrounded herself with first-rate jazz improvisers. We can hear them play fill-ins and countermelodies while she is singing. We can also hear improvised solos when Smith gives her jazz accompanists some space of their own. Though trumpeter Louis Armstrong went on to make hundreds of great instrumentals by himself, he also contributed memorable lines to Smith's recordings.

Elapsed Time

0' 00"   **Introduction** (16 beats using the final four measures of the 12-bar blues)
Armstrong uses his huge tone and melodic gifts to fashion an introduction. He is accompanied by piano.

0' 14"   **Improvised Introduction** (16 beats)
Armstrong plays and paraphrases the beginning of the piece.

0' 27"   **Verse** (32 beats)
Smith sings a portion of the piece that precedes the blues choruses. Armstrong improvises lines that fill the silences between her phrases.

0' 57"   **First Chorus** (12 groups of 4 slow beats)
Vocal is accompanied with piano and Armstrong's fills.

1' 35"   **Second Chorus** (12 groups of 4 slow beats)
Vocal is accompanied by fills that are improvised at the same time by piano and Armstrong.

Elapsed Time	
2' 15"	**Third Chorus** (12 groups of 4 slow beats)
2' 54"	**Ending**
	unaccompanied break by Armstrong
2' 58"	Armstrong is joined by piano tremolo of the finishing chord.

Bessie Smith,
Empress of the Blues.

Photo courtesy of Frank Driggs

POPULARITY OF EARLY JAZZ

The earliest jazz had a wide appeal, especially to young audiences and particularly to social dancers. This roughly parallels the kind of popularity that rock music had during the 1950s and 60s. But it contrasts dramatically with public response to modern jazz of later eras. Whereas modern jazz recordings rarely penetrated the hit parade, the Original Dixieland Jazz Band had several records that stayed near the top of the popularity charts. Early jazz giants such as Louis Armstrong and Jelly Roll Morton were known to a wide public.

New Orleans and Chicago styles did not just live and die with the 1920s. The music has persisted. For instance, there was a revival of interest in New Orleans combo jazz during the 1940s, and several players who had left music returned to careers in performing. The music at New Orleans' Preservation Hall, since 1962, has been so popular that they have always had to have several bands on hand. That way some could be on tour and at least one could be in residence. For many years it has been common to find a few good Dixieland bands in every major U.S. city. In addition, many regions of America sport yearly festivals of traditional jazz.

Louis Armstrong often sang during his band's performances. His vibrant personality and irrepressible humor were conveyed in every note. This warm-hearted manner endeared him to millions of listeners.

Photo by Bob Parent, courtesy of Don Parent

CHAPTER SUMMARY

1. The first forms of jazz resulted from blending improvisational approaches to ragtime, blues, spirituals, marches, and popular tunes.

2. The first jazz bands used the instruments of brass bands: trumpet, clarinet, trombone, tuba, drums, and saxophone.

3. The earliest jazz was not recorded. We can only infer how it sounded on the basis of recordings made by New Orleans players after they had moved to Chicago.

4. The first jazz group to record was the Original Dixieland Jazz Band in 1917.

5. Chicago was the jazz center of the world during the 1920s.

6. The earliest significant New Orleans pianist-composer was Jelly Roll Morton.

7. James P. Johnson was considered the "father" of stride piano.

8. Fats Waller was one of the most popular jazz musicians of the 1920s and 30s, as well as a prolific composer.

9. Waller brought a lightness and springy quality to stride style.

10. Earl Hines devised the "trumpet-style" of piano playing in which phrases are more "horn-like" than pianistic.

11. Louis Armstrong was one of the first combo players effectively to demonstrate solo improvisation instead of retaining the New Orleans tradition of collective improvisation.

12. Louis Armstrong possessed a larger tone, wider range, and better command of the trumpet than most early players. His solo improvisations were especially well constructed.

13. Bix Beiderbecke was one of the first "cool style" jazz improvisers.

EARLY JAZZ LISTENING

Numerous pieces by Louis Armstrong, Bix Beiderbecke, Earl Hines, James P. Johnson, Jelly Roll Morton, Fats Waller, and other early jazz musicians are in the *Smithsonian Collection of Classic Jazz* (RJ 0010, 5CDs) and *Riverside Collection of Classic Jazz* (Riverside/Fantasy 3RB 005-2, 3CDs).

SUPPLEMENTARY READING

Jazz Masters of New Orleans by Martin Williams (Macmillan, 1970; Da Capo, 1978)

Hear Me Talkin' to Ya by Nat Shapiro and Nat Hentoff (Rinehart, 1955; reprinted by Dover)

Really the Blues by Mezz Mezzrow (Random House, 1946; Anchor, 1972; Citadel, 1990)

Early Jazz by Gunther Schuller (Oxford, 1968)

The Essential Jazz Records, Vol. 1: Ragtime to Swing by Max Harrison, Charles Fox, and Eric Thacker (Mansell, 1984; Da Capo, 1988)

Mister Jelly Lord (Jelly Roll Morton biography) by Alan Lomax (University of California Press, 1973)

The World of Earl Hines by Stanley Dance (Scribner, 1975; Da Capo, 1983)

Jazz Masters of the Twenties by Richard Hadlock (Macmillan, 1965; DaCapo, 1986)

James P. Johnson: A Case of Mistaken Identity by Scott E. Brown and Robert Hilbert (Scarecrow, 1986)

Louis (Armstrong biography) by Max Jones and John Chilton (Little, Brown, 1971; Da Capo, 1988)

Satchmo: My Life in New Orleans by Louis Armstrong (Prentice-Hall, 1954; Da Capo, 1986)

Original Dixieland Jazz Band playing into acoustic recording horns. This was the method for making records before the advent of electric microphones.

Photo courtesy of William Ransom Hogan Jazz Archive, Tulane University

CHAPTER 5

SWING

Duke Ellington band of 1942   Courtesy of Frank Driggs

A looser, less stiff rhythmic feeling developed in jazz during the 1920s, causing jazz to swing more. This was a gradual change which continued into the 1940s. Most jazz from the mid-1930s to the mid-1940s is called swing music. Since much of it was played by bands of ten or more musicians, it is also called music of the "big band era." **Swing was the most popular style in jazz history**, and it attracted millions of dancers. Several of the big dance bands were very important in jazz because of their soloists and the ways the bands combined written with improvised parts. Before we examine those particulars, let's look at a few ways that swing differs from early jazz:

1. The preferred instrumentation for swing was **big band** rather than combo. This made for greater reliance on written arrangements during the swing era.
2. **Saxophones** were more common in swing.
3. **Bass viol** appeared more often in swing. (*Demo CD* Track 22)
4. **High-hat** cymbals were used more. (*Demo CD* Track 2)
5. Collective improvisation was rare in swing.
6. Overall **rhythmic feeling was smoother.**
7. Swing musicians usually showed a **higher level of instrumental proficiency** in terms of speed, agility, tone control, and playing in tune.

Big bands were made up of ten or more musicians whose instruments fall into three categories: brass, saxophones, and rhythm section. The brass section included trumpets and trombones. Although saxophones are also made of brass, they are technically called woodwinds because they originated from instruments traditionally made of wood (clarinet, flute, and oboe). They are also played in the manner of traditional wooden instruments. Because most saxophonists also play clarinet, and both sax and clarinet have cane reeds attached to their mouthpieces, the sax section was often called the "reed section." This label was retained in later decades, even when saxophonists began adding flute, a non-reed instrument.

(Listen to *Demo CD* Tracks 69–75.)

Alto (on left), tenor (on right), and baritone saxophone (lying down).

The alto and tenor saxophones were the most frequently used saxes. By the late 1930s, most bands had also adopted the baritone saxophone. The sax section contained from three to five musicians. Saxophonists did not usually play one instrument to the exclusion of the others. Some musicians, for instance, were required to alternate from clarinet to alto and baritone saxophones. Eventually a section of two altos, two tenors, and a baritone became standard.

The size of the trumpet section varied from two to five musicians. Most had three during the late 1930s and early 40s. The lead trumpeter usually sat in the middle. The trombone section ranged from one to five musicians, two or three being standard. The lead trombonist was in the center. (Listen to *Demo CD* Tracks 59 and 76.)

With the growth of big bands came an increase in the use of written arrangements. These had not been as necessary with small combos. As bands became bigger, it was more difficult to improvise a respectable performance, though some big bands did succeed in playing without written arrangements. Eventually, however, musicians had to learn to read and write arrangements to have a big enough repertory on hand. A newcomer had much less difficulty learning the music if a band worked from written arrangements rather than memorized routines.

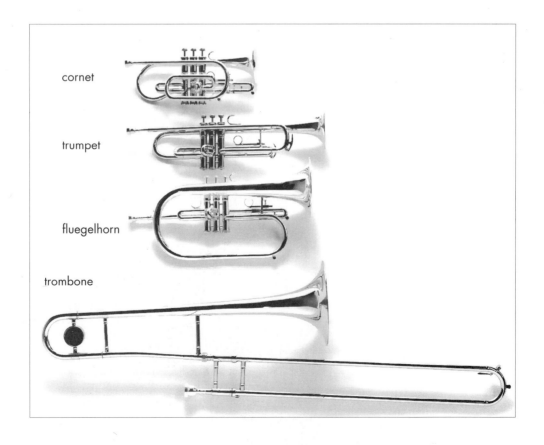

cornet

trumpet

fluegelhorn

trombone

The compositional devices employed in most of the arrangements were simple. Melodies were played by the entire band in unison or in harmony. Then jazz improvisation followed, accompanied both by the rhythm section and by figures scored for other members of the group. These figures were usually short, simple phrases called *riffs*. The melodies and accompanying figures were taken up in turn by one section of the band and then another. Saxes might state the "A" section, brass state the bridge, and so forth. Besides pop tune melodies, arrangements often contained variations on those themes. Some of those variations were actually as good as improvised solos. These were offered as passages for one section of the band to play while another accompanied them or remained silent. Sometimes, portions within the passages were passed back and forth. This sounded as though one section of the band posed a question and another section answered it. This technique is called call and response style.

Jimmy Blanton, Duke Ellington's bassist from 1939 to 1941. Not only was Blanton a superbly swinging timekeeper, but he was also a soloist Ellington used in the manner of a horn. This was revolutionary for its time, and Blanton was idolized by bassists for many years thereafter.

Photo courtesy of Frank Driggs

SWING RHYTHM SECTIONS

The rhythm section ordinarily contained piano, guitar, bass, and drums. **Rhythm guitar** (*Demo CD* Track 88) disappeared from most big bands during the late 40s. Although the banjo had been present in early-style bands, it dropped out of sight during the 1930s. Tuba had preceded string bass in some bands, but had been abandoned by the mid-1930s. Before the guitar and string bass became firmly established, guitarists often alternated on guitar and banjo, and bassists alternately played both tuba (brass bass) and string bass (bass viol).

The **pianist** in the rhythm section occasionally played melody instead of just chords and embellishments. Comping was not the common accompaniment style during the swing era, though Count Basie did use it. (*Demo CD* Track 20) Pianists of the swing era used stride style or played a chord on every beat or every other beat.

Guitar and bass were usually assigned timekeeping duties. The guitarist strummed one chord on each beat. This was known as *rhythm guitar style*. The **bassist** generally played a note on the first and third of every four beats, *two-beat style*, or on every beat, *walking style*. Bassists during the swing era remained in the background.

Most big band drummers during this period limited themselves to making the beat obvious for dancers and lending swing feeling to the band. It was a matter of simple timekeeping with occasional dramatic effects. Swing drummers tended not to play new or provocative rhythms that ran counter to the horn lines. This came with modern jazz during the 1940s, when drummers began offering a parallel line of activity instead of just keeping time.

Sonny Greer, Duke Ellington's drummer from 1919 to 1951. This photo shows some of the instruments used by swing era drummers. We can see only the top of the bass drum in the bottom center of our picture, but an assortment of attached instruments are clear: two cowbells and a woodblock mounted close to its rim, large tom-toms mounted to tilt toward Greer, four cymbals on stands. Greer is using wire brushes to strike his cymbals.

Photo by William P. Gottlieb

Roy Eldridge, the most daring trumpeter of the 1930s. Eldridge frequently improvised in the manner of a saxophonist by using long, swooping, scale-like lines. He also liked to dart into the highest register of his instrument and make his sound explode like fireworks. His style formed the beginning for Dizzy Gillespie's new bebop style.

Photo courtesy of Frank Driggs

ROY ELDRIDGE

Trumpeter Roy Eldridge (1911–1989) was one of the most advanced improvisers of the swing era. He is often considered a link between swing and modern jazz. Eldridge had a fiery, aggressive style and unprecedented mastery over the trumpet. His imaginative choice of notes and sax-like lines bridged the gap between the style of Louis Armstrong and the modern approach pioneered by Dizzy Gillespie. Eldridge also creatively varied the size, texture, and vibrato of his tone. Sometimes it was clear and warm, at other times brittle and edgy. His high-register playing had a sweeping scope. In that register, he gave his entrances a rhythmic feeling which suggested modern jazz inflections to come.

Roy Eldridge demonstrated that long, sinewy lines were possible on trumpet. These, though easy to execute on saxophone, do not lend themselves to the mechanics of the trumpet. Eldridge influenced modern trumpeters to cultivate greater instrumental facility and to improvise in more intricate and unpredictable ways than their early jazz counterparts. Eldridge's influence extended into the 1950s because Dizzy Gillespie built his own influential modern style upon the foundation of Eldridge's bristling high-register work, unorthodox choice of notes, and saxophone style of phrasing.

COLEMAN HAWKINS

The man generally considered to be the first important jazz tenor saxophonist is Coleman Hawkins (1904–1969). Prior to his arrival on the jazz scene in the 1920s, the saxophone was considered little more than a novelty. Hawkins' supercharged playing on it brought recognition to the horn. His command of the instrument and his deep, husky tone became a model for other saxophonists. As a result, tenor sax became one of the most popular instruments in jazz. (*Demo CD* Track 73) In fact, it symbolizes jazz for many people. Hawkins also demonstrated more interest in chord progressions than most other premodern saxophonists. He loved to play over complex chord progressions, such as those in his famous rendition of "Body and Soul." (*Jazz Classics CD* Track 24) He was less interested in devising new melodies than in investigating the chord progressions that could be added to a tune's original accompaniment. Because of his attitude, some listeners consider Hawkins primarily a harmonic improviser rather than a melodic improviser.

Coleman Hawkins, father of jazz tenor saxophone.

Photo courtesy of Duncan Schiedt

The 1938 Count Basie band, with the most swinging rhythm section in jazz: Basie (piano), Freddie Green (guitar), Walter Page (bass), and Jo Jones (drums). Trumpeter Buck Clayton is standing (with a cup mute in his horn). Tenor saxophonist Lester Young (far right) is resting. This photo was shot at a New York City night club called the Famous Door.

Photo courtesy of Frank Driggs

COUNT BASIE

Musicians generally agree that the most swinging big band was that of Count Basie (1904–1984). When compared with all others from the swing era, Basie's never seemed out of breath nor the least bit frantic, and it always seemed to swing more. Basie led a big band almost continuously from 1937 until his death. Every edition of the band had at least two players who made important contributions to jazz history. Some editions had four or five.

Basie was originally a stride-style pianist. Basie's touch was unique among jazz pianists. It was very light and extremely precise. His choice of notes was near perfect. His impeccable sense of timing was equivalent to a good drummer's. In fact, Basie originally began his musical career as a drummer, not a pianist. Succinct and compact statements are hallmarks of Basie's style. When he soloed, he artfully used silence to pace his lines.

Basie led the first rhythm section in jazz history that consistently swung in a smooth, relaxed way. That famous rhythm section consisted of Basie himself (piano), Freddie Green (rhythm guitar), Walter Page (string bass), and Jo Jones (drums). Among the special **qualities of the Basie rhythm section** were:

1. An excellent sense of tempo.
2. The ability to keep time and swing consistently without using a hard-driving, pressured approach.

3. Quiet, relaxed playing, which conveyed a feeling of ease.

4. Placing a fairly even amount of stress on each beat instead of on every other beat.

5. Emphasis on buoyancy rather than intensity.

Bassist **Walter Page** (1900–1957) contributed:

1. A supple walking bass sound. In fact he is considered to be one of the first masters of the walking style.

2. A strong, articulated sound with life in it.

3. Playing all beats evenly. (*Demo CD* Track 23)

4. Balancing his sound to mesh smoothly with piano, bass, and guitar.

Guitarist **Freddie Green** (1911–1987) was noted for:

1. His crisp strokes on unamplified guitar that sounded his rhythm chords with unerring steadiness and propulsive swing feeling. (*Demo CD* Track 88)

2. His close coordination with bass and drums.

Drummer **Jo Jones** (1911–1985) was distinguished for:

1. A loose, assured manner that was precise without being stiff.

2. Quieter bass drum playing than was common in the swing era. Jones sometimes omitted bass drum entirely, sometimes using it only for off-beat accents. (*Demo CD* Track 1)

3. Quiet use of wire brushes on high-hat. (*Demo CD* Track 2)

4. Ride rhythms played on high-hat continuously as the apparatus was opening and closing. Jones let his cymbals ring prominently between strokes, thereby creating a sustained sound that smoothed the timekeeping pattern instead of leaving each stroke as an abrupt sound.

The Basie rhythm section was well balanced among the sounds of each member. The four parts were so smoothly integrated that one listener was inspired to compare the effect to riding on ball bearings. If you listen carefully to recordings of the band, you will notice that it is unusual for one member to stick out. Guitar, bass, and drums are all carefully controlled to avoid disturbing the evenness and balance of sound.

In Basie's interjections, jazz piano had the bounce, syncopation, and flexibility of what became known as comping. This is playing accompanying chords as accents behind the soloist. (*Demo CD* Track 20) It requires the pianist to listen carefully and play interactively. Though he did not invent it, Basie is so thoroughly associated with comping that he might as well have. His comping was very sharp and lively. Basie comped so well and with such relaxed swing feeling that he provided the most-used model for it. (*Jazz Classics CD* Track 13) To appreciate how far ahead of its time Basie's comping was, consider this. Though Basie had been doing it for over ten years, many other pianists of the 1940s continued in the predominant styles of the 1920s and 30s, accompanying by (1) stride style (*Demo CD* Track 38), (2) playing a chord on each beat in the manner of a rhythm guitarist (*Demo CD* Track 88), or (3) playing flowery countermelodies and embellishments. But by the end of the 1940s, the other pianists had caught on, and comping had become central to modern jazz.

Kansas City Style

During the 1920s and 30s there was a thriving jazz scene in Kansas City, Missouri. A number of historically significant jazz musicians worked there and are associated with "Kansas City style jazz," though few were born there. Count Basie (from New Jersey) and Lester Young (from Louisiana) were the most famous. Their music was not as glossy or elaborate as that of their New York counterparts; it was lighter, more relaxed, and exceptionally swinging.

Kansas City style was not based on the interweaving lines of the collectively improvised New Orleans style. Arrangements were based instead on short musical phrases called **riffs** that are repeated again and again. Riffs serve two functions. Sometimes they are (1) theme statements, and sometimes they are (2) backgrounds for improvised solos. Some of these riffs were written down and became the basis for tunes. Many, though, were created spontaneously during a performance ("off the top of someone's head"), learned by ear, and kept in the heads of the players. Arrangements of this kind are called **head arrangements**, and they are basic to the Kansas City *riff band style*. For example, "Taxi War Dance" has no theme. It consists solely of riffs and improvisations over the chord progression accompaniment of "Willow Weep for Me." (See below.)

LISTENING GUIDE

Count Basie's "Taxi War Dance"

Introduction

CD Track	Elapsed Time	
12	0' 00"	*Four Measures*
		Basie's boogie-woogie left-hand figure with no bass, rhythm guitar, or drums accompaniment.
		Four Measures
		Trumpets punctuate in unison with piano as a set-up for the piece, all the while trombones are "walking" underneath them, and Jo Jones has begun playing ride rhythms.
13	0' 09"	**First Chorus (based on the chord progression of "Willow Weep for Me")**
		A Tenor saxophonist Lester Young opens his improvisation by quoting the first line of "Ol' Man River." Listen to Freddie Green playing rhythm

CD Track	Elapsed Time	
		guitar, Walter Page playing walking bass lines, and Jo Jones playing ride rhythms on opening and closing high-hat. Basie stops his boogie-woogie figures and moves to comping.
	0' 18"	**A** In first four bars Basie returns to his boogie-woogie piano figures under Young's solo. After that, Basie goes to comping. Note how Young's lines relate to these changes in accompaniment patterns.
	0' 27"	**B** Continuation of Young with rhythm section accompaniment.
	0' 37"	**A** Continuation (This is a good example of Basie's big band functioning as a combo, something for which they were particularly distinguished.)
14	0' 45"	**Two Measure Introduction to the Next Chorus**
		A return to the brass figure that originally opened the piece. Basie's boogie-woogie piano figure is also included. The walking trombones are missing, however.
	0' 47"	**Second Chorus** (A-A-B-A)
		A Trombonist Dicky Wells improvises a solo. He is very melodic and sounds like he is poking fun. Pay attention to how he bases his solo on simple phrases to be developed by repetitions and slight alterations. Note how clear and logical his lines are.
	0' 57"	**A** Solo continues with rhythm section accompaniment, again returning to a small combo performance.
	1' 05"	**B** Continuation.
	1' 14"	**A** Continuation.
15	1' 23"	**Third Chorus** (A-A-B-A)
		A *First Four Measures*
		Band returns, Basie abandons comping for patterned figures. Trombones call and trumpets respond.
	1' 27"	*Second Four Measures*
		Tenor saxophonist Buddy Tate begins a solo improvisation. He can be distinguished from Lester Young by having a coarser tone that is darker and has faster vibrato. Tate's execution is less poised and has less swinging rhythmic feeling.
	1' 32"	**A** Repeat of layout for first A-section.
	1' 41"	**B** Piano solo by Basie. Notice his light touch, use of the piano's upper register, and impeccable timing.
	1' 50"	**A** *First Four Measures*
		Trombones call and trumpets respond.
	1' 55"	*Second Four Measures*
		Tate solos with a rapid pattern repeated.
16	1' 59"	**Fourth Chorus** (A-A-B-A)
		A *First Four Measures*
		Basie plays a boogie-woogie figure underneath ensemble figures by trumpets and trombones.
17	2' 04"	*Second Four Measures*
		Tenor saxophonist Lester Young returns with a light feeling. He plays a solo in his instrument's upper register.

CD Track	Elapsed Time	
	2' 09"	**A** *First Four Measures*
		Repeat of the pattern used in the first A-section, but this time Young enters his solo space early by using a bit of the four-measure lead-in to get started.
	2' 13"	*Second Four Measures*
		Young completes his solo, remaining with upper–register tones.
	2' 17"	**B** Basie solos in the upper register, playing lightly and staccato.
	2' 27"	**A** *First Four Measures*
		Trombones call, and the trumpets respond with a simple, syncopated figure which uses alternation of muted and unmuted sound in rapid succession.
	2' 31"	*Second Four Measures*
		Lester Young improvises by rapidly alternating his tone quality.
18	2' 36"	**Ending**
		Two Measures
		Stop-time solo break for Count Basie.
	2' 38"	*Two Measures*
		Stop-time solo break for Lester Young (this is called "trading two's").
	2' 40"	*Two Measures*
		Walking bass unaccompanied.
	2' 42"	*Two Measures*
		Sticks on drums unaccompanied.
	2' 44"	*Two Measures*
		Brass play a tie-it-up figure, and Jo Jones strikes a cymbal and grabs it abruptly to prevent it from ringing. This technique effectively closes up the sounds and provides a dramatic means for ending a performance.

LESTER YOUNG

Many of the best jazz trumpeters and saxophonists of the 1930s and 40s played with Count Basie at one time or another. Basie's most notable soloist during this period was tenor saxophonist Lester Young (1909–1959). This musician was so good that he was nicknamed "Pres" (or "Prez"), short for president of tenor saxophone players. His style served as a model for modern jazz saxophonists, and an entire subcategory of modern jazz that was called "cool jazz." Even trumpeters and guitarists were inspired by the way Young improvised. He became one of the five most influential saxophonists in jazz history.

Young played lines which were fresher and more smoothly swinging than those of any previous improvisers. He paved the way for modern saxophone tone color, vibrato, rhythmic conception, and

Lester Young (Pres), the swing era tenor saxophonist who offered a model for the beginnings of modern jazz "bebop" and "cool" styles. The most melodic of all improvisers, Young generated lines that floated above the band with remarkable grace and a lilting swing feeling never heard before him. Shown here in 1941 at a New York night club called Kelly's Stables.

Photo courtesy of Frank Driggs

phrasing. **Young offered a clear alternative to the heavy tone, fast vibrato, and complicated style of Coleman Hawkins**. Young's light tone, slow vibrato, and loping, buoyant phrases became the model for an entire generation of saxophonists, who often copied his solos note for note.

To explore Lester Young's improvisatory style, let's compare it with Coleman Hawkins'. Often, where Hawkins seemed to be chugging, Young seemed to be floating. Hawkins made improvisation sound like hard work. Young made it seem easy, like talking. Whereas Hawkins accented hard and often directly on main beats, Young was more subtle. Furthermore, Young tended to accent off-beats and lightly stress portions of beats that made his lines swing with ease. Young's playing was not as intricate as Hawkins', but his melodic ideas were certainly as advanced. He just made it sound easier.

Young concerned himself with only a core of melodic material. He didn't incorporate afterthoughts into his phrases, as Hawkins was prone to do. He practiced deliberate restraint. He could pace a solo so well that it seemed an integral part of the written arrangement. His gift for inventing new, easily singable melodies while he improvised is unsurpassed in jazz history. He often improvised long lines which had a fresh, expansive feeling. There is an overriding sense of continuity in Young's improvisations that is very satisfying. Young possessed a musical storytelling talent which surfaced in nearly every improvisation. (*Jazz Classics CD* Tracks 13 and 20)

Billie Holiday, the most influential singer in jazz after the early 1930s.

Photo courtesy of Frank Driggs

BILLIE HOLIDAY

Billie Holiday (1915-1959) is the most influential singer associated with jazz since the early 1930s. Many vocalists began their careers imitating her. Some devoted albums to tunes they first heard Holiday sing. Nicknamed "Lady Day," she is also the singer most frequently cited by jazz musicians when asked what music they would take to a desert island. This is quite an endorsement because most jazz musicians prefer instrumental music and rarely name a vocal recording among their favorites.

Holiday did not possess the power of Bessie Smith, the deep, rich voice of Sarah Vaughan, or the speed and range of Ella Fitzgerald. Yet why is she so revered? First, she was original and fresh. Second, the depth and sincerity of emotion that she communicated are unparalleled. She made lyrics come alive. Holiday conveyed the song's meaning as though speaking directly to you. The agony she portrayed in sad songs could tear your heart out. Her renditions of "Gloomy Sunday," "Strange Fruit," and a tune she herself co-authored, "God Bless the Child," had intense effects on listeners. On the other hand, some of her late 1930s recordings convey a carefree spirit of joy unmatched by her contemporaries. No matter the mood, her tender, knowing delivery grabbed you right away. (Listen to her "She's Funny That Way" in SCCJ and her "Back in Your Own Back Yard" in the *Jazz Classics CD*.)

A third reason for Holiday's stature is jazz flavor. Though she was not really a blues singer—her repertory was mostly pop and show tunes—Holiday often formed her tones as a jazz hornman, with a whine that had blues flavor. Like jazz instrumentalists, she did not always give songs a straight reading, even though she had excellent diction. Instead, she varied her delivery creatively. One of the ways Holiday transformed songs was by manipulating their rhythms. Her method of intentionally delaying the arrival of certain words and phrases is almost indistinguishable from rhythmic displacements used by trumpeter Louis Armstrong, one of her main influences. (Listen to her "She's Funny That Way" in SCCJ.) This caused an engaging syncopation and swing feeling. The combination of her bluesy inflections, jazzy accents, and improvising gave jazz flavor to her music

Holiday toured and recorded with many of the top jazz musicians of the time, including Artie Shaw, Benny Goodman, and Count Basie. Her 1937 recording of "Carelessly" reached the #1 position on the popularity charts, and she had thirty-five other recordings reach the top twenty by 1945. She was prolific during the 1940s and 50s as well. Some listeners like her work of the 1930s the most. Others find her late recordings of the 1950s to be even more emotionally compelling. Not only did her life story inspire a popular movie (*Lady Sings the Blues*, 1972), but her recordings continue to sell today, more than forty years after her death.

LISTENING GUIDE

"Back in Your Own Back Yard" featuring Billie Holiday and Lester Young

Composed by Al Jolson; recorded January 12, 1938 by singer Billie Holiday, trumpeter Buck Clayton, tenor saxophonist Lester Young, pianist Teddy Wilson, bassist Walter Page, guitarist Freddie Green, drummer Jo Jones.

Jazz instrumentalists have often made part of their living by accompanying singers. And to satisfy a segment of their audience, the practice of carrying at least one singer was common for leaders of jazz bands as recently as the 1950s. Appearing with singers sometimes produced results that had jazz value, though it was not usually as artistically fulfilling as strictly instrumental music. Many jazz musicians consider it an imposition to have to accompany singers. They do it only to guarantee their livelihood. However, when asking musicians what music they themselves enjoy, one singer's name is often mentioned along with the names of instrumentalists—Billie Holiday.

This particular recording has more jazz in it than vocal features usually have. All the horn solos are outstanding. And if you listen carefully to Holiday's timing, you might even detect the influence of Louis Armstrong's rhythmic style. In other words, you might appreciate Holiday's part as jazz, too. Holiday did not scat sing or improvise in the manner of a jazz saxophonist. But she took liberties with the pitches and tone qualities of the notes in the song. And she took so much liberty with their timing that we might almost call her a jazz improviser. Those liberties were so creative, soulful, and swinging that she was held in high esteem even by musicians. Like Armstrong before her, Holiday in turn exerted considerable influence on other singers. And several of the tunes she recorded became standard repertory for jazz-oriented singers because her renditions were so stunning.

Though best known for solos he recorded with Count Basie, Lester Young is also highly acclaimed for his brief appearances on Billie Holiday records. The same can be said for trumpeter Buck Clayton. Particular recognition has been given to pianist Teddy Wilson, who organized numerous recording sessions for Holiday and played tastefully on all of them. Wilson is also known for work with Benny Goodman, where his grace and swing feeling remain a marvel for other musicians to hear. In this particular recording, Wilson is joined by the Count Basie rhythm section, minus Basie.

CD Track	Elapsed Time	
19	0' 00"	**Introduction** (32 beats)
		Buck Clayton trumpet improvisation, accompanied by piano, guitar, bass, drums, and sustained tones on tenor sax
	0' 12"	**Vocal Chorus** (A-A-B-A)
		Holiday's singing is accompanied by muted trumpet and piano improvising counterlines while guitar, bass, and drums play time keeping rhythms.
	0' 25"	*Second A-Section*
	0' 38"	*Bridge*
	0' 50"	*Final A-Section*

CD Track	Elapsed Time	
20	1' 02"	**Lester Young Tenor Sax Solo Improvisation** (A-A-B-A)
		Young devises a smooth solo line in a very relaxed manner, using notes mostly from the low and the middle registers of his horn.
		Accompaniment includes guitar and faint piano chords played in a simple and steady manner. A prominent accompaniment sound is the opening and closing high-hat played by the drummer.
	1' 14"	*Second A-Section*
	1' 27"	*Bridge*
		Notice the "kicks" and "bombs" from the drums, especially near the beginnings and endings of sections.
	1' 38"	*Final A-Section*
	1' 47"	Cup-muted trumpet and tenor sax play a preset figure together during the final 8 beats of this section.
	1' 50"	**Vocal Chorus** (A-A-B-A)
		Holiday's singing is accompanied by improvised piano countermelodies.
	2' 02"	*Second A-Section*
	2' 15"	*Bridge*
	2' 28"	*Final A-Section*
		Collectively improvised closing with lines coming from sax and unmuted trumpet

Teddy Wilson, the pianist who organized many of Billie Holiday's best recording sessions. The sensitivity, grace, and intelligence of his improvisations were unmatched in the 1930s.

Courtesy of Frank Driggs

Ella Fitzgerald,
the most outstanding
non-operatic singer in
the twentieth century and
a leading popularizer
of scat singing.

Photo courtesy of Frank Driggs

ELLA FITZGERALD

Ella Fitzgerald (1918-1996) is considered by many to be the most outstanding non-operatic singer of the twentieth century. She had near-flawless technique. Listeners were impressed by her grace and lilt. Mastery of swing eighth notes and perfect timing of syncopations gave her singing the rhythmic effect achieved by the best swing era hornmen. Delivered with such bounce and lightness, her phrases actually swung more than those of some modern trumpeters and saxophonists.

First achieving prominence in the mid-1930s, Fitzgerald had a #1 hit in her 1938 rendition of "A-Tisket-A-Tasket" with the Chick Webb Band. With this group she recorded, toured, and, for several years after Webb died, served as leader. By 1955, thirty-four of her other records had risen to popularity positions within the top twenty. Albums of her concert appearances climbed to high positions on the popularity charts during the 1960s and again in the 1980s.

Ella Fitzgerald's tone was pure and supple. Her command spanned the unusually wide range of about three octaves. Singing in tune proves difficult for many singers, but not for Fitzgerald. Her pitch was accurate, no matter the register or tempo of the material. Her articulation was exquisite. A remarkable agility conveyed an effortless feeling. She gave every note a lift. Her overall manner achieved great presence and warmth. Her combination of spirit and ease imparted a bright touch even to ballads, as though she were never really sad. A youthful quality always pervaded her work, even when she was in her seventies. Not inclined to the melodramatic attitude of so many other singers, Fitzgerald's effect is often called "cheerful," "exhuberant," or "ebullient." Many consider her creative peak to be the 1950s and 60s, yet she was still giving remarkable performances during the 1970s and 80s.

Though she did not invent it, Fitzgerald was scat singing's best known practitioner. Among the modern scat singers who followed, almost all cite her work as their first inspiration. Contained within her scat devices were stock phrases from late swing and early bop improvisers. On some recordings she functions as a horn, using nonsense syllables exclusively, no lyrics. Fitzgerald was quite melodic in her scats. This was due in part to (1) basing portions of her passages on set routines rather than completely fresh improvisations in every performance and (2) improvising more around the melody of the original tune than from the chords of its accompaniment.

Despite her scat singing's historic visibility, that work represents only a small fraction of her output. Fitzgerald gets high marks from listeners who like a singer to stick to the melody as written. Some of the greatest pop tune composers were eager to have her perform their songs because her readings were so true to their original intent. So, in addition to her exalted position in jazz, she also had a large following among pop music listeners.

ART TATUM

Art Tatum (1910–1956) is among the most widely admired pianists in jazz history. His music has survived his death by many years. With his impressive technical facility and unceasing energy, he still stands above all the very fast, imaginative pianists who have emerged since him. (*Jazz Classics CD* Track 21)

Tatum's style combines a variety of techniques. He often employed stride-style in his left hand with horn-like lines in his right hand. Tatum's playing was quite flowery, with long, fast runs which sometimes overlapped each other. These runs seemed to throw showers of notes upon the listener. The rhythms in these showers were often odd combinations, not merely strings of eighth notes and sixteenth notes. But despite their complexity, Tatum's runs have been memorized by hundreds of pianists, and they have been used to decorate solos in performances by jazz pianists and popular pianists alike.

He was also a master at spontaneously adding and changing chords during his performance of pop tunes. This is termed chord *substitution.* Generations of jazz pianists have followed him and learned this technique. Sometimes Tatum changed keys several times within a phrase and still managed to resolve the harmonic motion gracefully. Tatum was unpredictable rhythmically, too, and he frequently interrupted the direction of his own lines. He seemed to indulge his impulses and momentarily pursue musical tangents.

Art Tatum's impact on jazz history was enormous. The fast lines and added chords of Tatum were absorbed by saxophonists Don Byas

Art Tatum, the most widely admired piano virtuoso in jazz history.

Photo courtesy of Frank Driggs

and Charlie Parker. Tatum also influenced two pianists who were very important during the early days of modern jazz: Bud Powell and Lennie Tristano. Both Powell and Tristano, in turn, went on to influence numerous pianists of the 1950s, further extending the reach of Tatum's work.

LISTENING GUIDE

"Tiger Rag" featuring Art Tatum

Composed by the Original Dixieland Jazz Band; recorded March 21, 1933 by pianist Art Tatum

This is the first solo record by Tatum to be issued, and it is one of the fastest jazz piano improvisations on record. It goes by at about 370 beats per minute. Tatum was legendary for his dazzling speed. He was also known for changing the mood and direction abruptly in the middle of his improvisations. A third virtue was his changing a piece's harmonies by substituting new chords for old and adding more. This third aspect was particularly inspiring to modern jazz musicians of the 1940s. His performance on "Tiger Rag" demonstrates all those talents, and it shows why Tatum's playing stood as a peak that hundreds of pianists aspired to.

CD Track	Elapsed Time	
21	0' 00"	**Introduction**
		Tatum made up his own opening to the piece, in the style of French composer Claude Debussy. He plays it in a free rhythmic style that does not depend on a steady tempo. Instead it slows and quickens according to its own internal drama.
	0' 14"	**First Theme** (A-A-B-A, each section having 8 groups of 4 beats)
		Tempo begins at about 320 beats per minute. Tatum's left hand is playing bass notes on every other beat. His right hand plays melodic figures that cascade up and down the keyboard.
	0' 24"	*B-section* (two sections, each having 4 groups of 4 beats)
		Tatum's right hand continues to improvise while his left-hand accompaniment pattern switches to short, stabbing chords.
	0' 30"	*A-section* (8 groups of 4 beats)
		Left-hand accompaniment figure returns to bass notes on every other beat.
22	0' 35"	**Second Theme** (4 groups of 4 beats, 4 more groups of 4 beats, 8 groups of 4 beats and another 8 groups of 4 beats)
		This theme is in a new key and a new style. Tatum plays the brief melody in a chordal style, followed by a torrid run that is not accompanied. Then he plays more chords and another unaccompanied run. This is like the stop-time method of a New Orleans jazz band.

CD Track	Elapsed Time	
	0' 39"	The theme continues with chorded melody played by the right hand and the stride-style accompaniment of bass notes alternating with chords played by the left hand.
23	0' 50"	**Third Theme** (32 groups of 4 beats) This new theme is in a new key and a new style. The melody is familiar to some listeners as the part of the song that repeats again and again the phrase "Hold that tiger!" Tatum takes liberties with that melody. Listen for the trill played by his left hand in the bass register of the piano.
	0' 56"	Second half of theme begins.
	1' 00"	Stop-time break in the middle of the theme permits Tatum to showcase his impressive left-hand skill.
	1' 06"	The theme concludes with some of the sounds Tatum used in the end of his introduction.
	1' 11"	**Repeat of the Third Theme** (32 groups of 4 beats) Tatum improvises brilliantly with his right hand while his left hand plays stride-style accompaniment.
	1' 21"	A stop-time break is followed by a slightly different left-hand accompaniment style. Tatum uses his left hand to play a counter-melody while maintaining the stride-style accompaniment pattern at the same time.
	1' 24"	Second half of theme begins.
	1' 30"	As the theme ends, Tatum builds his improvisation to a frenzy. An immense two-handed tremolo leads into the next rendition of the third theme.
	1' 33"	**Another Repeat of the Third Theme** (32 groups of 4 beats) Tatum plays a riff by his right hand sounding chords. His left hand plays energetic walking bass lines. This gives the music a feeling of time units being composed of four pulses instead of two.
	1' 42"	A stop-time break midway through this theme is followed by more improvisation by Tatum's right hand. His left hand continues accompanying in the stride style.
	1' 48"	This theme ends with a three-note riff played seven times.
	1' 53"	**Another Repeat of the Third Theme** (32 groups of four beats) Tatum plays a descending run seven times. Then, over a stop-time break, that run is played an eighth time, but now it is stretched out to last longer.
	2' 04"	Second half of theme begins.
	2' 10"	This theme concludes with the three-note riff that ended the previous time. Tatum plays another descending run, and ends the performance by arriving at a single note on the bottom end of the piano keyboard.

BENNY GOODMAN

During the 1930s and 40s, clarinetist Benny Goodman (1909-1986) led the best-known jazz-oriented big band. His group had a very hard-driving sound and showcased Goodman's swinging and highly agile clarinet playing. His name was so well known, so often on the

Benny Goodman (standing in foreground, playing clarinet), the most popular jazz musician of the swing era. Pictured here leading his big dance band of 1936.

Photo courtesy of Duncan Schiedt

popularity charts, that he ranks above all but five other artists making recordings between 1890 and 1954. This means that Goodman was one of the most popular figures in the music industry as a whole, not just in jazz. Today he ranks with Louis Armstrong and Dave Brubeck as one of the best-known musicians in all of jazz history. In addition to his impact as a clarinetist, he influenced the course of jazz by providing exposure for other outstanding improvisers. His small combos were especially effective for bringing wide recognition to such swing era stand-outs as pianist Teddy Wilson, guitarist Charlie Christian, and vibraharpist Lionel Hampton. (Clarinet is on *Demo CD* Track 69. Vibraharp is on Track 97.)

DUKE ELLINGTON

Duke Ellington (1899–1974) is one of the most outstanding figures in jazz history. His contributions were threefold: he was significant as (1) a bandleader, (2) a pianist, and (3) a composer-arranger. He led one of the first jazz-oriented big bands, beginning in 1923, and only his death in 1974 ended the band's run. **Ellington's group was the most stable and longest-lived big band in jazz history.** Some of the musicians remained for twenty to thirty years at a stretch. His musicians had strong, unique styles of their own. Together they made up an all-star unit. Many of their improvisations were so good that they became permanent parts of the band's pieces, as though composed. Ellington knew their musical personalities so thoroughly that he wrote tunes especially for them. He imaginatively mixed and matched their work with his own. The result was a breadth and depth of repertory that was superior to every other jazz group in history.

Ellington was **the single most creative and prolific composer-arranger in jazz history.** He wrote more than two thousand compositions and many arrangements and rearrangements for them. He

The Duke Ellington Band of the 1930s, the vehicle for its leader's innovative composing and arranging ideas.

Photo courtesy of Cleveland Press Collection/Cleveland State University Archives

began composing and arranging before 1920 and continued productively until his death. Recording more than any other jazz group, the Ellington band and its leader's compositions can be heard in hundreds of 78 r.p.m. recordings and long-play albums.

As a piano soloist, Ellington performed often in the stride style, and he also performed in his own original style, which was still quite percussive though much sparser than the stride style. His playing sparkled and popped with unerring swing feeling. Ellington stood out for his unusual harmonies. He showed the same imagination, but with more restraint, in playing for his orchestra. His sidemen valued his accompanying for its vitality and the complementary way he framed their phrases. His comping was full of spirit, and his timing and taste were near perfect.

Ellington wrote many tunes, often in collaboration with his sidemen. Some of these became popular songs when lyrics were added. A few were hits when recorded by singers apart from the Ellington band. Among his best-known songs are "I'm Beginning to See the Light," "Solitude," "Mood Indigo," and "Don't Get Around Much Anymore." Nearly all jazz musicians have played at least one Ellington tune during their careers. Many have devoted entire albums to his music, more albums than have honored any other jazz composer.

Ellington also wrote hundreds of instrumentals. **Some of them paint musical portraits of famous personalities** such as the great stride pianist Willie "The Lion" Smith ("Portrait of the Lion") and the comedian Bert Williams ("Portrait of Bert Williams"). **Others paint musical pictures of places** such as "Warm Valley" and "Harlem Airshaft," or sensations such as "Transblucency."

Ellington also wrote many longer pieces. **He is widely acclaimed for having taken jazz into the format of "extended**

works," as these longer pieces were termed. His most respected such work is "Black, Brown, and Beige," a fifty-minute tone poem describing the history of the American Negro. Some of his longest pieces were film scores. A favorite of musicians and critics is his music for "Anatomy of a Murder," the Otto Preminger movie starring Jimmy Stewart.

An important element of the Ellington sound is what is called **voicing across sections of the band.** Most arrangers, including Ellington, routinely write passages that pit the sound of one section of the band, such as the saxes, against another section of the band, such as the brasses. But Ellington was innovative because he often wrote passages to be played by combinations of instruments drawn from different sections of the band. The most famous example is in his 1930 recording of "Mood Indigo." There he voiced clarinet with muted trumpet and muted trombone. This piece combined instruments from three different sections of the band: trumpet section, trombone section, and saxophone section. In his 1940 recording of "Concerto for Cootie," he voiced pizzicato bass notes in unison with the horns. This was unusual because bass was primarily assigned to a timekeeping role as a member of the rhythm section and rarely played melody parts.

Another notable technique employed by Ellington was placing a **wordless vocal** in an arrangement. Sometimes called *instrumentalized voice,* this became identified with Ellington. He was applauded for its use in his 1927 recording of "Creole Love Call" and his 1946 recording of "Transblucency."

Cootie Williams, Duke Ellington's star trumpeter who specialized in growl-style use of the plunger mute. Ellington featured his unmuted playing on "Harlem Airshaft."

Photo courtesy of New York Public Library

Ellington was also famous for his exotic "jungle sounds." These originated with his jobs playing for floor shows at New York nightclubs that wanted stylized presentations of African atmosphere. To do this, he wrote parts for trumpeter Bubber Miley and trombonist "Tricky Sam" Nanton playing into plunger mutes, achieving what has become known as *growl style* (*Demo CD* Track 67). He also used clarinets playing unusual harmonies in an intense, wailing fashion. Even years later when he was no longer playing for these floor shows, he continued to employ these exotic sounds. They contributed to his group's reputation as a "hot band."

LISTENING GUIDE

Duke Ellington's "Harlem Airshaft"

Introduction

CD Track	Elapsed Time	
25	0' 00"	*Four Measures*

The brass instruments call in harmonized, sustained tones, and the saxes respond with an active figure. Then, while they are silent, you can hear a full rhythm section sound with prominent rhythm guitar, walking bass, and Sonny Greer using brushes on snare drum for timekeeping. Ellington inserts a brief piano fill.

0' 5"   *Four Measures*

Saxes now have the lead. Listen to their harmony. Notice more piano fills.

0' 10"   *Four Measures*

Now the trombones take the lead for about a measure and a half with the baritone saxophone coming in with a response at the end of that second measure. Trombones instantaneously return for two measures of punching figures.

26   0' 15"   **First Chorus** (A-A-B-A)

(The remainder of the piece follows a repeating, thirty-two bar A-A-B-A form.)

A   Saxes play a simple melody in unison while muted trumpets repeat a more complex background figure in harmony as an answering embellishment.

0' 25"   **A**   Repeat the above.

27   0' 35"   **B**   Saxes take the foreground by playing a harmonized part in the high register, alternating their calling with trombonist Joe "Tricky Sam" Nanton responding in plunger-muted growl style. Then saxes tie it up with a quick, little, low-register figure at the end of the bridge.

0' 45"   **A**   Repeat of A, but this time with a tie-it-up figure from the trumpets to get ready for the upcoming stop-time. Sonny Greer ends the figure by striking a cymbal, then quickly grabs it to prevent ringing. (The sound and timing of this technique is effective for closing a musical idea in an abrupt way.)

28   0' 55"   **Second Chorus** (A-A-B-A)

A   *First Four Measures*

The rhythm section stops playing. This creates a four-measure stop-time break. The saxes use it to play a high-register, harmonized part

CD Track	Elapsed Time	
		with sustained tones. This evokes a suspended feeling, partly because the rhythm section is no longer stating each beat, and partly because there is suddenly very little movement in the sax sound. Then Sonny Greer uses sticks to play rolls and rim shots, "breaking things up," to enhance the band's transition from the suspension to a rough and tumble trumpet solo by Cootie Williams.
29	1' 00"	*Second Four Measures*
		Cootie Williams opens his trumpet improvisation by percussively stating the same note repeatedly in an off-the-beat fashion. He creates excitement by using the high register and by shaking his tones as they end. Notice the sax activity underneath Williams.
	1' 06"	**A** Same strategy as for the first A-section. Williams continues with more repeated and shaken high notes, and Greer uses cymbal clasp to end this section of the piece.
	1' 16"	**B** Sax part becomes more intricate, repeating a climbing figure while Williams continues his improvisation against sax lines. Greer's cymbal clasp ends this section, too.
	1' 25"	**A** Same strategy as for the first and second A-sections. Notice how Williams dramatically slides down from his last high note. Listen to Greer's activity. It almost constitutes another line added to those of Williams and the saxes.
30	1' 35"	**Third Chorus** (A-A-B-A)
		A Trombones play a harmonized melody in the foreground while clarinetist Barney Bigard improvises around it, and saxes play yet another series of interjections underneath. Pay attention to Bigard's swoops and the New Orleans flavor of his playing. Imagine having to invent all those lines and colorations to spontaneously embroider the trombone and sax parts without clashing. This is not an ordinary jazz solo.
	1' 45"	**A** Same formula as for the first A-section.
	1' 54"	**B** Trumpets join trombones to repeat a sustained tone while Bigard continues his improvisation and answers them. Saxes make periodic interjections. Listen to Bigard's shake at the end of the bridge.
	2' 04"	**A** Same formula as for the first A-section. Notice Bigard's blue notes. Drummer Sonny Greer becomes louder, striking high-hat while it is in partially opened position.
31	2' 14"	**Fourth Chorus** (A-A-B-A)
		(Though it starts softly, this chorus gets louder and louder, gradually raising excitement for the climax.)
		A Band softly plays a syncopated, low-register melody while Bigard's solo from the previous chorus overlaps into the first three measures of this one, with him entering the clarinet's lower register. Listen to the rhythm guitar and Jimmy Blanton's driving bass sound. They are easier to hear now that the band has quieted down. Cootie Williams begins a muted trumpet solo where Bigard leaves off. Williams starts softly, but, as he proceeds, note how he changes the size and texture of his tone.
	2' 23"	**A** Pay attention to the finish of his solo in which Williams taps out the last four notes in the manner of a drummer.
	2' 33"	**B** The arrangement builds excitement by increasing loudness, adding instrumental activity, and going higher in register. The band calls, and Bigard repeatedly climbs out of the ensemble sound in response. The brass sound

CD Track	Elapsed Time		
			becomes clearer. Note the relationship between Bigard's improvised figures and the composed ones being played by the rest of the band. It all fits together despite the spontaneity.
	2' 43"	**A**	Saxes call, and the brass answer repeatedly. A high level of excitement is reached. Bigard is improvising throughout the sounds of several written themes. Saxes repeat a new riff of their own. Bigard enters the high register. Brass begin repeating a new riff of their own. The several levels of competing activity threaten to result in chaos by becoming more and more active at the end, but it all is resolved just in time to prevent an explosion. It ends with the brass sustaining a chord and the baritone sax sounding a low note at the finish.

ELLINGTON'S REPERTORY

Diversity and breadth characterized Ellington's music. The pieces in Ellington's repertory were filled with variety, and the lack of repetition within each piece is striking. Ellington's arrangements presented a larger number of different themes and rhythmic figures than those of other swing bands. Accompanying figures also reflected a greater assortment than was customary. In addition, Ellington's overall repertory was also diverse. It was so varied that we can summarize it as a number of separate books: (1) an impressionistic book with arrangements that place more emphasis on orchestral colors and shading than on swinging; (2) a book of romantic ballads; (3) a book of exotic pieces; (4) a concert book in which each piece is a long work with much less improvisation than was usually found in his music; (5) a book of concertos in which each piece frames the style of one Ellington sideman; (6) a book of swinging instrumentals, each with jazz solos, catchy ensemble themes, and punching accompaniment figures; (7) a book of music for sacred concerts. This was a context that brought Ellington to present new shows and use choirs, new vocal soloists, organ, and dancers. It inspired writing for different moods, such as that of prayer. It also inspired extensive lyrics.

Duke Ellington's contributions were indeed vast. You could explore a few hundred selections and then realize that Ellington also composed several operas, a couple of ballets, and about ten musical shows. We should also remember that the Ellington band's music never really fell into any fixed category—early jazz, swing, or modern. It was always unique. Ellington created a jazz classification that was practically his own. And it maintained its creative energy for more than four decades.

The influence of Ellington's music was also vast. Other big bands played his compositions and were influenced by his writing style as early as the 1930s. There was an echo of Ellington in the work of several outstanding arrangers of the 1950s and 60s. Revivals

Johnny Hodges,
Duke Ellington's star
soloist, the most widely
imitated alto saxophonis
of the swing era. Even
modern giants like John
Coltrane were influenced
by his style.

Photo by Lee Tanner

of Ellington's work were frequent during the 1980s and 90s. Even a few avant-garde bands and composers of this period drew upon Ellington for inspiration. Ellington's piano style was also influential. His approach inspired a number of players, including the highly individualistic modernists Thelonious Monk and Cecil Taylor.

THE POPULARITY OF SWING

Certain jazz musicians were as well known to the general public during the swing era as rock stars are today. For example, Benny Goodman, Count Basie, and Duke Ellington were household words during the 1930s and 40s. The public knew them as leaders of dance bands more than as jazz musicians. Still, they were better known than the jazz giants of later eras. Even some of their soloists were well known and not just by jazz buffs. The big bands, famous and not so famous, employed hundreds of jazz musicians. This made it easier at that time for musicians to find work as performers. Unfortunately, however, most of the jobs with big bands did not permit much improvisation for all but a few star soloists because these groups worked largely from written arrangements. Opportunities to improvise were generous in smaller combos, yet steady employment in jazz combos was difficult to find.

Though big bands went hand in hand with the swing era, *big band style does not necessarily mean swing style. There were also jazz-oriented big bands before and after the swing era.* Many of these sounded very different from swing bands. Big band style doesn't necessarily mean jazz style, either. In the 1930s and 1940s, ten to sixteen musicians was the standard size of bands of all types. After that, the standard size decreased to about three to eight musicians.

Also during the swing era, journalists and musicians distinguished between bands that emphasized jazz improvisation and those that did not. For example, the very popular Glenn Miller big band was a swinging band. It had a handful of hit records that contained brief jazz improvisations. But the Miller band emphasized pretty arrangements and vocals more than improvised jazz solos. Therefore, despite its swinging qualities, the band was sometimes classified as a *sweet band*. This distinguished it from the *hot band* or *swing band* classification. Bands such as Count Basie's and Duke Ellington's fell into these categories because they had more solo improvisations.

Like rock combos since the 1950s, *one of the most important functions for swing bands of the 1930s and 40s was to provide dance music.* Jazz functioned as dance music more during the swing era than it ever did thereafter. Also like popular rock combos, swing era big bands usually used elaborate costumes and showy staging, and most of them routinely carried several singers. The visual appeal of the performance, including the personality and looks of the singers, was a primary attraction for a sizable portion of the audience. Most swing era hits contained vocals. Many that did not have singing were at least based on songs that listeners knew. This indicates that *jazz value was not the primary appeal of the pieces to the wider public. Such popularity simply reflects the same appeal that songs have had throughout history.* Only occasionally during the swing era were jazz musicians given paid opportunities to perform just for listening, as later became customary. In summary, the popular success of jazz bands during the swing era was partly a result of their appeal to the eyes and feet of fans instead of to the ears alone.

CHAPTER SUMMARY

1. Swing differs from early jazz in
   a. greater use of written arrangements
   b. less emphasis on ragtime-like pieces
   c. rejection of collective improvisation in favor of solo improvisation

    d. increased use of string bass instead of tuba

    e. greater swing feeling

    f. increased use of high-hat cymbals

    g. replacement of banjo with guitar

    h. emphasis on big band over small-group instrumentation

    i. saxophone becoming the predominant instrument

2. Important big bands were led by pianists Duke Ellington and Count Basie, and clarinetist Benny Goodman.

3. Ellington was the most creative and prolific composer-arranger in jazz history.

4. Basie's rhythm section played lightly and swung with great ease.

5. The most influential saxophonists were Coleman Hawkins and Lester Young.

6. The most influential pianists were Art Tatum and Teddy Wilson.

7. Tatum possessed phenomenal speed. He was known for spontaneously changing and adding chords in pop tune accompaniments.

8. Roy Eldridge paved the way for modern jazz trumpeter Dizzy Gillespie by improvising fiery, saxophone-like lines on trumpet.

SUPPLEMENTARY LISTENING

Masters of Jazz, Vol. 3: Big Bands of the '30s and '40s (Rhino 72470)

Smithsonian Collection of Classic Jazz (RJ 0010) contains renditions of "Body and Soul" by Coleman Hawkins, "Willow Weep For Me" by Art Tatum, "Breakfast Feud" by Benny Goodman, "I Can't Believe That You're in Love With Me" by Roy Eldridge, "Lester Leaps In" by Lester Young and Count Basie, "Doggin' Around" by the Count Basie big band with Lester Young, "Ko-Ko" and "Concerto for Cootie" by Duke Ellington, plus other examples of swing era jazz (phone 800-419-5606).

The Jazz Classics Cassette for Jazz Styles: History and Analysis (ISBN 0-13-012695-0) contains these pieces by Duke Ellington: "Transblucency," "Cottontail," and "Prelude to a Kiss." It also contains "Lester Leaps In" by Count Basie and Lester Young. The CD format (ISBN 0-13-012693-4) has all but "Lester Leaps In." Order by phone: 800-947-7700.

Lester Young — *The "Kansas City" Sessions* (Commodore/GRP: CMD-402)

Count Basie — *The Complete Decca Recordings* (Decca Jazz/GRP: GRD3-611)

Duke Ellington — *The Blanton-Webster Band* (RCA Bluebird: 5691-2-RB)

SUPPLEMENTARY READING

Benny Goodman by Bruce Crowther (Apollo, 1988)

Benny Goodman and the Swing Era by James Lincoln Collier (Oxford, 1989)

Jazz Masters of the Thirties by Rex Stewart (Macmillan, 1972; Da Capo, 1980)

The Swing Era by Gunther Schuller (Oxford, 1989)

Goin' to Kansas City by Nathan Pearson (University of Illinois, 1987)

Good Morning Blues (autobiography) by Count Basie (Random House, 1985)

You Fight for Your Life: A Biography of Lester Young by Frank Buchman-Moller (Greenwood, 1990)

Lester Young by Lewis Porter (Twayne, 1985)

Song of the Hawk: The Life and Recordings of Coleman Hawkins by John Chilton (University of Michigan Press, 1990)

Music Is My Mistress (autobiography) by Duke Ellington (Doubleday, 1973; Da Capo, 1976)

The World of Duke Ellington by Stanley Dance (Scribner, 1970; Da Capo, 1980)

Duke Ellington by James Lincoln Collier (Oxford, 1987)

The World of Swing by Stanley Dance (Scribner, 1974; Da Capo, 1979)

The World of Count Basie by Stanley Dance (Scribner, 1981; Da Capo, 1985)

CHAPTER 6

BEBOP

Charlie Parker and Miles Davis, 1947   Photo by William P. Gottlieb

Modern jazz became a recognizable sound in the 1940s. It grew from roots laid down in the 1930s by saxophonists Coleman Hawkins and Lester Young, pianists Art Tatum and Nat Cole, trumpeter Roy Eldridge, and the Count Basie rhythm section. Early jazz and swing styles are often considered the "classic period." New styles which have emerged since 1940 are often classified as modern jazz. The first well-known modern jazz musicians were alto saxophonist Charlie Parker, pianist Thelonious Monk, and trumpeter Dizzy Gillespie. By the middle 1940s, they had inspired a legion of other creative musicians including trumpeter Miles Davis and pianist Bud Powell. By the late 1940s, Parker and Gillespie had also influenced the music in several big bands.

Modern jazz did not burst on the jazz scene suddenly. It developed gradually through the work of swing era musicians. Parker and Gillespie themselves began their careers playing improvisations in a swing era style. They expanded on swing styles and gradually developed new techniques. Their work eventually became a recognizably different style, though it was still linked to its roots in the swing era. Modern jazz improvisers were also inspired by contemporary classical music, particularly the work of Bela Bartok and Igor Stravinsky. Rather than being a reaction against swing styles, modern jazz developed smoothly *from* swing styles.

Bebop (or just "bop") is the name of the first modern jazz style. It was considerably less popular than swing, and it failed to attract dancers. However, it did contribute impressive soloists who gained followers for decades to come. The first bebop soloists created a new vocabulary of musical phrases and distinctive methods of matching improvisation to chord progressions. This became the standard jazz language for the next forty years. Even during the 1990s, musicians frequently evaluated new players according to their ability to play bebop. Mastery of this style was considered the foundation for competence as a jazz improviser.

Bebop differed from swing in a number of performance aspects:

1. Preferred instrumentation for bebop was the small combo instead of big band.
2. Average tempo was faster in bebop.
3. Clarinet was rare in bebop.
4. Display of instrumental virtuosity was a higher priority for bebop players.
5. Rhythm guitar was rare.
6. Less emphasis was placed on arrangements in bebop.

Bebop differed from swing in a number of stylistic respects:

1. Melodies were more complex in bebop.
2. Harmonies were more complex in bebop.
3. Accompaniment rhythms were more varied in bebop.
4. Comping replaced stride style and simple, on-the-beat chording. (*Demo CD* Tracks 20 and 38)
5. Drummers played their timekeeping rhythms primarily on suspended cymbal, rather than snare drum, high-hat, or bass drum. (*Demo CD* Track 3)
6. Bebop musicians enjoyed leaving phrases in tunes suspended or unresolved.
7. Bebop was a more agitated style than swing was.
8. Bebop improvisation was more complex because it contained
   a. more themes per solo
   b. less similarity among themes
   c. more excursions outside the tune's original key
   d. a greater scope of rhythmic development
9. Surprise was more highly valued in bebop.

Bebop improvisations were composed mostly of melody lines which seemed jumpy, full of twists and turns. The contours of the lines were jagged. There were often large intervals between the notes and abrupt changes of direction. The rhythms in those lines were quick and unpredictable, with heavy emphasis on syncopation.

Bebop musicians did more than embellish the melody during their improvisations. They departed completely from the melodies and retained only the chord progressions of a song's accompaniment. Often they enriched a progression by adding new chords. Art Tatum had gotten in the habit of changing accompaniment harmonies for melodies that traditionally had been accompanied in only one particular way. He also had added chords to existing progressions. Coleman Hawkins had loved to improvise on complicated chord progressions and to add chords to the pieces he played. In these ways, Tatum and Hawkins prepared the way for the wide use of these techniques in bebop style.

A bebop combo playing in a New York City club (left to right): Charlie Mingus (bass viol), Roy Haynes (drums), Thelonious Monk (piano), and Charlie Parker (alto sax).

Photo by Bob Parent, courtesy of Don Parent

Max Roach, the leading bebop drummer. Roach improvised more drum sounds than swing-style drummers used for timekeeping. This made bebop more spontaneous and exciting.

Photo by Herman Leonard, courtesy of Robert Asen — Metronome Collection

Bebop players often wrote original tunes using the accompaniment chord progressions of popular tunes. Many of these new tunes went without names. The leader just called out the key and the name of the tune which provided the chord progression. In that way, members of the rhythm section could immediately play a tune they might never have previously heard. This technique was not new to bebop. It had been used in swing and early jazz. The chord progression for the twelve-bar blues had been used in that way for decades. And Count Basie's recordings of the 1930s are filled with loosely arranged performances in which riffs and improvisations are placed atop the accompaniments of such popular songs as "Lady Be Good," "Honeysuckle Rose," and "I Got Rhythm." (*Demo CD* Track 33) This practice provided a common ground for jam sessions because all the participants knew the chord progressions to these popular songs. The practice merely became more common during the bebop era because the emphasis in bebop was on improvisation by small combos rather than set arrangements by big bands.

There were differences in drumming style, too. By comparison with swing-style, (1) bebop drummers more frequently kicked and prodded the soloist, in addition to playing timekeeping sounds. (*Demo CD* Track 8) (2) They moved away from the heavy ways of timekeeping. For instance, the bebop drummer (a) feathered the bass drum instead of pounding it. Sometimes he did not use it for timekeeping at all. (b) Timekeeping was primarily done on the suspended ride cymbal. (*Demo CD* Track 3) And (c) bebop drummers snapped shut the high-hat crisply on every other beat. (*Demo CD* Track 2) (3) Bebop drummers got into the habit of creating an almost continuous "chatter" that increased the excitement of the performance.

Much of this was generated on the snare drum, and it took the form of pops and crackles that seemed to provide a commentary on what else was happening in the band. Surprises came from the bass drum, too. This was called "dropping bombs."

CHARLIE PARKER

The musician who contributed most to the development of bebop was alto saxophonist Charlie Parker (1920–1955), nicknamed "Bird." Jazz musicians and historians feel that he is the most important saxophonist in jazz history. Many musicologists consider Parker to be one of the most brilliant figures in twentieth-century music. Going beyond the advances made by Lester Young, Coleman Hawkins, and Art Tatum, he built an entire system by his improvisations and compositions. The system had new ways of selecting notes that fit around the notes in the accompaniment chords. It also had new ways of accenting notes so that the phrases have a highly syncopated, sometimes off-balance character.

Charlie Parker astonished other musicians with his tremendous fertility of melodic imagination, unprecedented mastery of the saxophone, and the dizzying pace with which he was able to improvise. (*Jazz Classics CD* Track 34) By comparison with swing-style players, Parker sounded more hurried. He sounded like a modern composer who was improvising at lightning speed, not an easygoing romantic. Parker's solos were densely packed with ideas. During his improvisations, his mind seemed to be bubbling over with little melodies. It was as though he had so much energy and enthusiasm that he could barely contain himself. As a result he sprinkled his solos with double-time and quadruple-time figures. Even in ballad renditions, he tended to ornament slow lines with double-time figures. Soon after Parker's mid-1940s recordings appeared, other musicians followed suit. There was an increase in the average tempo, the amount of double-timing, and the amount of melodic ideas in improvisations. This trend had begun during the swing era, but it was furthered by the example that Parker set.

Parker's tone quality departed from standard swing era models. Rather than making it lush and sweet, Parker made his sound dry and biting. His tone fit his fast, serious attitude.

Charlie Parker's improvisations were inspired by many sources. He devised his lines by many of the same methods that classical composers use. He also drew phrases from such sources as the solos of Louis Armstrong and Lester Young, the melodies of blues singers and early jazz hornmen, pop tunes, and traditional themes from opera and classical music.

Parker wrote many tunes himself. Their character set the flavor for bebop as much as his improvisations did. Though not melody-like in the pop tune sense, they were catchy lines in a jazz vein. This was the musical language of bebop. Most were accompanied by chord progressions borrowed from popular songs. Many used accompaniments of the twelve-bar blues chord progression.

The phrases of Parker's tunes were memorized and analyzed by hundreds of jazz soloists. They were played at jam sessions for decades after he introduced them.

Parker had an immense impact on jazz. Bebop trumpeter Dizzy Gillespie cites Parker as a primary influence on his own style, and bebop pianist Bud Powell modelled some of his lines after Parker's. Methods of improvisation devised by Parker were adopted by numerous saxophonists during the 1940s and 50s. So many musicians imitated him that jazz journalists soon complained about a lack of originality and freshness among musicians at that time. Musicians of the 1990s studied Parker's improvisations as a foundation for developing their own styles. His work was treated by jazz musicians with as much respect as the works of J. S. Bach and Ludwig van Beethoven were treated among classical musicians. Jazz clubs were named for Parker—Birdland in New York and Birdhouse in Chicago. Parker's melodic inventiveness is so stunning that bebop singers performed his pieces with lyrics which had been written for his melodies as well as his improvisations. During the 1970s, a group called Supersax began using five saxes and rhythm section to play harmonized transcriptions of Parker's improvised solos. Supersax was able to treat his solos as compositions in their own right because Parker's work was so rich with catchy ideas.

Charlie Parker, the most significant saxophonist of the 20th century and an inventor of bebop. His tunes and improvisations have been memorized and analyzed by thousands of modern jazz musicians.

Photo by Bob Parent, courtesy of Don Parent

LISTENING GUIDE

Charlie Parker's "Ko-Ko"

Recorded November 26, 1945 by Charlie Parker (alto sax), Dizzy Gillespie (cup-muted trumpet and piano), Curley Russell (bass), Max Roach (drums).

This is the most widely acclaimed improvisation of Charlie Parker on record. Almost all of this recording contains spontaneous work. The piece has no theme, and we never hear the theme to "Cherokee," the pop tune from which "Ko-Ko"'s progression of accompaniment chords was borrowed. Most of what we hear is a saxophone solo guided by those chords in their 64-measure A-A-B-A format. The only written parts are the brief figures played together by trumpet and sax at the beginning and end.

The solo style and accompaniment style typify bebop. Parker's improvisation is filled with fast, intricate phrases and abrupt changes of direction. It is well constructed and melodic. Listeners might not perceive those virtues, however, unless they speed up their hearing and attend to each note in Parker's line. Max Roach's accompaniment often contains a commentary on Parker's solo that consists of sudden "kicks" from the snare drum and "bombs" from the bass drum. Timekeeping is provided mostly by walking patterns played by the bassist and ride rhythms made by the drummer striking the ride cymbal with his drum stick. The piano comping is by trumpeter Dizzy Gillespie, not a full-time pianist. Gillespie feeds the chords to Parker and that's about all.

CD Track	Elapsed Time	
33	0' 00"	**Introduction**
		Alto sax and cup-muted trumpet play in unison, accompanied by drummer playing timekeeping rhythms on the snare drum by use of wire brushes.
	0' 06"	improvised trumpet solo in a cup mute
	0' 13"	improvised alto sax solo
	0' 19"	Sax and trumpet play a harmonized figure that ties up the introductory remarks.
	0' 22"	Explicit timekeeping rhythms stop while a figure is played by trumpet with sax playing it an octave lower.
		Charlie Parker Alto Saxophone Solo
		First Chorus (A-A-B-A)
34	0' 26"	sax solo improvisation following the chords to "Cherokee"; timekeeping by bassist walking, pianist comping, and drummer striking ride cymbal with drum stick in a steady pattern
	0' 38"	*Second A-Section*
	0' 50"	*Bridge*
	1' 03"	*Last A-Section*
		Notice the kicks and bombs from the drums.
	1' 16"	**Second Chorus** (A-A-B-A)
	1' 29"	*Second A-Section*
	1' 41"	*Bridge*
		many kicks from snare drum

CD Track	Elapsed Time	
	1' 54"	*Last A-Section of Second Solo Chorus*
35	2' 07"	**Drum Solo by Max Roach**
		Ending
	2' 29"	muted trumpet figure with alto sax an octave below it; no bass or piano, just drums accompaniment
	2' 36"	muted trumpet improvisation, accompanied only by cymbals and drums
	2' 49"	highly syncopated figure played in harmony by trumpet and sax, with the final two notes underscored by drums
	2' 52"	Piece ends with a very brief note (a "stinger") played by drummer crisply snapping shut his high-hat in unison with a note from the bass.

DIZZY GILLESPIE

Louis Armstrong was the major jazz trumpet virtuoso of the late 1920s and early 30s. Roy Eldridge held a similar position after that. Then Dizzy Gillespie (1917–1993) appeared on the scene. His innovative melodic concepts and high-register playing were not only phenomenal for the 1940s, but have rarely been matched since. *(Jazz Classics CD* Track 39) But Gillespie's awe-inspiring command of the trumpet accounts for only part of his impact. Much of his influence stems from his stirring musical ideas.

Dizzy Gillespie's harmonic skills were startling, and he flaunted them. His phrases were full of surprises and playful changes of direction. His work bristled with excitement. He would weave in and out of different keys within a single phrase. He always managed to resolve his line's logic to fit with the ways the chords changed in his accompaniment. He often zoomed up to the trumpet's high register during the middle of a phrase and still managed to connect the melodic ideas logically. Sometimes he interspersed quotes from non-jazz pieces such as the opera "Carmen" or the pop tune "We're in the Money." He would use the quote as a point of departure for developing his own phrases. He sometimes increased tension by building a line higher and higher with staccato syncopated notes and then released the tension by coming down with legato lines.

Gillespie exerted sweeping influence on modern jazz. His pet phrases became stock clichés for two generations of jazz trumpeters, pianists, guitarists, saxophonists, and trombonists. Several established trumpeters of the 1940s originally derived their styles from premodern sources. But when they heard Gillespie's approach, they began imitating him. He was only a year or two older, but he influenced them as a classic model rather than a contemporary.

Gillespie also made lasting contributions as a composer. His "Groovin' High" and "A Night in Tunisia" became jazz standards that

The Dizzy Gillespie Big Band, with pianist John Lewis and bassist Ray Brown (who became founding members of the Modern Jazz Quartet) and Miles Davis (second trumpeter from the left). Their recording of "Things to Come" demonstrated that the fast-paced and difficult bebop style could be played by a large band.

Photo by William P. Gottlieb

are still played frequently. After being recorded with lyrics, they gained wider audiences in the 1980s. Afro-Cuban music was one of Gillespie's special interests, and he explored it in his big band numbers "Manteca," "Cubano Be," and "Cubano Bop." These pieces are among the earliest appearances of Latin American music in modern jazz.

After co-leading a combo with Charlie Parker and leading a few small bands of his own, Gillespie began a series of bebop big bands. He kept his big bands going through most of the late 1940s, then formed others once in a while thereafter. His combos and big bands featured a number of powerful players, many of whom went on to lead significant groups of their own.

LISTENING GUIDE

"Things to Come" by Dizzy Gillespie Big Band

Composed by Dizzy Gillespie and Gil Fuller; recorded July 9, 1946 by the Dizzy Gillespie big band (5 saxes, 3 trombones, 5 trumpets, vibraharp, piano, bass, and drums), featuring Gillespie on trumpet, Milt Jackson on vibraharp, John Brown on alto sax; rhythm section = John Lewis (piano), Ray Brown (bass), Kenny Clarke (drums).

This is the most spectacular example of big band bebop on record. The music is so intricate and the pace is so fast that even musicians themselves have a hard time believing their ears the first time they hear it. Small bands customarily played intricate lines at quick tempos, a reputation of bebop. But big bands were traditionally less flexible because coordinating 16 musicians is much harder than coordinating 5.

"Things to Come" was developed by Gil Fuller from a combo piece of Gillespie's called "Bebop." This recording even contains parts of his difficult trumpet improvisation from the "Bebop" recording, here written for four trumpets to play at the same time. Aside from the energetic solo improvisations by trumpeter Gillespie and alto saxophonist John Brown, we hear a vibraharp solo from Milt Jackson, who became the featured soloist with the well-known Modern Jazz Quartet. We also hear a considerable amount of very inventive bebop drumming from Kenny Clarke, one of the original pioneers of bebop.

CD Track	Elapsed Time	
36	0' 00"	**Introduction**
		Complex line played together by the trumpets with drummer underscoring some of their rhythms.
		A phrase by the saxes. An exclamation by the brass instruments. Brief drum solo. No timekeeping rhythms yet from drums or bass. Other complex lines from brasses jut out at us.
		Main Theme (A-A-B-A)
37	0' 08"	*First A-Section*
		Saxes state the melody while trumpets and trombones punctuate it, and bass and drums play timekeeping rhythms.
	0' 14"	*Second A-Section*
		Saxes state the melody while trumpets and trombones punctuate it, and bass and drums play timekeeping rhythms.
	0' 20"	*Bridge*
		Trumpets carry a melody while saxes accompany them.
	0' 26"	*Final A-Section*
		Saxes state the melody while trumpets and trombones punctuate it, and bass and drums play timekeeping rhythms.
38	0' 32"	**Interlude**
		Previous timekeeping rhythms stop in bass and drums. Drummer plays tom-toms under trumpets. Difficult brass lines.
	0' 34"	Saxes play a phrase 3 times.
	0' 37"	Trumpets play another line on top of third sax phrase.
	0' 40"	Dizzy Gillespie begins his solo improvisation without any accompaniment.
		Dizzy Gillespie Trumpet Improvisation (A-A-B-A)
39	0' 42"	*First A-Section*
		The band joins him at the beginning of the A-A-B-A form. Timekeeping rhythms resume in bass and drums.
		Sax figures accompany Gillespie. Brass occasionally add an exclamation.
	0' 48"	*Second A-Section*
	0' 53"	*Bridge*
	0' 59"	*Final A-Section*

CD Track	Elapsed Time	
		Milt Jackson Vibraharp Improvisation (A-A-B-A)
		Accompaniment: piano comping, bass walking, and drummer playing time-keeping rhythms.
40	1' 05"	*First A-Section*
	1' 11"	*Second A-Section*
	1' 16"	*Bridge*
	1' 22"	*Final A-Section*
		Second Chorus of Vibraharp Solo
	1' 28"	*First A-Section*
		Accompaniment: piano, bass, and drums, plus countermelodies from other instruments. Trumpets call in unison, and trombones echo them in harmony.
	1' 33"	*Second A-Section*
		Accompaniment is by piano, bass, and drums, plus countermelodies from other instruments. Trumpets call in unison, and trombones answer in harmony.
	1' 39"	*Bridge*
		Saxes sustain chords.
	1' 44"	*Final A-Section*
		Accompaniment is by piano, bass, and drums, plus countermelodies from other instruments. Trumpets call in unison, and trombones echo in harmony.
	1' 49"	**Interlude**
		John Brown Alto Sax Improvisation
41	1' 54"	*First A-Section*
		Brass punctuations accompany sax solo.
	2' 01"	*Second A-Section*
		Brass punctuations accompany sax solo.
		Full Band
	2' 07"	*Bridge*
		Trumpets state theme and saxes answer, then accompany them.
	2' 13"	*Final A-Section*
		Saxes play the melody, accompanied by occasional brass punctuations.
42	2' 18"	**Ending**
		Complex trumpet and sax phrases dart about with much drumming activity interspersed.
	2' 26"	Timekeeping stops, saxes sustain, and Dizzy Gillespie plays the octave key notes and a flat fifth interval.
	2' 33"	Timekeeping stops, saxes sustain, and trombone plays the octave key notes and a flat fifth interval.
	2' 37"	Saxes fall together in pitch and then slide up together. Saxes are joined by a loud brass chord.
	2' 41"	Band plays loud chord.
	2' 43"	Gillespie slides up in pitch to play a note high over the others.

THELONIOUS MONK

Thelonious Monk (1917–1982) was a pianist who wrote compositions whose melodies were unorthodox and whose accompaniment chords severely challenged improvisers. His compositions influenced the flavor of much modern jazz. Several musicians have devoted entire albums to his music. A few touring bands have constructed their repertories primarily from his compositions. Like his compositional style, his approach to piano improvising was also influential. Many people consider Monk a creative genius responsible for significant directions taken by modern jazz.

Monk's tunes have a logic and symmetry all their own. Unlike the tunes of many popular composers, his are so perfectly structured that they cannot withstand tampering. Monk was expert at placing accents in irregular order. He was also especially skilled in ending phrases on the least expected notes, yet making the piece sound as though those phrase endings had been expected all along.

As a pianist, Monk was a curious mixture. He used stride piano techniques, horn-like lines, and very dissonant chord voicings. He was famous for the blunt, strident way he struck the keyboard. As an accompanist, his work was not like conventional bebop comping style. Nor was it like the light and bouncing approach that evolved from Count Basie's methods. He would play a note here, a dissonant chord there. In addition to these irregularities, Monk often stopped comping for long passages, leaving the soloist to improvise with only bass and drums for accompaniment.

Monk's music conveys a sense of unsettling deliberation. He uses notes so sparingly that silence is almost as important as sound. The agonizing care he devotes to choosing each individual note and rhythm contrasts with the long, horn-like improvisations of most other pianists. His music is not smooth. His piano improvisations convey a sense that he is struggling to decide on every note, and then

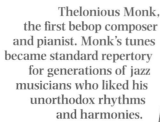

Thelonious Monk, the first bebop composer and pianist. Monk's tunes became standard repertory for generations of jazz musicians who liked his unorthodox rhythms and harmonies.

Photo by William P. Gottlieb

he reaches that decision just barely in time to play it. Nothing is produced casually or routinely. Each phrase is played very emphatically, and with much consideration for its maximum rhythmic effect. Monk's approach is very intense and percussive. He often strikes a note or chord several times in a row, as though knocking on a door. His music does not evoke the easy rise and fall of tensions associated with most jazz lines. Perhaps that's why listeners disagree about whether Monk's music swings.

Monk was one of the most original of all jazz improvisers. His lines often display jagged contours, and the construction for some of his improvisations is quite playful. In his harmonies, Monk is particularly known for combinations of tones that clash resoundingly with each other. It has been joked that Monk could make an in-tune piano sound out of tune. Combined with an uneven rhythmic style, these harmonic characteristics made his music quite jarring. But this is what he wanted.

BUD POWELL

Bud Powell (1924–1966) is the most imitated of all bebop pianists. He crafted his approach from Art Tatum's, with other borrowings from the styles of Billy Kyle, Nat Cole, and Thelonious Monk. Atop these foundations, Powell incorporated the style and phrases of Charlie Parker and Dizzy Gillespie. The result was one of the first modern jazz piano styles.

Bebop pianists mastered **comping.** This is a technique of spontaneous chording that flexibly interacts with the improvised solo lines. This accompaniment technique had been demonstrated by Count Basie as early as the mid-1930s. Swing piano styles had begun to take advantage of the widening use of string bass. As a result, pianists placed less emphasis on the left hand for supplying chords under their own right-hand solo lines. They eventually phased out the practice of providing one-note-at-a-time bass lines for themselves. By the time bebop was well underway, pianists had almost entirely abandoned the left hand's bass functions that were so common in the styles of stride, boogie woogie, and swing piano players. A new left-hand style evolved which was to characterize jazz piano for several decades.

Powell de-emphasized the activity of the left hand, thereby departing from the stride tradition and the "chomp, chomp, chomp, chomp" style of chording used by many swing pianists. This served to lighten the way pianists had begun playing, even more than the streamlining introduced by Teddy Wilson and Nat Cole. In place of the striding left-hand figures, **Powell's left hand inserted brief, sporadically placed two- and three-note chords that reduced his statement of harmony to the barest minimum.** Sometimes the chords sustained for a few beats. Sometimes there was no left-hand sound at all. This comping style became standard for modern jazz pianists accompanying their own solo lines. This development was almost as significant within the history of solo piano as the

Bud Powell, the most influential bebop pianist. His approach combined piano styles of Art Tatum, Nat Cole, and Thelonious Monk with the horn styles of Charlie Parker and Dizzy Gillespie.

Photo by Bob Parent, courtesy of Don Parent

emergence of comping had been for rhythm section pianists. In other words, **the breakthrough that Count Basie had made in lightening the manner in which a pianist supplied chords and support for an improvising soloist was paralleled by the way Powell lightened the manner in which a pianist accompanied his own solo lines.**

In his prime, Powell had the speed and dexterity to create piano solos that almost matched the high-powered inventions of Parker and Gillespie. (*Jazz Classics CD* Track 45) He mastered the erratically syncopated rhythms of bebop and charged through his solos with terrific force. **Powell was the model for hundreds of pianists during the 1940s and 50s, as James P. Johnson had been during the 1920s and Earl Hines had been after Johnson.**

DEXTER GORDON

Dexter Gordon (1923–1990) was the first tenor saxophonist to be recognized as a bebop player. He was making important recordings in this new style as early as 1945. Though strongly influenced by Lester Young and Charlie Parker, Gordon used a tone that was deep and dark, not light or hollow like Young's. And his improvisations were not as unpredictable and jumpy as Parker's. Although Gordon's style was quite aggressive, his work conveyed great ease. There was a sense of authority and majesty in his playing. He used a large

Dexter Gordon, the first bebop tenor saxophonist. Known for very logical and melodic solos, his style was widely imitated, especially among "hard bop" players of the 1950s. Gordon's approach provided a link between Lester Young's style of the 1930s and John Coltrane's style of the 1950s. Gordon remained an important figure on the jazz scene until his death in 1990. He was the saxophone playing star of the movie *'Round Midnight*.

Photo by Bill Smith

variety of melodic devices to create his lines. His phrase lengths and rhythms contained more variety than those of most other tenor saxophonists in bop. Gordon loved to quote from pop tunes and bugle calls. He was known for developing his solos by making firm statements and following through on them. (*Jazz Classic CD* Track 46) His improvisations contained remarkable logic and continuity, a tendency that became even more conspicuous during the 1960s and 70s. He offered phrase after phrase of complete musical ideas, each of which was well rounded and meaty. Gordon influenced many tenor saxophonists whose styles in the 1950s were classified as "hard bop." He had a strong recording career from the 1940s into the 1980s, and his playing displayed depth of imagination and swing feeling all that time.

LISTENING GUIDE

Dexter Gordon's "Dexter Digs In"

Composed by Dexter Gordon; recorded January 29, 1946 by Dexter Gordon (tenor sax), Leonard Hawkins (trumpet), Bud Powell (piano), Curley Russell (bass), and Max Roach (drums).

This recording typifies combo bebop of the 1940s and 50s. The main soloist here is Dexter Gordon, the leading tenor saxophonist in bebop. He was the first on his instrument to devise a style that was sufficiently distinct from swing era models to be called bebop. Pianist Bud Powell was the most important pianist in bebop and became the model for hundreds of others in the 1940s and 50s. (Even Herbie Hancock and Chick Corea studied his work when developing their own styles.) Drummer Max Roach was the most prominent bebop drummer, and he can be heard here adding a variety of sounds that are not related to timekeeping. These extra sounds help us distinguish bebop drumming styles from earlier approaches in which spontaneous musical comments were less frequent.

The band uses a stock format for this performance. The chord progression is organized with each chorus presented in an A-A-B-A manner. After a brief introduction, the melody is played in unison by trumpet and saxophone. Then no melody is used for the bridge, but the pianist improvises a solo instead. The melody is then played again in unison by trumpet and sax, as in the first two renditions of the A-section. The saxophonist improvises a solo for a complete chorus. Then the saxophone and trumpet use an entire chorus by taking turns improvising for half a section apiece. This is called "trading fours" because the soloists alternate improvising the length of time taken by four groups of four beats. (Musicians refer to each group of beats as a "measure" or a "bar.") Sax and trumpet then return to the theme. However, on this recording they do not complete it, apparently because after two renditions of the A-section they had run too close to the 3-minute limit for the 78 r.p.m. records. In a night club performance of the same tune, they would have included the bridge and the final A-section.

CD Track	Elapsed Time	
43	0' 00"	**Introduction** Tenor sax plays without accompaniment.
	0' 04"	**Theme** (A-A-B-A) Trumpet and tenor sax play melody in unison, accompanied by piano comping, walking bass, and drummer using the standard timekeeping methods as well as punctuating sporadically by striking his snare drum or bass drum at unexpected moments.
	0' 14"	*Second A-Section* Trumpet and sax continue.
	0' 23"	*Bridge* Bud Powell solo piano improvisation
	0' 32"	*Final A-Section* Trumpet and tenor sax play melody in unison.

CD Track	Elapsed Time	
44	0' 41"	**Second Chorus** (A-A-B-A)
		trumpet solo improvisation
	0' 50"	*Second A-Section*
45	1' 00"	*Bridge*
		Bud Powell solo piano improvisation
	1' 09"	*Final A-Section*
		Powell continues.
46	1' 19"	**Third Chorus** (A-A-B-A)
		Dexter Gordon solo tenor sax improvisation
47	1' 58"	**Fourth Chorus** (A-A-B-A)
		Sax and trumpet are trading fours.
		First Half of First A-Section
		sax improvisation
	2' 02"	*Second Half of First A-Section*
		trumpet improvisation
	2' 06"	*First Half of Second A-Section*
		sax improvisation
	2' 11"	*Second Half of Second A-Section*
		trumpet improvisation
	2' 16"	*First Half of Bridge*
		sax improvisation
	2' 21"	*Second Half of Bridge*
		trumpet improvisation
	2' 25"	*First Half of Final A-Section*
		sax improvisation
	2' 30"	*Second Half of Final A-Section*
		trumpet improvisation
48	2' 35"	**Theme** (A-A)
		First A-Section
		Trumpet and tenor saxophone play melody in unison.
	2' 44"	*Second A-Section*
		Trumpet and sax continue.
	2' 53"	**Ending** (No Bridge or Final A-Section)
		Drums and cymbals tie it up.

Sarah Vaughan, the best-known singer associated with bop. Noted for recasting melodies by seamlessly changing their pitches and rhythms, she extracted the maximum drama and sensuality from each phrase.

Photo by Popsie Randolf, courtesy of Frank Driggs

SARAH VAUGHAN

The best-known singer to emerge from the bop era was Sarah Vaughan (1924-1990). Recording with the top instrumentalists, including Dizzy Gillespie, Tadd Dameron, and Clifford Brown, she achieved a position of respect among musicians that sustained throughout her long career. Like Ella Fitzgerald, she also had a large following outside of the jazz audience. "Nature Boy" and "It's Magic" were hits for her in 1948; then her "Broken Hearted Melody" became a million-seller in 1959.

Vaughan's tone quality was darker and more richly textured than Billie Holiday's and Ella Fitzgerald's. As the years passed, her pitch range deepened into tenor and almost baritone range. (Listen to her "My Funny Valentine" in SCCJ.)

Vaughan's voice control is a source of envy among singers. She showed none of the abruptness or lost tone quality and pitch control that typify most pop singers when they shift registers. She could glide through several octaves seamlessly. Like opera singers, she favored a quick and prominent vibrato, and she milked every note for its last vibration. Also as in opera, she emphasized the maximum drama that could be extracted from each phrase.

Vaughan, a professional pianist with a working knowledge of modern harmony, was an accomplished scat singer. But like other jazz singers, she rarely performed scat improvisations. Instead, she usually chose to sing the original words. The focus of her creativity was in recasting the rhythms and embellishing the pitches. These departures exceeded mere ornamentation, but they did not take the liberties that constitute scat singing.

Straight readings of tunes were not Vaughan's routine practice. She improvised extensively with the timing of words, as though the lyrics were elastic and could be stretched to occur almost anywhere in relation to the passing beats. At the same time she also played with the enunciation of the words and their tone's pitch and timbre. The effect is exceedingly sensual. She drew us in by toying with almost every phrase. The result was that each of her renditions became an intimate experience. Ballad performances account for her greatest achievements. The slow-paced tunes were excellent vehicles for her mastery of nuance. She luxuriated in the depth and richness of her voice and took listeners along in this celebration of sound for its own sake.

Most singers lose tone and energy as they age. Yet Vaughan's tone quality, range, and technique actually increased over the years. Her performances were impeccable during all phases of her career, with her greatest virtuosity displayed during her final twenty years.

STAN GETZ

Stan Getz (1927–1991) was one of the most distinctive tenor saxophonists to emerge during the 1940s. He did not rely as heavily on Lester Young's ideas as most other bebop saxophonists did, and he used few of Charlie Parker's and Dizzy Gillespie's pet phrases. He developed an original melodic and rhythmic vocabulary instead. His phrasing and accenting were less varied and syncopated than Parker's and Gillespie's. At times classical music seems to have influenced him more than bebop did. Some of his improvisations are quite pretty, and less like bebop than like classical music. That side of his style fit with his light, fluffy tone and graceful approach to playing the saxophone. Partly because of this, many listeners categorize the Getz style as "cool jazz," not bebop.

Getz was one of the few bebop musicians to become known outside a small circle of musicians and jazz fans. He could play hard-driving jazz that was envied by the best of his peers. But his greatest impact with the public was made with slow, pretty pieces. They showcased his sensitivity and tapped his talent for melody played with elegance and tenderness. His first hit came with a solo he played in a Woody Herman big band performance during the late 1940s: "Early Autumn." His other hits were in a similar vein. His 1952 "Moonlight in Vermont" with guitarist Johnny Smith was one of them. His 1962 "Desafinado" with guitarist Charlie Byrd was a major event in the popularization of bossa nova. This was a kind of music that combined jazz with Brazilian styles, and it had considerable popularity. During the mid-1960s almost every jazz musician recorded at least one piece in the style, and Getz recorded several albums of bossa novas. His 1964 recording of the bossa nova "Girl From Ipanema," with its vocal by Astrud Gilberto, outsold almost every previous modern jazz record.

Stan Getz, the most popular jazz tenor saxophonist of the 1950s and 60s. Though he first emerged during the bebop era of the 1940s, some listeners consider him a "cool jazz" or, "bossa nova" player instead of a bebop stylist. But despite any resemblance to established trends, he really had his own style, and it was fresh and graceful.

Photo by Charles Behnke

THE POPULARITY OF BEBOP

With the arrival of bebop, the status of jazz began to resemble that of classical chamber music more than that of American popular music. It became a serious art music. Its performance required highly sophisticated skills, and it was appreciated by a relatively small elite. Jazz had always required special skills because of its demand for so much spontaneous creativity. As far as American popular music went, it had long been an elite art form. Yet bebop crystallized those tendencies, removed jazz even further from most of American popular music, and turned it into a fine art music.

Bebop was not nearly as popular as swing had been. When Charlie Parker died in 1955, he was an obscure figure compared to Benny Goodman, whose name was a household word. And yet Parker was musically a more significant force in jazz than Goodman. Several swing records sold more than a million copies. No bebop instrumentals ever came close to that. There are several possible explanations for this.

One reason why bebop was less popular than swing was that it had **less visual appeal.** Most swing bands carried singers, and many also carried dancers and showy staging. Bop combos, on the other hand, rarely carried any of this. To appreciate modern jazz, people had to listen instead of watch.

Another factor is that, by comparison with swing, **bebop had a scarcity of singers.** The bebop listener was rarely offered song lyrics or the good looks and personality of the singer delivering them. More than ever before, jazz fans now had to follow melodies that had no words. This made jazz more abstract and less enjoyable to the casual listener. Singers have always been more popular than instrumentalists. Lyrics are in a language that is common to both the performer and the listener. Jazz instrumentals, on the other hand, are in a language that is known to only a tiny portion of the listening public. In addition, the human voice produces a sound that is far more familiar to listeners than that of any instrument.

Listeners have historically shown that they prefer relatively uncomplicated music. Furthermore, they like music to be fairly predictable. They especially like themes that they can sing along with, remember, and hum by themselves. **In comparison to swing, bebop is much more complicated and unpredictable. The written melodies in many bebop performances are difficult to follow.** A sizable percentage of bebop tunes are so complicated that, even if listeners know them, it is hard to sing along with them.

Another factor that made bebop more challenging to understand is **the change in ratio between written and improvised music.** Swing bands framed short improvisations inside extended arrangements. The arrangements included much repetition which made the music easy to digest. On the other hand, bebop combos featured improvisers who played long solos after a melody was stated. There was much less reference material. The listener was more on his own.

Remember, too, that the large amount of arranged material in a swing band performance stayed the same in every performance, recorded or live. This offered even more familiarity to the listener. Bebop performances, on the other hand, were created anew each time a tune was played. Again, this is because the emphasis was mostly on improvisation. The smaller amount of repetition in the bebop performance would therefore present a greater listening challenge.

Still, despite the lesser popularity of bebop, there were a few groups and a few records that did become commercial successes. That music had some of the same features as swing. Also note that Charlie Parker's best-selling records were those he made of well-known songs with prewritten orchestral accompaniments.

It should be clear by now that a style's popularity is not based on its quality. Instead **the degree of popularity of a style of music can largely be attributed to differences in performance practices and in the ways each style treats the basic elements of music.** In comparing bebop to swing, these performance practices are relevant: appearance, amount of improvisation, repetition, the amount of framing for improvisation, and presence of words in the music.

The musical elements of melody, harmony, and rhythm are also treated differently in the two styles. Bebop offered higher, faster, more complex playing. Bebop featured more variety in rhythms, in melody lines and in accompaniments. Bebop used richer chords, more chord changes, and a more elaborate relationship between the notes of the melody and the notes of the accompanying chords.

Modern jazz continued the jazz tradition of influencing American popular music and symphonic music. But it seemed to carve its own sturdy path for musicians and a small audience of non-musicians. Bebop became the parent for a series of other fascinating modern styles, which were also less popular than swing. Jazz did not regain its popularity until the 1970s when a jazz-rock fusion brought millions of new fans.

The Modern Jazz Quartet: pianist John Lewis, vibra-harpist Milt Jackson, bassist Percy Heath, and drummer Kenny Clarke. Formed from members of Dizzy Gillespie's big band — all but Heath are heard on Gillespie's 1946 "Things to Come" record — this group became associated with "cool jazz" because it played soft jazz that was polished and restrained. Their work has often been likened to classical chamber music.

Photo by Bob Parent, courtesy of Don Parent

CHAPTER SUMMARY

1. Bebop differed from swing by using smaller bands; richer chords; more chord changes; drier, more biting tone qualities; and faster playing with more surprises.

2. The originators of bebop were alto saxophonist Charlie Parker, trumpeter Dizzy Gillespie, and pianist Thelonious Monk.

3. Parker wrote numerous tunes based on the accompaniment harmonies for popular songs and twelve-bar blues. These became standard repertory for generations of jazz musicians.

4. Gillespie devised an unorthodox trumpet style and led a string of outstanding combos and big bands.

5. Monk played piano in a very spare manner that was filled with unusual rhythms and harmonies. He wrote tunes that were difficult because of their odd accents and chord progressions.

6. The ideas of Art Tatum, Charlie Parker, and Dizzy Gillespie appeared in the piano style of Bud Powell. Powell was widely imitated, and he significantly altered jazz piano style by reducing the activity of the left hand.

7. Bebop drummers differed from swing drummers by increasing the frequency and spontaneity of kicks and prods, feathering the bass drum instead of pounding it, playing timekeeping rhythms on a suspended cymbal, and snapping the high-hat shut sharply on the second and fourth beats.

8. Bebop styles and their offshoots were less popular than swing styles because they used fewer popular tunes and singers. They also relied less on arrangements. Solos and accompaniments were more complicated. Consequently there was less predictability in the music.

BEBOP LISTENING

The Complete Bud Powell on Verve, from 1949–56 (Verve 314 521 669-2).

Bud Powell's 1947 rendition of "Somebody Loves Me" is in the *Smithsonian Collection of Classic Jazz*. His 1951 rendition of "Night in Tunisia" is in the revised edition of the *Smithsonian Collection of Classic Jazz*.

Thelonious Monk — *Genius of Modern Music, Vols. 1 and 2*, from 1947–52 (Blue Note 81510/81511).

Dexter Gordon — *Dexter Rides Again*, from 1945–71 (Savoy/Denon SV-0120/CY-78812).

Stan Getz is well represented on *Jazz Samba*, from 1962 (Verve 314 521 413-2), *Getz/Gilberto*, from 1964 (Verve 314 521 414-2), *Stan Getz at Storyville*, from 1951 (Roulette 94507), *Stan Getz and J.J. Johnson at the Opera House*, from 1957 (Verve 831272).

Dizzy Gillespie — *The Complete RCA Victor Recordings*, 1937–49 (RCA Bluebird 667528) and *Shaw 'Nuff*, from 1945–46 (Musicraft 70053).

Many of Charlie Parker's most significant recordings are on *The Genius of Charlie Parker* and *The Charlie Parker Story* (Savoy/Denon SV 0104 and 0105).

Original recordings by Monk, Gillespie, Parker, Davis and other bebop players are in the *Smithsonian Collection of Classic Jazz* available by mail from Smithsonian Books and Records (phone 800-419-5606).

SUPPLEMENTARY READING

The Charlie Parker Companion: Six Decades of Commentary by Carl Woideck (Schirmer, 1998)

Bird: The Legend of Charlie Parker by Robert Reisner (Citadel, 1962; DaCapo, 1975)

To Be or Not To Bop (autobiography) by Dizzy Gillespie (Doubleday, 1979)

Jazz Masters of the Forties by Ira Gitler (Macmillan, 1966; DaCapo, 1983)

Bebop: The Music and the Players by Thomas Owens (Oxford, 1995)

Charlie Parker: His Music and Life by Carl Woideck (Univ. Michigan, 1996)

Stan Getz: A Life in Jazz by Donald L. Maggin (William Morrow, 1996)

Straight, No Chaser: The Life and Genius of Thelonious Monk by Leslie Gourse (Schirmer, 1997)

CHAPTER 7

COOL JAZZ

Gerry Mulligan, Larry Bunker, Chet Baker, Lee Konitz   Photo by William Claxton

The term "cool jazz" refers to modern jazz that tends to be softer and easier than the bebop of Charlie Parker and Dizzy Gillespie. "Cool jazz" avoids roughness and brassiness. The term "cool" has been applied to the music of saxophonist Lester Young and some of the musicians whom he and Count Basie influenced. Though musicians inspired by Basie and Young were found in almost all regions of America, many of them were based in California during the 1950s. Because of this, "West Coast Jazz" came to designate soft bop and Basie-Young disciples who devised new styles there. New York, Chicago, and Boston were also centers of innovation in cool jazz.

LENNIE TRISTANO

Lennie Tristano (1919–1978) was a pianist, composer, and bandleader. He created a modern alternative to bebop during the 1940s in Chicago and New York. Tristano's music was just as complex as bebop, but it differed from bebop. (*Jazz Classics CD* Track 50) He avoided the pet phrases of Charlie Parker and Dizzy Gillespie. Tristano preferred very long phrases, and his lines were smoother and less jumpy than those of Parker and Gillespie. Also, he did not swing his music in the customary bebop manner. Like bebop, his lines did not resemble popular songs: they had no easily "singable" quality to them.

In creating a style of his own, Lennie Tristano began by learning the work of the great masters. Art Tatum and Lester Young were particularly important influences. In developing mastery of piano playing, Tristano learned how to play Tatum's difficult and impressive runs. He also made himself and his students learn Lester Young's solo improvisations by carefully listening to recordings. The 18th-century composer Johann Sebastian Bach was also important to him. Tristano regarded Bach so highly that he required his students to practice Bach compositions and learn to improvise in that style.

Lennie Tristano, pianist-composer who invented a modern jazz alternative to the bebop style of Bud Powell. Though often considered part of "cool jazz," Tristano's playing conveys a surging intensity.

Courtesy of Frank Driggs

LISTENING GUIDE

"Subconscious-Lee" featuring Lee Konitz and Lennie Tristano

Composed by Lee Konitz; recorded January 11, 1949 in New York City by Lee Konitz (alto sax), Billy Bauer (guitar), Lennie Tristano (piano), Arnold Fishkin (bass), and Shelly Manne (drums).

"Subconscious-Lee" was written by Lee Konitz in the style of Lennie Tristano, his teacher and the pianist on this recording. The piece follows the chord progression of the pop tune "What Is This Thing Called Love." The style of the melody and improvisations differs significantly from bebop in its pattern of accent, its extreme absence of space, its lack of variety in the lengths of notes, and its very quiet and smooth rhythm section sound. The tone of Konitz is lightweight, dry, and airy. The drummer uses brushes instead of sticks to play timekeeping rhythms. And he plays them on the snare drum in a smooth, slurred fashion, instead of on the cymbal in the more percussive manner of bebop drummers.

During the late 1940s and the early 1950s, many musicians liked this style more than they liked bebop. They were impressed by the comprehensive mastery Tristano's musicians had over their instruments. Many were awed by the speed, precision, and grace with which they played. The sounds were more uniform, the articulation was cleaner, and the music was less brassy and explosive than in bebop. On the other hand, the choice of notes was often more adventuresome harmonically than in bebop, and the Tristano-inspired lines were less melodic than Charlie Parker's.

In this performance, there is no introduction. The theme occupies the entire first chorus of the "What Is This Thing Called Love" chord progression. Then each musician is featured for a complete chorus. The final chorus is broken into four parts. The first is a Tristano solo improvisation of 8 measures (termed 8 "bars" by musicians). The second is a Bauer solo improvisation of another 8 bars. (Musicians term such a sequence "trading eights.") The third is a Konitz improvisation and the fourth is a Tristano improvisation. The ending is a new 8-bar line played by sax and guitar.

CD Track	Elapsed Time	
49	0' 00"	**Theme** played in unison by alto and guitar, accompanied by walking bass, timekeeping rhythms played by wire brushes on snare drum, and piano comping.
50	0' 32"	**Piano Solo Improvisation** by Lennie Tristano
51	1' 03"	**Guitar Solo Improvisation** by Billy Bauer
52	1' 34"	**Alto Sax Solo** by Lee Konitz
53	2' 05"	**Piano Solo** by Lennie Tristano (First A-Section of Form)
54	2' 13"	**Guitar Solo** by Billy Bauer (Second A-Section of Form)
55	2' 21"	**Alto Sax Solo** by Lee Konitz (Bridge of Form)
56	2' 29"	**Piano Solo** by Lennie Tristano (Final A-Section of Form)
57	2' 36"	**Ending:** New Line Played in Octaves by Alto Sax and Guitar

LEE KONITZ

Tristano's most talented student during the 1940s was alto saxophonist Lee Konitz (b. 1927). Tristano joined Konitz and made recordings which still dazzle listeners today. By the late 1940s, Lee Konitz had developed a new jazz saxophone style. (*Jazz Classics CD* Tracks 52 and 55) His speed and agility were very impressive and frequently compared to Parker's. Technically, these two alto saxophonists were in a class by themselves, outplaying all others. They were both masters of technique, but they played in different styles. This is an important point in jazz history: *Konitz's style was inspired by Tristano, while most other young alto saxophonists at that time were imitating Charlie Parker.*

Both Parker and Konitz steered away from the warm, syrupy lushness of older alto saxophonists Benny Carter and Johnny Hodges. But Konitz went further from swing era models than Parker: Konitz played with a light, dry, airy tone. He employed a slow vibrato and preferred the alto saxophone's upper register. His sound on the alto saxophone is comparable to Lester Young's on tenor. This represented a contrast with the biting, bittersweet sound of Charlie Parker. Also, Konitz did not like to sneak quotes from pop tunes into his playing the way Parker did. Konitz also differed from Parker in his rhythm and in the way he treated individual notes. He used less off-beat rhythm. Almost all the notes in his lines were slurred together, and he avoided hard, sudden attacks. The overall effect of the Konitz style typified "cool" jazz.

BIRTH OF THE COOL

In 1949 and 1950, trumpeter Miles Davis organized recording sessions of a nine-piece band in New York. It became known as the Miles Davis Nonet or the "Birth of the Cool" band. The group was formed partly from members of the Claude Thornhill big band. The concept for the music was inspired by the arranging style of Gil Evans, who had worked with Thornhill during the 1940s. In addition to Davis on trumpet, the nonet included Lee Konitz, who had played alto saxophone for Thornhill, and baritone saxophonist Gerry Mulligan, who had played and written for Thornhill. These three hornmen all employed lightweight tone qualities and preferred subdued effects. The nonet used a standard rhythm section of piano, bass, and drums. But Davis added something rather unusual. He added French horn and tuba along with a trombone, and he had no tenor saxophone or guitar. The overall effect was much more subdued than the sounds of big jazz bands had been. For this reason it was ultimately referred to as "cool jazz."

Lee Konitz, the leading alto saxophonist in cool jazz. Inspired by Lennie Tristano's piano style, Konitz offered a modern jazz alternative to the bebop sax style of Charlie Parker.

Photo by Bob Parent, courtesy of Don Parent

GERRY MULLIGAN

Gerry Mulligan (1927–1996) was Miles Davis' baritone saxophonist and primary composer-arranger on the Birth of the Cool recordings. He used a soft, dry, lightweight tone quality whose texture has been compared to tweed cloth. His approach was simpler and more direct than bebop. Rhythmically, Mulligan's improvisations were less jagged than those of Charlie Parker and Dizzy Gillespie. His choice of notes suggested great deliberation rather than wild exuberance. His phrases were coolly logical and systematically developed. He rarely squeezed a lot of notes into them. Mulligan's compositions were simpler than Tristano's and less intense than bebop pieces. Some are quite song-like, and they share the same gentleness one hears in his improvisations. These features of his style combine with his subdued tone quality to place his music squarely in the "cool" category.

The "Birth of the Cool" band led by trumpeter
Miles Davis (with alto saxophonist Lee Konitz and
baritone saxophonist Gerry Mulligan at his left).

Photo by Popsie Randolf, courtesy of Frank Driggs

In 1952, Mulligan moved to California and launched a series of
piano-less quartets. He played baritone saxophone, and was joined
by another horn, bass, and drums. Let's take a moment to consider
what it means to have a jazz group without a chording instrument.
Normally a piano provides chords to the soloists. These chords act as
a sort of an anchor, always reminding the horn players of where
they are in the harmony that accompanies the tune. In some ways
the piano chords direct the flow and texture of the music. A comping
pianist complicates the sound considerably. Therefore the absence of
piano in Mulligan's groups was partly responsible for the band's
light, simple sound texture. It also highlighted the bass, which
pianos often drown out. His drummers also contributed to this effect
by playing conservatively, often using wire brushes instead of sticks
to strike the drums and cymbals. All of these aspects together made
Mulligan's band sound "cool." Though Mulligan was based on the
West Coast for only about three years, his music came to stand for
what journalists mean by the term "**West Coast Jazz.**" Long after
returning to the New York area, Mulligan maintained his piano-less
format, and many listeners still considered him to be "**West Coast
Cool**" style.

Baritone saxophonist Gerry Mulligan and trumpeter Chet Baker were distinguished for their dry, subdued approach to modern jazz.

Photo by William Claxton

DAVE BRUBECK

Pianist Dave Brubeck (b. 1920) led the best known of all cool jazz groups. He performed in the San Francisco area during the 1940s and early 1950s. He achieved widespread international fame leading a quartet from 1951 to 1967 with California-born alto saxophonist Paul Desmond, a bassist, and a drummer.

The rhythmic feeling in a lot of Brubeck's playing has much in common with classical music. However, Brubeck never was a classical pianist. He simply stayed away from sounding like bebop players, either in his melody or his rhythm. This made him sound more "classical." In fact, sometimes he and Desmond improvised duets that sounded like the two-part inventions of J. S. Bach, accompanied by bass and drums. He is highly inventive, constantly making up his own improvised melodies. In other words, Brubeck is a modern jazz musician who does not use the bebop language, and who likes to play around with classical styles.

Dave Brubeck Quartet (drummer Joe Morello, bassist Gene Wright, pianist Dave Brubeck, alto saxophonist Paul Desmond), the most popular small group in jazz history.

Photo by Bob Parent, courtesy of Don Parent

Brubeck's popularity may also be partly due to his "classical" sound. His compositions and improvisations are simple and tuneful. They are easier to follow than the jumpy and explosive phrases in bebop. His creations are orderly and clear, making the listener's job easy. In addition, most of Brubeck's pieces are pretty, and they convey a light and pleasant mood.

Brubeck was also an innovator with rhythm. His use of unusual meters brought him much publicity. It also influenced other jazz musicians. During the 1960s his quartet crafted a number of tunes and improvisations in odd meters such as three, five, and seven beats to the measure, instead of the usual four. His albums *Time Out* and *Time Further Out,* which explored those meters, were immensely popular. *Time Out* contained "Take Five," a funky and engaging little theme whose accompaniment was a simple, repeated rhythm in meter of five. During the 1990s, people were still asking jazz groups to play it.

In the period 1955 to 1985, Brubeck ranked second in record sales among all jazz recording artists. During the 1950s and 60s, his name became almost as synonymous with jazz as Louis Armstrong and Duke Ellington. His quartet's music provided an introduction to jazz for millions of new listeners, including a whole generation of college students.

STAN KENTON

Stan Kenton (1912–1979) led the best-known succession of big bands in modern jazz. He presented repertories that spanned several eras and featured numerous styles. His name first became well known during the 1940s while he was leading a big band in the swing era style. A number of cool style musicians played in his bands. Kenton's music of the late 1940s and early 50s is also linked to cool jazz by arranging style. He was influenced by Claude Thornhill, after whom Miles Davis had modelled the "Birth of the Cool" band style.

In addition Kenton used a few arrangements by Gerry Mulligan, who had provided arrangements for the Davis band. Despite the connections with "cool" jazz, Kenton dubbed his music **"progressive jazz,"** and some have also called it "big band bop."

Kenton created a distinctive band style that is immediately recognizable. He turned out a large body of dance music. But the most impressive work he presented was nonswinging concert music which vividly exposed rich, modern harmonies. It was separate from the dance band tradition of big band jazz. The rhythmic feeling of classical music was common in his sound. The musicianship of his players was very high. The precision of his performances was almost equal to the sterling standards of symphony orchestras. Usually performed without vibrato, his brass and saxophone parts had a dry quality that some listeners call "transparent." Some pieces featured trumpet parts which were high-pitched, loud, and often included five-note chords. These sounds were combined with saxophone lines written in long strings of rapid notes which came up from under the trumpet and trombone sounds like fountains.

Though Kenton's performances usually ranged from the softest to the loudest of sounds, Kenton earned a reputation for leading the loudest big band. This was partly due to the number of brass instruments. It was common to find five trumpets and five trombones in a Kenton band. Additionally, some Kenton trombonists doubled on tuba, and one version of his band carried four mellophoniums. These instruments were trumpet-French horn hybrids which were specially made for Kenton.

Another trademark of the Kenton band sound was its glossy trombone tones. The music frequently featured harmonized parts for five trombones that were performed very smoothly. Kenton's trombone soloists preferred high-register work, and they graced the beginnings of many tones with long, climbing smears. They used a meticulously controlled vibrato which started slow and then quickened dramatically near the tone's end. Their approach was extroverted, but in a well-manicured way rather than the rough, guttural way of earlier jazz trombonists.

To help put Kenton's sound in perspective, let's compare it with Basie's. While Basie's band conveyed an easygoing and swinging feeling, Kenton's conveyed a solemn and weighty feeling that is quite serious. Kenton's sound resembles twentieth-century concert music written for trumpets, trombones, and saxophones with rhythm section. Sometimes other instruments associated with symphony orchestras were added—strings, French horns, and tuba. Latin American percussion instruments were also added during a number of different phases in Kenton's career. The band's character is based more on elaborate arrangements than on the simplicity and swing feeling associated with Basie. Remember that the Basie band of the late 1930s functioned much as a big combo. Solo improvisation was primary, and many of the horn backgrounds were almost incidental to the music. Kenton's approach contrasts with Basie's because its effect was frequently similar to a brass choir, not a big jazz combo. The Kenton bands usually emphasized composition more than improvisation.

Among Kenton's major contributions to jazz history were his skill at public relations and his motivation and talent for finding and leading creative modern musicians and composers. Lying behind this contribution is the fact that, because of his band's great popularity during the 1940s, Kenton became financially free enough to invest in musical experiments. He channeled this freedom into hiring relatively unknown writers and encouraging ambitious compositions which had little chance of realizing commercial success. Improvisers had enjoyed these kinds of opportunities throughout jazz history, but composers had not. He must also be credited with tenacity and durability. Though he began leading bands in 1941, when the big band era was still flourishing, he continued into the 1960s and 70s, when big bands were out of fashion. Moreover, he was one of the founders of the college stage band movement which is today the enormous jazz education establishment represented by Kenton-sized jazz bands in almost every high school and college. This movement in schools continued the big band tradition in jazz long after regularly touring big bands disappeared.

Stan Kenton's 1947 band, a platform for ambitious concert works, the most popular of all modern big bands, and a source for many "cool jazz" players. The five trumpets, five trombones instrumentation was popularized by Kenton and adopted by college "stage bands" thereafter. (A trumpeter closest to the drummer is mostly hidden in this photo of a rehearsal with Kenton seated at the piano.)

Photo by William P. Gottlieb

THE POPULARITY OF COOL JAZZ

A few players in the "cool" category are the most popular musicians in modern jazz. Trumpeter Miles Davis and saxophonist Stan Getz could pack nightclubs and concert halls. The Dave Brubeck Quartet was among the first groups in jazz that were sufficiently popular to tour regularly as concert artists. They appeared on college campuses and in recital halls which before them had presented only classical musicians. But only a few non-vocal cool jazz groups were this popular. For instance, Lennie Tristano and Lee Konitz were not known outside of well-informed jazz fans.

CHAPTER SUMMARY

1. Cool jazz is a term for modern styles that sound more subdued than the bebop of Charlie Parker and Dizzy Gillespie.

2. Count Basie and Lester Young were important influences on the cool jazz styles.

3. Pianist Lennie Tristano, alto saxophonist Lee Konitz, and trumpeter Miles Davis were among the first jazz musicians to devise styles that came to be called "cool."

4. The nine-piece band that Miles Davis recorded in 1949 and 1950 became known as the "Birth of the Cool" band.

5. Lee Konitz and baritone saxophonist Gerry Mulligan played in the "Birth of the Cool Band" with Miles Davis.

6. While in California Mulligan began leading a series of quartets that did not use piano. Because of their location and sound, he is still identified with the label "West Coast Jazz" or "cool jazz."

7. Pianist Dave Brubeck was the most famous cool jazz musician. His quartet performed and recorded from 1951 to 1967.

8. Stan Kenton led the best-known string of modern jazz big bands. Many of his musicians were associated with cool jazz.

COOL JAZZ LISTENING

Miles Davis — *Birth of the Cool* (Capitol 927862)

Stan Kenton — *New Concepts of Artistry in Rhythm* (Capitol 92865)

Kenton Showcase (Creative World 1026)

Lennie Tristano — *Intuition* (Capitol Jazz 52771)

Lee Konitz — *Subconscious-Lee* (Fantasy OJC-186) has excellent recordings of Lee Konitz and Lennie Tristano from 1949.

Konitz Meets Mulligan (Pacific Jazz 46847)

The Smithsonian Collection of Classic Jazz contains one piece by Lennie Tristano with Lee Konitz and one piece by the Miles Davis Nonet with Konitz and Gerry Mulligan.

The Best of the Gerry Mulligan Quartet with Chet Baker (Pacific Jazz 95481; 1952–1953)

Two Dave Brubeck Quartet albums that contain representative material are:

Jazz at Oberlin (Fantasy OJC-046) and
Time Out (CBS CK65122)

SUPPLEMENTARY READING

West Coast Jazz by Ted Gioia (Oxford, 1992)

Jazz West Coast by Robert Gordon (Quartet, 1986)

Stan Kenton: Artistry in Rhythm by William F. Lee (Creative Press of Los Angeles, 1980)

Gerry Mulligan and Miles Davis are discussed in *Jazz Masters of the Fifties* by Joe Goldberg (Macmillan, 1965; reprinted by DaCapo)

Lennie Tristano and Lee Konitz are discussed in *Jazz Masters of the Forties* by Ira Gitler (Macmillan, 1962; Da Capo, 1983)

Listen: Gerry Mulligan by Jerome Klinkowitz (Schirmer, 1991)

It's About Time: The Dave Brubeck Story by Fred M. Hall (University of Arkansas, 1996)

CHAPTER 8

HARD BOP

Cannonball Adderley   Photo by Popsie Randolf, courtesy of Frank Driggs

A number of jazz styles emerged during the 1950s and 60s. Most of them, including many of the "cool" styles, were variants on bebop. Though musicians tended to refer to all these styles as simply "bop" or "bebop," journalists and publicists coined new names such as hard bop, funky jazz, mainstream, post-bop, and soul jazz. The label "funky jazz" was attached most frequently to earthy, blues-drenched, gospelish pieces by Horace Silver, Cannonball Adderley, and others. The bluesy quality influenced a number of players who were popular in the 1960s and

70s. The small slice of this music called "funky jazz" was more popular than almost any other segment of modern jazz.

Let's look at several styles that coexisted with "funky jazz" and were sometimes performed by the same musicians who included funky pieces in their repertory. This stream of styles has no single, widely accepted name. "Hard bop" is the designation we use in this textbook. The sounds of most styles within this stream differ little from the sounds of bebop. But when they do differ, these trends frequently can be observed:

1. Drummers play with more activity.
2. Tone colors are darker, weightier, and rougher.
3. Chord progressions in the accompaniment are less frequently identical to those of pop tunes.
4. There is somewhat less of the start-and-stop quality that leaves the listener off balance.
5. There is a hard-driving feeling that pushes relentlessly, with an emphasis on consistent swinging.
6. Piano comping has more variety in rhythms and chord voicings.

Art Blakey, hard bop drummer and bandleader. Blakey's groups played with hard-driving, unrelenting force, always swinging with super-charged energy. For four decades Blakey continued to hire the top players, including Clifford Brown, Wayne Shorter, Freddie Hubbard, Wynton Marsalis, and others.

Photo by Bernie Thrasher, courtesy of Robert Asen—Metronome Collection

These traits first appeared during the early 1950s in the work of trumpeter Clifford Brown and the bands led by drummer Art Blakey. Later they persisted in the music of other bands which included those same musicians. They also survived in the music of their associates and followers. The musicians playing with Horace Silver worked within this style into the 1990s.

The sounds of hard bop were not found in only one particular geographic region. For example, forerunners of hard bop tenor sax styles included Los Angeles-based as well as New York-based players. In addition, Philadelphia and Detroit contributed many vital players, and so did Indianapolis.

The hard bop category also includes a second wave of players. This wave went beyond hard bop in creating its own stream of styles. These players made their mark in the 1960s and derived their approaches even less directly from bebop than did those players mentioned above. Much of their music draws upon sources outside hard bop. With the notable exception of saxophonist John Coltrane, who died in 1967, the most prominent in this wave were still active in the 1990s. They remained models for aspiring jazz musicians to imitate. The outstanding tenor saxophonists in this category are Joe Henderson and Wayne Shorter. The top trumpeter is Freddie Hubbard. The pianists are McCoy Tyner, Herbie Hancock, Chick Corea, and Keith Jarrett. The drummers are Tony Williams and Elvin Jones. You may know some of these names because of other styles they developed later. Such versatility is common to jazz giants. For example, Herbie Hancock contributed significantly to hard bop during the early 1960s and then created new styles in jazz-rock fusion of the 1970s and 80s.

HORACE SILVER

Horace Silver (b. 1928) is one of the biggest names in hard bop, a reputation derived mostly from his work as a composer and bandleader. But he also developed an original and substantial piano style. By the 1960s, he had replaced bebop's emphasis on long, bobbing lines with his own brief, catchy phrases. Virtuosity is not essential to Silver's style. He almost never plays fast for long stretches. Compactness and clarity are far higher priorities in his playing than speed and agility. His ideas unfold with a logic that is clear even to the inexperienced listener. Silver made considerable use of silence and was very clever in timing the starting and stopping points of his phrases. His solos are like his tunes—filled with simple ideas that are hummable and easy to remember. Each melodic segment is played in a forceful, percussive way. It is as though, while improvising, Silver keeps on composing at the same level of creativity and clarity that he maintains in his writing.

As an accompanist, Horace Silver initially drew from bebop style. By the late 1950s, however, he had perfected a new style of accompaniment. His accompaniment patterns sounded like structured set-ups for his soloists. This differed from the normal practice of spontaneous chording which responded to the twists and turns of solo improvisations. In this way, the soloists in Silver's bands were supported by backgrounds similar to those in big bands. Remember that big bands use written arrangements to supply the same accompaniment figures each time the soloist improvises on a piece. This gave Silver's music more continuity than was common in most modern groups. These accompaniments were also a restriction, however, since they limited the range of moods an improvising soloist could create. But Silver's accompaniments gave listeners something easier to hear, and this may account for his greater popularity.

Horace Silver was hard bop's most prolific composer. For the Blue Note record company alone, he composed almost all the tunes on over twenty-five years' worth of his bands' albums. Silver put together arrangements that were generally more elaborate than those of other hard bop groups. They often contained written melodies in the middle of a piece, as well as Latin American rhythms and hints of gospel music. Silver often assigned notes to trumpet and tenor saxophone, creating harmony that made it sound as though his quintet contained more than five musicians. In addition to using this technique, Silver often wrote bass figures and played them on the piano in unison with his bassist. These figures had an engaging quality which expanded the limited scope of bebop bass lines. It is partly for these reasons that his quintet was easily distinguishable from other bebop or hard bop groups. In addition, Silver's quintet performances were consistently swinging and polished, and they featured many of the best musicians of the 1950s and 60s. Silver remained active in the 1990s and continued to tour and record in his original style.

Horace Silver, the leading pianist-composer-bandleader in hard bop. Prolific and versatile, Silver composed catchy themes and arranged them for his quintets. His music swung with an appealing crispness and bounce.

Photo by Bob Parent, courtesy of Don Parent

MILES DAVIS

Jazz trumpeter and bandleader Miles Davis (1926–1991) played a pivotal role in the history of modern jazz. For fifty years he showed the foresight to anticipate trends in jazz styles well before they became widespread. During this period Davis created a very diverse body of music, which defined jazz for three different generations of listeners. His recordings won the near universal admiration of fellow jazz musicians. A significant slice of modern jazz history is documented in Davis-led recording sessions because he picked out the key innovators of each period for his bands and let them direct the course of his music in everchanging ways.

Unlike most artists, Davis never became limited to one particular band style. Among his most important contributions are

1. Creating an original and substantial **trumpet style**. This was first evident in recordings he made with Charlie Parker's group in the mid-1940s. It influenced many trumpeters of the cool jazz and hard bop styles.

2. Producing a large body of recordings with many distinctive, **high-quality performances**. His recordings served as textbooks for modern musicians in the way that recordings of Louis Armstrong and Lester Young had served earlier generations.

3. Making a **significant change** during the 1960s in his original trumpet style. In the 1980s, this variation became the basis for trumpet styles of Wynton Marsalis, Terence Blanchard, Wallace Roney, and others.

4. Being part of the "Birth of the Cool" recording sessions of 1949 and 1950 that combined Claude Thornhill's and Gil Evans' styles of orchestration with the subdued approaches of Gerry Mulligan, Lee Konitz, and himself: "**cool jazz**."

5. Pioneering "**modal jazz**" on the *Kind of Blue* album in 1959.

6. Pioneering the predominant group approaches and individual instrumental **styles of the 1980s and 1990s** (such as Marsalis and Wallace Roney) with his quintet of 1965–68.

7. Pioneering **jazz-rock fusion** styles with an original mixture of elements from "modal jazz," rock, and funk music on his *Bitches Brew* album of 1969.

Miles Davis did not invent entire jazz idioms himself. He organized bands of key innovators at early moments in the development of bop, cool jazz, modal jazz, and jazz-rock fusion. Davis' musicians often produced the best work of their careers while in his bands. They speak highly about his help in their own development and his wise editing of their music. There is a feeling of intelligent, well-measured musical creation in most Davis recordings.

Paul Chambers (bass), Cannonball Adderley (alto sax), Miles Davis (trumpet), and John Coltrane (tenor sax). Each man was a modern jazz giant on his respective instrument, and all were present on the historic *Milestones* and *Kind of Blue* recording sessions. Pictured here at the 1958 Newport Jazz Festival.

Photo courtesy of Frank Driggs

LISTENING GUIDE

"Two Bass Hit" featuring Cannonball Adderley and John Coltrane

Recorded in 1958 by Miles Davis (trumpet; no solo), Cannonball Adderley (alto sax), John Coltrane (tenor sax), Red Garland (piano), Paul Chambers (bass), Philly Joe Jones (drums).

The material for this performance was adapted from a piece originally written in the 1940s by pianist John Lewis for the Dizzy Gillespie big band. The title is a play on words, referring to the presence of two bassists in Gillespie's band as well as baseball terminology. Lewis recorded other versions of this piece under the title "La Ronde."

This recording was selected for several reasons:

1. to demonstrate hard bop drumming as exemplified by Philly Joe Jones, illustrating particularly well his

   a. supercharged, highly interactive manner

   b. crisp use of sticks on snare drum, especially at 4' 32"

   c. melodically conceived fills that are woven into breaks occurring between phrases of theme statements by the horns, especially at 43" to 57"

   d. coordination with accompaniment rhythms of the pianist, especially at 2' 01" and 3' 03"

   e. running commentary on the sax solos (this seems to pop and crackle, thereby increasing the excitement of Coltrane's and Adderley's work)

2. to demonstrate the mid-1950s style of tenor saxophonist John Coltrane, captured in a hard-swinging context. This particular style

preceded a string of innovative approaches that Coltrane began developing after this recording session.

3. to demonstrate the alto saxophone style of Cannonball Adderley with one of his best solos on record.

4. to offer a sample of what many musicians consider to be one of the best Miles Davis albums: *Milestones*.

CD Track	Elapsed Time	
58	0' 00"	**Introduction** (32 beats)
		Unison statements by trumpet, alto sax, tenor sax, piano, and bass alternate with drumming statements.
		Melody
	0' 07"	*A-section (4 groups of 4 beats)*
		Horns play a phrase, and piano echoes it. Bass is walking.
	0' 10"	*A-section repeats with variations*
	0' 14"	*B-section (8 groups of 4 beats)*
		Unison statements by trumpet, alto sax, tenor sax, piano, and bass alternate with drums.
	0' 21"	*A-section, with variations*
	0' 25"	*A-section, with variations*
	0' 28"	*C-section (8 groups of 4 beats)*
		Horns and piano play in unison.
	0' 36"	*D-section (8 groups of 4 beats)*
		Horns play in unison. Piano accents.
	0' 43"	*E-section (16 groups of 4 beats)*
		Horns, piano, and bass play stop-times under drum solo.
59		**John Coltrane Tenor Sax Improvisation**
	0' 57"	**1st Chorus** (Form Switches to 12-bar blues)
		Accompaniment includes: piano comping, walking bass, high-hat snapping shut sharply on every other beat, "chatter" made by drum sticks striking the snare drum, ride rhythms played by a drum stick striking the ride cymbal.
	1' 07"	*2nd Chorus*
	1' 18"	*3rd Chorus*
	1' 29"	*4th Chorus*
	1' 39"	*5th Chorus*
		Piano drops out.
	1' 50"	*6th Chorus*
	2' 01"	*7th Chorus*
		Piano returns, punctuating in unison with drums.
	2' 12"	*8th Chorus*
60		**Cannonball Adderley Alto Sax Improvisation**
		Notice the new sax's brighter tone quality and higher pitch.
	2' 23"	*1st Chorus*
		Accompaniment has piano and drums coordinated to begin this new solo. Walking bass continues.

CD Track	Elapsed Time	
	2' 33"	2nd Chorus
	2' 43"	3rd Chorus
		Piano drops out.
	2' 53"	4th Chorus
	3' 03"	5th Chorus
		Piano returns, punctuating in unison with drums.
	3' 14"	6th Chorus
		Piano plays preset rhythms with drums.
	3' 25"	7th Chorus
	3' 37"	8th Chorus
	3' 48"	9th Chorus
		Piano begins this chorus by playing four strokes in unison with the drummer, then piano stops playing.
	3' 59"	10th Chorus
	4' 10"	11th Chorus
		Trumpet plays descending scale to accompany sax solo.
	4' 22"	12th Chorus
		Trumpet plays descending scale to accompany sax solo. Drumming becomes highly active.
61	4' 32"	**Philly Joe Jones Drum Solo** (32 beats)
62	4' 39"	**Horns Play Melody**
		Horns play a phrase, and piano echoes it.
	4' 50"	Horns and bass sustain tones while drums continue.
63	4' 57"	**Drum Solo** (32 beats)
	5' 05"	**Horns Return**
		Horns play the same note three times in unison.
	5' 10"	**End**
		Drums and cymbals end the piece.

THE CLASSIC MILES DAVIS QUINTET

Miles Davis made many of his historically significant recordings as a bandleader for the Prestige record company. Musicians tend to prefer *Steamin'*, *Cookin'*, *Workin'*, and *Relaxin'*, all recorded in 1956 with tenor saxophonist John Coltrane, pianist Red Garland, bassist Paul Chambers, and drummer "Philly Joe" Jones. The style and energy of those recording sessions were particularly evident again in *Milestones*, an album he made for Columbia record company in 1958, with the same musicians plus alto saxophonist Cannonball Adderley. (See above.)

Though Miles Davis had long been linked with cool jazz, the band on these recordings sounds more like hard bop and later styles.

The musicians play with blistering intensity. Their work has an unusual freshness and excitement that combined to make these among the most striking jazz performances since the groundbreaking Parker-Gillespie records of the previous decade.

These recordings signalled the first time that many jazz fans heard John Coltrane's tenor saxophone. His work with Davis was so original that he would still qualify as a jazz giant if he had never done anything else. Still, some journalists considered these early recordings to be merely a development stage for Coltrane.

The classic quintet, with the addition of Cannonball Adderley, was responsible for a landmark event in jazz history. With their recording of the tune "Milestones" in 1958, they broke away from the practice of guiding improvisations solely by chord progressions. Most of the tunes Davis had recorded before 1958 were pop tunes or bebop compositions with frequently changing chords in their accompaniment. But instead of using frequently changing chords to guide their improvisations on "Milestones," the musicians used different scales. The first was in effect for 64 beats, the second for another 64 beats, followed by a return to the first for the final 32 beats. Basing a tune on scales allowed improvisers new types of freedom. They had fewer demands placed on their attention, so they could more easily concentrate on piecing together interesting melodies and rhythms. After the *Milestones* album (containing "Milestones") was released, this approach—the absence of changing chords—became popular among modern jazz musicians. This trend became especially popular following the release of Davis' very modal album *Kind of Blue*, recorded in 1959.

THE MILES DAVIS TRUMPET STYLE

Miles Davis created an unmistakable sound with his trumpet. It is so distinctive that we can instantly pick it out, even in the crowded mix of a rock record or the background music for a movie. He was such a uniquely creative thinker that he altered what listeners came to expect from jazz trumpet. His personal sound seems almost independent of the instrument. It is so much his own that to call it "Miles Davis" might be more accurate than to call it "jazz trumpet."

The uniqueness of the Davis style can be divided into at least seven components. The first two are manners of handling the trumpet sound. The most obvious is his expressively toying with pitch and tone quality at the beginnings and ends of notes.

A second component of Davis' highly personal style comes from using a Harmon mute. This resulted in a wispy sound that is delicate and intimate. He used this mute much more than other trumpeters. (See illustrations on pages 218–219. Listen to *Demo CD* Track 65 and *Classics CD* Tracks 65 and 69.)

A third component of the Davis style is an unusually skillful timing and dramatic construction of melodic figures. Davis was a master of self-restraint. His placement of silence is at least as significant as his choice of notes, and he often let several beats pass without

Miles Davis playing trumpet with Harmon mute. The sound that Davis produced when playing into this mute was so personal he might as well have patented it.

Photo by Bill Smith

playing. (*Jazz Classics CD* Track 65) During the moments he was not sounding his own notes, the sound of bass, drums, and piano came through clearly, further establishing the mood. The success of this very lean approach depends on the steadiness of swing feeling and overall musicality of the rhythm section. The silences in his own solos were filled in a highly musical, well-paced manner because Davis always hired the best accompanists.

More than most improvisers, Davis gave the impression that he was editing his solos very carefully while performing them, clarifying his ideas in his mind before letting them go through his horn. As Lester Young did on the tenor saxophone, Davis pared his thinking down to a bare core of melodic material; and like Young's solos, the best Davis improvisations seem to "tell a story."

A fourth component of the Davis style can be identified by comparing rhythmic concepts. Most modern trumpeters play swinging lines staying close to a strict tempo and swing feeling, even when they play slow tunes. These players practice a very precise subdivision of each beat. Miles Davis, on the other hand, not only improvised swinging melodic figures, but he also sometimes played outside of strict tempo and away from the swing feeling. This introduced a further element of rhythmic freedom.

A fifth component is an acute sensitivity in paraphrasing. The Davis paraphrases of popular songs were constructed in such fresh ways that the finished products were like new melodies.

A sixth component is Davis' simplicity. He could play with bebop-style complexity. But, instead, he often constructed solos of brief, simple phrases. Many of his improvisations on blues and slow pieces consist of only a few notes. These notes were chosen and timed so well and played so expressively that the effect is dramatic.

A seventh component is his handling of tone quality and pitch range. During the 1940s and 50s, Davis played with a tone quality that was lighter, softer, and less brassy than that of most other trumpeters. He used almost no vibrato; he favored the trumpet's middle register over its flashier high register; and he rarely double-timed. His style was gentle by comparison with the styles of most other modern trumpeters.

LISTENING GUIDE

"Blue in Green" featuring Miles Davis and Bill Evans

Composed by Bill Evans, though often mistakenly credited to Miles Davis; recorded in 1959 by Miles Davis (Harmon-muted trumpet), John Coltrane (tenor sax), Bill Evans (piano), Paul Chambers (bass), and Jimmy Cobb (drums); originally released on *Kind of Blue* (Columbia PC 8163)

This selection demonstrates

1. the chord voicing and ballad style of pianist Bill Evans
2. the unique tone qualities and musical character achieved by trumpeter Miles Davis playing through a Harmon mute
3. the very personal manner that Miles Davis originated for playing slow pieces and generating calm, reflective moods
4. the unique touch that tenor saxophonist John Coltrane used for treating slow meditative pieces
5. a sample of *Kind of Blue*, the album that is most frequently cited by jazz musicians and critics in lists of all-time favorites

CD Track	Elapsed Time	
		Introduction
64	0' 00"	Bill Evans plays gently on piano, accompanied by the bassist sounding one note on each chord. Each chord lasts two beats.
65	0' 17"	**First Chorus**
		Miles Davis plays the melody on Harmon-muted trumpet. The harmonic pace shifts to one chord for every four beats. Davis' manner is very relaxed, almost lagging behind the beat on purpose. The drummer is dragging wire brushes around the surface of the snare drum (achieving an almost continuous "shhhhhhss" effect).

CD Track	Elapsed Time	
	1' 00"	**Second Chorus**
		Davis takes more liberties with the melody. Bass improvises counterlines.
66	1' 43"	**Third Chorus**
		Improvised piano solo by Bill Evans. He doubles the harmonic pace so that each chord lasts for two beats.
	2' 04"	**Fourth Chorus**
		Piano solo continues.
67	2' 25"	**Fifth Chorus**
		John Coltrane tenor sax improvisation. He begins in the high register and plays a solo that uses very few notes. This is one of the most elegant Coltrane improvisations on record.
	2' 47"	**Sixth Chorus**
		Sax solo continues.
68	3' 07"	**Seventh Chorus**
		New piano solo by Evans. Original melody is played almost verbatim. But the pace has doubled so each chord lasts only one beat.
	3' 17"	**Eighth Chorus**
		Piano solo continues with Evans improvising upon the melody.
69	3' 27"	**Ninth Chorus**
		improvised trumpet solo, with the pace of chord movement so slow that each chord lasts four beats
	4' 09"	**Tenth Chorus**
		Davis continues soloing, and Evans punctuates and complements the solo with improvised piano chords. Bass plays only a few notes instead of a regular pattern.
70	4' 49"	**Eleventh Chorus**
		Evans plays the melody on piano at four times the pace of the preceding chorus; that is, each chord lasts one beat.
	4' 54"	Drummer rubs his brushes on the snare drum then drops out. Bass drops out.
	5' 01"	Bass returns, now bowing instead of plucking his strings.
	5' 04"	**Twelfth Chorus**
	5' 16"	**Conclusion**
		Bowed bass concludes Evans' phrase.

CLIFFORD BROWN

The modern styles of trumpet playing began in the 1940s with Dizzy Gillespie, who influenced Miles Davis and Fats Navarro. However, it was the successor to these men who had the greatest impact on hard bop. His name was Clifford Brown (1930–1956), and he drew his style largely from Navarro. Among musicians, Brown is probably the most widely admired trumpeter since the swing era. However he is not widely known outside the inner circles of modern jazz musicians, and he recorded only from 1952 to 1956.

Brown used a wider, more deliberate vibrato than Gillespie or Davis. Brown's slow vibrato may be responsible for its renewed use by jazz trumpeters in the 1950s and 60s. Another distinguishing mark of Brown's style is the overall contour of his solos. Brown tended to jump into the high register less often than Gillespie. The contours of Brown's lines are also usually smoother than Gillespie's, and he did not tend to make as many peculiar note choices as Gillespie. His improvisations were more melodic and pretty.

Let's consider several reasons why musicians were so impressed with Clifford Brown's playing. Most important was that Brown managed to convey relaxation in his playing, even when playing complicated melodic figures. This has at least two possible causes: his masterful control over the trumpet and his attempt to refine bebop instead of blazing new trails as Parker and Gillespie had. Brown also preferred to swing rather than to try to throw off his listeners with surprise after surprise, as bebop soloists often did. Brown developed a repertory of his own phrases which led him gracefully through the chord progressions. These techniques, his fluid manner, and easy swing feeling influenced numerous other trumpeters. Brown's contributions then became a stock vocabulary for other hard bop players. (*Jazz Classics CD* Track 72)

Clifford Brown, the favorite trumpeter for most jazz musicians of the 1950s. An exceptionally melodic improviser, Brown had a pretty tone and unprecedented playing speed and agility.

Photo by Bob Parent, courtesy of Don Parent

Clifford Brown's music projected a joyful spirit. This, together with the lilt and bounce in his lines, was contagious. He could generate long, flowing lines at furious tempos and still maintain the warmth and ease of his wide, glowing tone. Most other trumpeters were amazed at Brown's dazzling speed and agility. Also, he did what is almost impossible at those frantic speeds: he kept very accurate pitch, what musicians call "playing in tune." He also kept his swing feeling relaxed. His firm command of accurate articulation was unparalleled in modern jazz. The result was that meaty phrases came tumbling from his horn, chorus after chorus after chorus. This happy feeling, along with his pretty sound and fertile imagination, strongly influenced an entire generation of modern trumpeters.

LISTENING GUIDE

"Gertrude's Bounce" featuring Clifford Brown and Sonny Rollins

Recorded January 4, 1956 in New York City by Clifford Brown (trumpet), Sonny Rollins (tenor saxophone), Richie Powell (piano), George Morrow (bass), and Max Roach (drums).

This is a superb performance by one of the top groups in mid-1950s jazz, the Clifford Brown-Max Roach Quintet with Sonny Rollins. Each soloist's improvisations are distinctly fluid, melodic, and swinging, despite the challenge placed by the brisk tempo. The band pianist, Richie Powell, composed its main theme, which, along with all the solo improvisations, is based on the progression of accompaniment chords for George Gershwin's "I Got Rhythm." (This is a 32-bar A-A-B-A song form explained on *Demonstration CD* Track 33.) The 13-bar introduction, also used as an ending, is pitched in a higher key and follows a fresh progression of chords, organized in a group of 4 bars, repeated once, followed by a 1-bar transition, and a new group of 4 bars. (See Elements of Music Appendix for explanation of these technical terms.)

This music was recorded about the time when the term "hard bop" began to distinguish much post-Charlie Parker/Dizzy Gillespie music from other styles. However, if we compare this with music by Art Blakey or Cannonball Adderley, we may understand how sounds classified as "hard bop" sometimes differ little from bebop. Here are some notable similarities. With the exception of a few odd chords, particularly in the tune's bridge, the composition continues bebop's practice of borrowing pop tune progressions. The drummer here is Max Roach, the leading drummer in 1940s bebop. The band's trumpeter Clifford Brown derived his style largely from bebop master Fats Navarro. The saxophonist Sonny Rollins was deeply influenced by bebop founder Charlie Parker. Lastly, this performance sounds more swinging and less weighty than most music that is designated "hard bop," such as Art Blakey's work. It is also considerably less funky than the hard bop of Cannonball Adderley and Horace Silver.

CD Track	Elapsed Time	
71	0' 00"	**Introduction** by trumpet and sax in harmony, accompanied by bass and drums
	0' 13"	**Melody** by trumpet and sax in unison, piano on bridge
72	0' 46"	**Clifford Brown Trumpet Solo** (2 choruses long)
73	1' 48"	**Sonny Rollins Tenor Sax Solo** (1 chorus long)
74	2' 19"	**Richie Powell Piano Solo** (1 chorus long)
75	2' 50"	**Max Roach Drum Solo** (1 chorus long)
	3' 19"	**Melody** by trumpet and sax in unison, piano on bridge
	3' 50"	**Ending** (same as introduction)
	3' 57"	**Fade-out**

FREDDIE HUBBARD

Miles Davis and Clifford Brown remained models for aspiring trumpeters to imitate long after they first became known among musicians. But by the 1970s, the majority of young trumpeters were imitating another model: Freddie Hubbard. Though his early playing drew from Clifford Brown and Miles Davis, Hubbard (b. 1938) had developed his own original approach by the early 1960s. His playing style departed from bebop and was compatible with "free jazz" approaches of the 1960s and "jazz-rock" approaches of the 1970s.

A number of characteristics can help us distinguish Hubbard from Brown and Davis. Although he incorporated some Davis techniques of altering his tone quality and pitch, Hubbard refused to stray from the beat the way Davis liked to. Instead, Hubbard stuck close to the beat and liked to double-time. Also, in contrast to the more solemn and methodical manner of Davis, much of Hubbard's work sounds offhanded and playful. There is a looseness to his approach that implies great creative freedom and flexibility. Instead of following through on every idea, he does not hesitate to interrupt himself to pursue a new one. His style bristles with excitement; even his ballad renditions reveal great verve. Like saxophonist John Coltrane, he avoids stock bebop phrases. Instead he will spontaneously construct and rework figures from odd combinations of notes and rhythms. In this way he was daring and impulsive. The richness and range of his imagination combined with his free manner to build a new vocabulary for jazz trumpet style.

Freddie Hubbard is almost universally envied among trumpeters for his outstanding mastery of the instrument. His tone is clear and well focused. His intonation is excellent. His articulation is crisp. He can improvise coherently at brisk tempos and sound as though he still has plenty of strength and agility in reserve. Like Brown's, Hubbard's sense of time was very precise.

Freddie Hubbard, the most imitated trumpeter of the 1970s. He followed Miles Davis and Clifford Brown by devising an original style that was compatible with hard bop and jazz-rock.

Photo by Paula Ross

CANNONBALL ADDERLEY

Cannonball Adderley (1928–1975) was one of the best improvisers to play alto saxophone after Charlie Parker died. In a few respects, Adderley's style is like Parker's: very flowing, supercharged with energy, and unpredictable. But Adderley's first inspiration was not Parker but the swing era styles of Pete Brown and Benny Carter.

Cannonball Adderley's tone quality on the alto saxophone was so deep and full that listeners sometimes mistook it for a tenor saxophone. Together with the vibrato Adderley used, the effect of his tone was warm and glowing. He colored this huge tone with blue notes and wails. The result was an earthy, legato style that has been called "blues drenched." In contrast to the serious urgency of most hard bop, Adderley's playing suggests fun. He loved to double-time, and he often put snippets of pop tunes into his improvised lines. Often he dug into an improvisation and spun inspired lines, with a dense rush of activity and zigzagging directions. (*Jazz Classics CD* Track 60) But Adderley was not always bouncy and lighthearted. He could also be calm and meditative. For instance, his solos on the Davis album *Kind of Blue* sound very reflective. They are among the most original improvisations he recorded.

On and off during the 1950s, 60s, and 70s, Cannonball Adderley co-led a series of bands with his brother, cornetist Nat Adderley. The groups enjoyed a large following and continued until Cannonball's death in 1975. Many pieces in the band's repertory were categorized "funky jazz": "Jive Samba," "Work Song," "Sack o' Woe," "Walk Tall," "Country Preacher," and their biggest hit, "Mercy, Mercy, Mercy." Though most of its repertory was swinging music in the bebop style, the group was best known for its funk hits. These tunes, their style and feeling, anticipated jazz-rock fusion.

Cannonball Adderley, hard bop alto saxophonist-bandleader-composer. One of the top improvisers in the 1950s and 60s, Adderley also became an important figure in funky jazz. The bands he co-led with his brother Nat Adderley (also pictured here) had a number of hit records that helped define the bluesy, soulful, gospelish approach.

Photo by Herman Leonard, courtesy of Robert Asen—Metronome Collection

SONNY ROLLINS

There were many excellent tenor saxophonists who played hard bop. Although an entire book could be written about them, we will consider two stand-outs—John Coltrane and Sonny Rollins. Coltrane created an original hard bop style that was documented in recordings he made in the 1950s while with the combo of Miles Davis. Rollins had his creative peak during the 1950s and remains the favorite jazz tenor of many musicians.

Sonny Rollins (b. 1930) began recording in 1949 and was second only to Stan Getz as the most popular tenor saxophonist of the 1950s. Though he is known today for his originality, Rollins was among the first group of musicians to use Charlie Parker's alto sax style on tenor saxophone. His name is often mentioned along with Charlie Parker and John Coltrane when saxophonists themselves list their favorites.

People admired Rollins for the way he started with simple melodic ideas and then developed them. In this way he produced solos that drew a listener in and told a musical story. He has such a powerful musical mind that he avoids musical clichés, even at high speeds. When playing fast, most jazz musicians tend to use easily fingered patterns instead of original melodic ideas. Not Rollins.

During the 1950s, the Rollins tone quality was hard, rough, and dry. Some listeners called it "brittle." His vibrato was slow and very deliberate. While most bebop tenor saxophonists used a smooth *legato* style phrasing, Rollins frequently used a choppy *staccato* style phrasing. Often he would attack bluntly, move to legato and back again to staccato. He delivered his phrases without ornamentation or any other kind of softening. The overall effect of his playing was brusque and aggressive, though not necessarily explosive or blistering.

Clifford Brown (left) and
Sonny Rollins (right), the
top hornmen in hard bop
of the 1950s.

Photo by Chuck Stewart

Sonny Rollins is a giant in the history of improvisers. He mastered the rhythmic devices necessary to swing, and he swung whenever he wished. But he also purposely deviated from the tempo at times, as if he were inside the beat one moment and ignoring it the next. Rollins treated a piece as though its tempo, chord progressions, and melody were mere toys to be played with. He redesigned them from moment to moment without necessarily respecting their original flavor.

Some listeners feel that Rollins' career reached its peak during the 1950s. They feel he did his most lyrical playing with Miles Davis and his most swinging playing with Clifford Brown. Whether you agree or not, there is no question that his recordings in the 1950s stand as landmarks in the history of tenor saxophone style.

During the 1960s, Rollins streamlined his style and explored less conventional approaches to improvisation. During the 1970s and 80s, Rollins played in ways that differed significantly from his style of the 1950s and 60s. He adopted a sound that was broader, coarser, and more guttural. In addition, he played with less speed and crispness. In contrast to his earlier style, his playing became simpler and funkier. Rollins kept the singing quality in his playing, but now his roots in Charlie Parker were barely detectable.

The tunes he performed in the 1970s and 80s were simpler, too, and their accompaniments sounded like disco, funk, and Latin

American dance styles. Although Rollins occasionally returned to more bebop-like playing, he now preferred to play in his new style. In fact, it was so gutsy and so much like popular music that it fit perfectly with the style of the Rolling Stones. That popular blues-oriented rock and roll group used him on one of their recordings. So twenty years after being the top hard bop tenor player, Sonny Rollins had mastered a new style and gained a broader audience.

JOHN COLTRANE

John Coltrane (1926–1967) is among the ten most important figures in jazz history. He had profound impact as a tenor and soprano saxophonist, composer, and bandleader. Hundreds of Coltrane imitators could be found among saxophonists of the 1960s, 70s, 80s, and 90s. His improvisational concepts and compositions were used not only by saxophonists but also by pianists, trumpeters, and guitarists. The combo sound that his quartet perfected became a major force during the few years the quartet toured, and it has remained an influential model ever since the group disbanded. The immense force of Coltrane's music has inspired poetry, sculpture, and modern dance. Even a church was founded in Coltrane's name.

Coltrane had developed a very individual style by 1955, when he first recorded with Miles Davis. By then, his roots were far less evident than his own fresh ideas. His approach was unusually vigorous. His tone was rough-textured and biting, huge and dark. Coltrane gave it a massive core and a searing intensity. It was full and penetrating in every register, from the lowest notes to the highest. He played with remarkable speed and agility, possibly as much as any other saxophonist in jazz history. Coltrane's impressive command over the tenor saxophone inspired hundreds of other saxophonists to work very hard on instrumental proficiency. Like Charlie Parker before him, Coltrane stimulated a taste for rapid, densely packed solo improvisations among young players.

Coltrane's pre-1960s playing showed a fascination for chord changes. His system involved putting chords together that sounded odd next to each other. Then, when he improvised solos, Coltrane devoured the chord changes. He tried to play every note in every chord and every scale that might be compatible with it. This was a historically significant contribution to the evolution of jazz styles. Journalist Ira Gitler described Coltrane's furiously paced streams of notes as "sheets of sound." (*Jazz Classics CD* Track 59)

The classic example of Coltrane's rapid playing over frequently changing chords was the title track on his *Giant Steps* album, recorded in 1959. Chords in it seldom last more than two fleeting beats, and each chord stakes out new territory. Coltrane originally wrote "Giant Steps" as an exercise to gain mastery over a difficult and unconventional situation for an improviser.

Coltrane exerted a striking effect on his listeners. People who hated his music argued in print with those who were impressed by it. Some felt that jazz history ended with Coltrane, whereas today many

John Coltrane, the most influential saxophonist in the second fifty years of jazz history.

Photo by Bob Parent, courtesy of Don Parent

feel it only just started with him. So many saxophonists in the 1970s and 80s were imitating him that journalists of this period were complaining about a general lack of originality just as they had done with the wave of Charlie Parker followers that rose during the 1950s. Saxophonist Andrew White was so inspired by Coltrane's music that he listened very carefully to more than six hundred recorded Coltrane solos and wrote down every note in each one.

Each of Coltrane's style periods caused many musicians to try out the techniques that Coltrane had used. First it was multi-noted playing and difficult chord progressions. Coltrane's way of replacing the chord changes from standard tunes was widely imitated. Musicians wrote tunes in which chords moved in ways similar to Coltrane's. Then it was modal style, as discussed in the next chapter. After that, it was simultaneous collective improvisation and the creation of frantic turbulence that emphasized textures more than the development of melody-like lines. Sometimes it appeared as though an entire community of jazz musicians had decided that Coltrane was their guide, and they waited to see what he was going to do next before they acted on their own. Even important musicians who were already known for considerable originality felt the impact of Coltrane's work.

THE POPULARITY OF HARD BOP

Like bebop musicians, hard bop musicians found that the public tended to neglect their music. Only a few managed to make steady livelihoods from performing jazz. The historically significant bands of Clifford Brown were unknown except to musicians and a small population of fans. During the 1950s, Sonny Rollins and John Coltrane were well known by jazz fans but almost unknown otherwise. The few hard bop pieces that found their way onto jukeboxes were mostly simple, funky compositions arranged with lots of very repetitive accompaniment rhythms and less improvisation than was found in most hard bop performances. Some of these accounted for brief periods of success enjoyed by Cannonball Adderley and Horace Silver, especially during the 1960s and 70s. But the highest record sales went to the organ-guitar-drums groups of Jimmy Smith and the piano-bass-drums group of Ramsey Lewis. These are players whose music is much simpler and helps define funky jazz. Musicians and critics do not ordinarily consider their music to be as serious as that of the other players we have discussed.

CHAPTER SUMMARY

1. Hard bop evolved directly from bebop during the 1950s, mainly among East Coast and Midwest musicians.

2. When hard bop differs from bebop, it is simpler; has more variety in accompaniment patterns; fewer pop tune chord progressions; darker, weightier tone qualities; and more emphasis on hard swinging.

3. Funky jazz is a subcategory of hard bop. It is characterized by bluesy inflections of pitch and gospel-type harmonies. Several pieces performed by the bands of Horace Silver and Cannonball Adderley were popular because of their funky qualities and simple, catchy melodies.

4. The most prominent figures in hard bop were drummer-bandleader Art Blakey; pianist-composer Horace Silver; trumpeters Clifford Brown, Miles Davis, and Freddie Hubbard; alto saxophonist-bandleader Cannonball Adderley; and tenor saxophonists Sonny Rollins and John Coltrane.

5. Miles Davis was a pivotal bandleader in bebop, cool jazz, modal jazz, and jazz-rock fusion. His trumpet style is very distinctive in many ways that are widely admired.

6. John Coltrane was the most influential saxophonist in jazz after Charlie Parker. He was also important for several styles of composing.

HARD BOP LISTENING

The Smithsonian Collection of Classic Jazz has renditions of "Pent-Up House" by Sonny Rollins and Clifford Brown, "Blue Seven" by Sonny Rollins, and "So What" by Miles Davis, John Coltrane, and Cannonball Adderley.

Cannonball Adderley — *Cannonball and Coltrane,* from 1959 (Emarcy 834588-2) and *Mercy, Mercy, Mercy,* from 1966 (Capitol 29915)

The *Jazz Classics Compact Disc for Jazz Styles: History and Analysis* (ISBN 0-13-012693-4; phone 800-947-7700) contains the complete 1959 recording of "Flamenco Sketches" by Miles Davis, John Coltrane, Cannonball Adderley, and Bill Evans; the complete 1963 recording of "The Promise" by John Coltrane, McCoy Tyner, and Elvin Jones; and the complete 1967 recording of "Masqualero" by Miles Davis, Wayne Shorter, and Herbie Hancock.

Freddie Hubbard is well represented on Herbie Hancock's albums *Empyrean Isles* (Blue Note 84175, from 1964) and *Maiden Voyage* (Blue Note 7243-4-98796-2-1, from 1965).

Horace Silver is well represented by his own albums *Horace-Scope* (Blue Note 84042, from 1960) and *Cape Verdean Blues* (Blue Note 84220, from 1965).

Art Blakey recordings that typify his hard bop bands include: *A Night at Birdland* (Blue Note 46519/20, from 1954) and *Mosaic* (Blue Note 46523, from 1961).

Sonny Rollins and Clifford Brown recorded some of their best work on *Sonny Rollins Plus Four* (Fantasy OJC-243, from 1956).

SUPPLEMENTARY READING

Jazz Masters of the Fifties by Joe Goldberg (Macmillan, 1965; reprinted by Collier and by DaCapo)

Miles Davis: The Autobiography (Simon and Schuster, 1989)

Sonny Rollins by Charles Blancq (Twayne, 1983)

Chasin' the Trane (biography of John Coltrane) by J.C. Thomas (Doubleday, 1975; reprinted by DaCapo)

Coltrane: A Biography by C.O. Simpkins (Black Classic, 1989)

Milestones (biography of Miles Davis) by Jack Chambers (DeCapo, 1998)

Miles Davis: A Biography by Ian Carr (Morrow, 1982)

John Coltrane: His Life and Music by Lewis Porter (Univ. Mich Pr, 1997)

CHAPTER 9

AVANT-GARDE OF THE 1960S AND 70S

Cecil Taylor

Photo by Grace Bell

The term "avant-garde" refers to the advance group of creators in any field of art or music. It designates individuals who are ahead of everybody else in developing the newest, freshest styles. All of the style chapters in this book are about innovators rather than imitators. So all the chapters could justify having "avant-garde" in their title; yet this is the only chapter titled "avant-garde." There are two reasons for this. First, the term has been applied in recent writing about jazz history as though it were a style by itself. New kinds of jazz in the 1960s and 70s were classified by a single term such as "avant-garde" or "the new thing," instead of original names such as Dixieland, swing, or bebop. Second, this textbook needs a chapter to discuss several significant modern styles that don't really fit in the other chapters. So the full

145

title for this chapter ought to be "avant-garde jazz musicians of the 1960s and 70s not treated elsewhere." Keep in mind that, as in the rest of the book, we are only looking at a few of the most prominent musicians of the period. There were other outstanding players during this period whom we don't have the space to discuss.

"Free jazz" is a classification that is sometimes applied to a few avant-garde jazz styles of the 1960s. It is most closely associated with **Ornette Coleman** and **Cecil Taylor.** *"Free jazz" gets its name from the fact that the musicians are improvising jazz that is free from preset chord progressions.* The term has also been applied to improvisation that is free from conventional practices of any kind, not just preset chord progressions. But the term can be deceiving because very little of the music is entirely free of tempo or key. It is rarely free of distinctions between soloists and accompanists. Moreover, a lot of the so-called "free" music does contain preset aspects such as a written or memorized melody, a definite order for soloists, and so forth.

A model for this music is a 1960 album by Ornette Coleman called *Free Jazz.* This recording contains music by two bands of musicians who are all playing at the same time and trying to improvise without following preset key, melody, or chord progressions. During the 1960s and 70s, a number of other modern jazz musicians tried collective free improvisation. Much of it was high-energy, high-density playing that contained no bebop phrasing or swing feeling. Similar styles appeared during the 1970s and 80s. Some of the inspiration for this came from John Coltrane, because he was the most prominent bandleader to try this approach.

Most free jazz groups omitted piano. There are several reasons for this. Historically the jazz pianist had assumed a role of providing chord progressions. Yet the restrictions created by preset chord progressions were exactly what free players were trying to free themselves from. Another reason is that few pianists were comfortable improvising without the suggestion of chords or key. It was as though, having been the harmonic gatekeepers for so long, they did not want to function when preset chord progressions were removed.

The role of the drummer in a free jazz group was significantly different from that in more conventional groups. *Instead of functioning as a timekeeper, sometimes the drummer provided only an undercurrent of drum sounds.* He used all the different instruments of the drum set to create a continuous variety of shadings. All four limbs were devoted to generating textures that popped and crackled. Free jazz drummers produced sound patterns that were less predictable than those of their counterparts in swing and bebop. *This was a major departure from the drumming traditions of marching band and dance band.*

Three qualities associated with free jazz have nothing to do with the absence of chord progressions: (1) **More extensive manipulations of pitch and tone quality**. Ultra-high-register playing was common, with the addition of shrieks, squawks, wails, gurgles, and squeals. Rough, hoarse tone qualities were also common. (2) **The creation of textures often seemed more important than the** development of melodies. **The "free jazz" label was often applied to music of high energy and dense textures which maintained turbulent activity for long periods**. In fact high-energy, dense-textured playing was sometimes dubbed "free jazz" even when the music was not free of key, set chord progression, or steady tempo. (3) **The free players' concept of melody displayed a loosening of bebop melodic and rhythmic practices that had been standard for jazz musicians since the 1940s**. Phrasing was often more fragmented. Sustained tones were alternated with screeches and moans. There was more of an unfinished quality in free style than in bebop style performances.

Some avant-garde jazz players of the 1960s and 70s pursued **non-European musical approaches which don't rely much on chord progressions. This includes some types of music from Africa, Indonesia, China, the Middle East, and India**. Like free jazz, many of these non-European forms of music did not use chord instruments. So it was logical for such development to have occurred with free players who also stayed away from piano and guitar. This interest led to combining jazz with music of non-European cultures, sometimes termed **Third World music** or **World music**. This resulted in kinds of music that are simpler than bebop.

One of the leading saxophonists in "free" jazz, Albert Ayler inspired John Coltrane during the 1960s.

Photo by Bill Smith

You can see from this discussion that free jazz players have developed new ways of playing their instrument as well as playing in a group. Free jazz players also opened themselves to music from other cultures.

ORNETTE COLEMAN

Alto saxophonist Ornette Coleman (b. 1930) was one of the most influential forces in jazz of the 1960s and 70s. Some consider him to have been as historically significant as Charlie Parker. In addition to being an important improviser, Coleman is also one of the freshest, most prolific post-bop composers. His style is quite original, and he has an exceptional gift for melody. Some of his tunes are quite catchy, despite their unusual rhythmic and harmonic qualities. A few are strikingly playful.

Though Coleman's music is known for its freedom from preset accompaniment chords, that's about all it's free of. The music actually has quite a bit of self-imposed structure. The musicians usually play at the same tempo throughout a given piece. They use written and memorized tunes during some portion of each performance. Though Coleman freely changes keys while he is improvising, he usually stays in each one long enough for us to hear that he is indeed in a particular key. And there is nothing haphazard about the freedoms with which Coleman and his musicians play. They are limited by their decision to listen to each other carefully, and they plan out their music while they improvise. Coleman's brand of free jazz also uses instruments in conventional solo and accompaniment roles. In his trio, for instance, there is interaction between saxophonist, bassist and drummer, but there is little doubt that Coleman is the soloist. (Listen to *Jazz Classics CD* Track 76.)

Coleman attempts a difficult task when he rejects preset chord changes and the supportive sound of a pianist's comping. Without the rise and fall of musical tension indicated by chord changes, Coleman has little to support and inspire his creations. Every moment is taxing his imagination, calling upon him to fill it with an interesting line. He brought us an especially abstract form of musical experience by doing away with chord patterns that repeat again and again in cycles.

CECIL TAYLOR

Cecil Taylor (b. 1929) is a pianist, composer, and bandleader who developed a unique and specialized style of modern jazz during the late 1950s and early 60s. His style is not merely different, innovative, or unconventional. Rather, it is **a major alternative to the dominant modern jazz styles**.

Taylor does not play with modern jazz swing feeling. He frequently emphasizes musical textures rather than musical lines. His rhythm is intense and very complex rather than light and swinging.

Ornette Coleman, the best known of the so-called "free jazz" musicians who improvised without following preset chord progressions. His sax style influenced numerous avant-garde musicians of the 1960s, 70s, and 80s. Pictured here in 1960 playing a white plastic alto saxophone because he could not afford to buy a more expensive instrument made out of brass (though he began to like the difference in sound afforded by this plastic instrument).

Photo by Bob Parent, courtesy of Don Parent

Taylor often generates notes in layered groups. This creates the fascinating effect of **textures of sound** rather than singable phrases. The textures are rich in internal movement. They shimmer and explode. In fact, much of Taylor's music is percussive and violent, with few moments of serenity. Many of his performances seem to draw on a continuous source of high energy. They maintain a feverish intensity for long periods.

During the late 1950s, Taylor based his improvisations on tunes and chord changes, and he employed bebop-style bassists and drummers. Then during the 1960s he began playing without preset chord progressions or constant tempo. He preplanned only what he called "unit structures." These were phrases and overall concepts about the architecture that the piece should assume. His preparation for performance does involve extensive rehearsal, and he does provide his musicians with pitches and rhythms to play. However, he does not specify the exact order of themes or a synchronization of them, their timing, or tempo. In addition, he requires his musicians to improvise some passages completely freely. These improvisations are not guided by preset themes or chord progressions. In other words, Taylor's music is not entirely free-form, but it is free of the preset forms that most jazz musicians use.

Taylor plays a very unconventional role as pianist in his groups. His comping is jagged and dense. It does not provide the springboard for soloists that other styles of comping provide. Instead it often sounds more like a separate and contrasting activity. It increases the density of the group sound more than it complements, mimics, or anticipates the rhythms of the soloist in a particularly obvious way.

Listeners who enjoy Taylor find that his playing is a spiritually uplifting experience. They do not listen to him to relax. Listening to him requires a different kind of mental openness. A listener must be ready to be carried along by the energy without being put off by dissonance or lack of swing. To enjoy Taylor's playing takes a special effort, but there is real reward for those who bother.

Pianist Cecil Taylor with bassist Buell Neidlinger pictured here in 1956 as Taylor was beginning to devise the most unorthodox style of piano improvisation ever to emerge from the jazz tradition. It was a non-swinging, densely textured sound.

Photo by Bob Parent, courtesy of Don Parent

MODAL JAZZ

During the late 1950s, Miles Davis recorded improvisations guided by the notes in scales. He did this to get away from improvising in ways that are guided by the notes in progressions of chords. In chord progression-based improvisation, whenever a chord changes, there are new notes that the improviser becomes restricted to playing. In bebop styles, the chords changed rapidly, and improvisers were confronted with a dizzying string of decisions. This did not allow them to relax. Davis reasoned that the character of the improvisation would change if a single chord were in effect for a long time or if improvisers could choose their notes from those in a single scale (known as a mode) that was in effect for a long time. The most famous example of this music is the Miles Davis album *Kind of Blue* with tenor saxophonist John Coltrane and pianist Bill Evans. This approach was dubbed "modal jazz," and it proved to be highly influential.

Scale-based pieces by John Coltrane and his disciples were even more influential than those by Miles Davis. One of Coltrane's most famous "modal" performances can be heard on the title track of his 1960 album *My Favorite Things.* The strategies Coltrane used to construct his performance of "My Favorite Things" became a model format. First he played the melody while his pianist and bassist used the tune's original chords as accompaniment. Then Coltrane abandoned the original chords and based his solo improvisation on a two-chord repeating pattern played by the piano. Those two chords together contained all the notes in the scale that guided his improvisation. It was much easier than "Giant Steps," with its ever-changing accompaniment chords. This new approach became popular with improvising musicians. In fact, many prominent modern jazz combos played only this kind of jazz between the late 1960s and the mid-1970s. (*Jazz Classics CD* Track 79 is a modal improvisation.)

Some jazz of this period was turbulent and not swinging. It featured several musicians improvising different lines at the same time by playing densely packed, rough-textured streams of notes that swirled around. Though it was loosely guided by preset scales, some listeners considered it "free jazz." One of the most widely discussed and influential examples of this style is the *Ascension* album that John Coltrane recorded in 1965. Inspired by Ornette Coleman's 1960 album *Free Jazz*, Coltrane hired four other saxophonists, two trumpeters, and rhythm section to maintain feverish activity through most of the performance. The results did not sound like most music that uses preset organization even though Coltrane had preset a series of four scales to guide the improvisations. After this, Coltrane recorded other albums using similar approaches with smaller bands. Because of these works, Coltrane's name became associated specifically with free jazz, though he never played entirely free from any preset arrangement of harmonies. Coltrane's work was clearly "avant-garde," but not really "free" jazz.

The John Coltrane Quartet of 1962 with pianist McCoy Tyner, bassist Jimmy Garrison, and drummer Elvin Jones. Each was a giant on his respective instrument who influenced styles for decades thereafter.

Photo courtesy of Duncan Schiedt

LISTENING GUIDE

"Your Lady" by John Coltrane

Composed by John Coltrane; recorded November 18, 1963 at Birdland in New York City by John Coltrane (soprano saxophone), McCoy Tyner (piano), Jimmy Garrison (bass), Elvin Jones (drums); from the album *Live at Birdland* (available on CD as Impulse/GRP: GRD-165).

This recording is included for several reasons. The style of accompaniment provided by this rhythm section constituted a new approach in jazz. The combination of unusual parts was particularly unique. The very active playing of drummer Elvin Jones often dispensed with regularly repeating patterns. On the other hand, the bass part was a very simple pattern that repeated almost continuously. The chords used here by pianist McCoy Tyner became the main sound preferred by pianists of the 1970s. The piece illustrates basing jazz improvisation on the notes in a single scale instead of on a progression of different chords. The pivot of that harmony was reiterated constantly by the bass. Coltrane's soprano saxophone playing that is sampled here became a model for hundreds of musicians in the three decades that followed. By the 1990s, his impact had not let up at all. Many saxophonists bought soprano saxophones because they heard Coltrane's playing. His influence could be heard on thousands of records, by jazz bands and jazz-rock fusion bands.

CD Track	Elapsed Time	
77	0' 00"	**Introduction**
		Bassist plays repeating rhythmic figure that anchors the piece's basic unit of 3 pulses. Drums and cymbals generate complex patterns around it.
	0' 13"	Pianist begins syncopated chording.
78		**Theme Statement**
	0' 28"	Melody is played by soprano sax, without piano accompaniment.
	0' 49"	Rhythm section plays accompaniment patterns without sax.
	1' 04"	Melody played again by soprano sax, without piano accompaniment.
79		**Soprano Sax Improvisation**
	1' 26"	Piano returns and sax improvisation begins.
	2' 11"	Drumming becomes particularly full under sax solo. Bassist continues repeating its pedal point.
	2' 14"	Piano drops out.
80		**Theme Statement**
	4' 30"	Sax plays melody again.
	4' 49"	Piano returns. Sax begins another improvisation.
	5' 30"	Sax plays melody again without piano.
	5' 54"	Piano returns. Sax stops.
		Ending
	6' 20"	Piano stops.
	6' 35"	Bass and drums end the piece.

John Coltrane, the most influential saxophonist after Charlie Parker. Pictured here playing soprano sax, the instrument he popularized during the 1960s. Coltrane's tunes and improvisations became textbooks for jazz musicians.

Photo supplied by Bill Smith

Bill Evans, the most influential pianist of the 1960s and 70s. He popularized the jazz use of harmonies based on modes and adapted the chords of French composers Claude Debussy and Maurice Ravel. Evans was also known for rhythmic practices in which he often avoided accenting the most obvious beats.

Photo by Chuck Stewart

BILL EVANS

The most influential pianist in jazz after Bud Powell was Bill Evans (1929–1980). His style is not rough and wild like most avant-garde jazz styles of the 1960s. Much of Evans' music is smooth and pretty, despite its highly explorative nature. Because of this, many people do not consider it avant-garde. The playing is too polished, and the innovations are too subtle to jar them. However, Miles Davis hired Evans in 1958 precisely because Evans was avant-garde, and Davis wanted to change the style of his music in directions that Evans was taking. Davis knew that Evans was devising ways of constructing harmonies around the flavors of certain scales called modes. Evans was showing the jazz world how improvisations could be developed in terms of scales. To do this he used harmonies that sounded quite different from bebop. He did this with popular songs as well as bebop tunes. Evans had built this jazz system from harmonies used by Claude Debussy and Maurice Ravel, who were French composers of piano music and symphonic music during the first part of the twentieth century. His unique combination of these methods influenced many pianists. Such well-known pianists as Herbie Hancock, Chick Corea, and Keith Jarrett all derived important aspects of their harmonic approaches from the model that Evans provided. Davis got what he sought from Evans, and the character of Davis' subsequent music reflected this. The music on the 1959 Davis-Evans album *Kind of Blue* became a textbook for the new approach. The melodies, harmonies, and concepts in that album were still being imitated by other musicians during the 1990s.

Bill Evans was not only avant-garde in a harmonic way. He was also avant-garde in a rhythmic way. Evans perfected a very involved manner of phrasing his improvisations without stressing notes that land on the most obvious beats. Instead of frequently accenting notes at times where we tend to clap our hands or tap our feet, Evans accented at other moments. Moreover, he often began a phrase in a way that was staggered across a series of beats. He could displace his phrases for entire passages and never land resoundingly on a strong beat. When he was doing this, his rhythms did not directly state the pulse, though he always kept it in mind while he was improvising. This means that you might not be able to hear the beat unless you pay close attention to the notes of the bassist or drummer accompanying Evans. This style was called *non-obvious pulse* or *floating pulse.* Though this kind of thinking was evident in his 1950s recordings, Evans developed it most in the 1960s and 70s. He could play in the bebop manner, and he occasionally did. And he could swing conventionally. But he frequently chose not to. Instead he often played in a way in which he floated across the beats very subtly. His rhythmic manner departed from bop. But, because his manner was so highly organized and subtle, most listeners were not aware of how avant-garde it was.

Another aspect of the Bill Evans style is also relatively unique in the history of jazz piano playing. His tone and conception often sound delicate without being fragile. On slow pieces he often created a harp-like effect by sounding single tones and letting them ring, as though to savor each vibration before proceeding to the next note. (*Jazz Classics CD* Track 68) Though he possessed considerable dexterity, his work was never flashy, and he steered clear of conveying an aggressively percussive manner.

Evans crafted his improvisations with exacting deliberation. (*Jazz Classics CD* Track 81) Often he would take a phrase or a rhythmic idea and then develop several choruses of lines from that single idea. During his performances, an unheard, continuous self-editing was going on. This resulted in sparing the listener his false starts and discarded ideas. Though he had a creative imagination, he never improvised solos that merely strung together ideas at the same rate they popped into his head. The results of these deliberations could be an exhilarating experience for the listener. However, they reflected the well-honed craftsmanship of a performer working in the manner of a classical composer more than the carefree abandon and rush of ideas which we associate with jazz improvisation. Because of this his music was sometimes called "brooding" or "introspective" instead of "swinging" or "light-hearted."

LISTENING GUIDE

"Solar" by Bill Evans

Composed by Chuck Wayne; recorded June, 25, 1961 at the Village Vanguard in New York City by Bill Evans (piano), Scott LaFaro (bass), and Paul Motian (drums).

Bill Evans had several different stylistic phases in his career. *The Concise Guide Classics Cassette* and *CD* samples two of them. The first is "Blue in Green," where his piano voicings, modal thinking, and very spare solo style all contribute to the overall effect. It is taken from *Kind of Blue*, the 1959 Miles Davis album. The second, "Solar," was selected to provide the clearest example of the unique approach that bassist Scott LaFaro developed when playing with Bill Evans. LaFaro does not walk during this performance. Also, his rhythms contain very little repetition. Unlike traditional bass playing that provides a very predictable foundation for the soloists, LaFaro's role can be considered an ever-changing counteractivity. Sometimes it even seems to go its own way, independent of Bill Evans' piano playing, as in the first few choruses.

This performance of "Solar" also illustrates subtle ways of phrasing that Evans used after the 1950s. Termed "non-obvious pulse" or "phrasing across the bar line," these approaches are particularly evident in the fifth and the seventh choruses. In the fifth chorus, almost all the accents in Evans' line are on the off-beat, and all three of his phrases are staggered across several measures. They are rhythmically displaced, never starting or clearly ending on a strong beat. Evans seems to stretch figures out so they sound half-time, yet he sometimes comes back to a feeling that is almost double-time. The rhythms that Evans uses are so subtle in their relationship to the underlying pulse that we lose track of that pulse unless we cue on the drummer's timekeeping rhythms. Evans thoroughly blurs the conventional rhythmic signposts here. This gives the listener more of a floating feeling. This was a new kind of jazz piano style, and this recording is one of the clearest examples of it.

The composition was written by guitarist Chuck Wayne, though it has always been mistakenly credited to Miles Davis. It is twelve measures long, but it does not follow the chord progression of a typical blues.

CD Track	Elapsed Time	
81	0' 00"	**First Chorus**
		Melody Statement
		Evans begins alone, playing the first phrase of the melody in octaves. Then he is joined by LaFaro and Motian, and he plays the second phrase in harmony and the remaining phrases in octaves. LaFaro improvises melody lines of his own, in the style of the "Solar" melody. LaFaro's lines occasionally quote phrases from the original melody and mimic Evans' lines. They also contain figures that state the pulse and outline notes in the chords.

CD Track	Elapsed Time	

In the first five choruses, piano and bass interweave their separate melodies. They take turns coming in and out of the foreground of the music. This is very different from the usual format in which piano melody is accompanied by walking bass. Though LaFaro's lines are usually somewhat subordinate to Evans', they are more dense, more varied, and closer to the foreground than bass parts had traditionally been.

82   0' 15"   Second Chorus

Evans Restates the Melody

All piano phrases are harmonized. LaFaro functions alternately as creator of countermelodies and as embellisher of beats.

83   0' 30"   Third Chorus

Evans begins his solo improvisation by voicing all his lines in octaves and not comping for himself. While Evans departs from the melody as he improvises, LaFaro paraphrases it. This amounts to a two-part invention with drums and cymbals accompaniment.

0' 43"   Fourth Chorus

Evans and LaFaro continue to improvise counterlines to each other, LaFaro occasionally quoting the melody.

84   0' 56"   Fifth Chorus

LaFaro moves to a less melodic and more rhythmic role. Evans improvises in ways which intentionally blur the rhythmic pulse.

1' 09"   Sixth Chorus

1' 22"   Seventh Chorus

1' 36"   Eighth Chorus

85   1' 49"   Ninth Chorus

Beginning in the fourth measure, Evans constructs about twelve measures' worth of lines from quarter-note triplet figures.

1' 60"   Tenth Chorus

86   2' 13"   Eleventh Chorus

After the fourth measure, Evans stops voicing his lines in octaves and begins to play one note at a time instead. He generates solo lines with his right hand and comps for himself with his left hand. Note how soft, light, and infrequent his left-hand chords are. This pattern persists until the sixteenth chorus.

2' 27"   Twelfth Chorus

2' 38"   Thirteenth Chorus

2' 50"   Fourteenth Chorus

3' 04"   Fifteenth Chorus

87   3' 17"   Sixteenth Chorus

Evans paraphrases the melody, using locked-hands block chording.

THE POPULARITY OF AVANT-GARDE JAZZ

The styles of Ornette Coleman and Cecil Taylor are among the most exciting and challenging styles in history. From their earliest years, these groups had a devoted following. However, their music was not wanted by most jazz clubs or record companies. Their following was just too small. No album by Ornette Coleman or Cecil Taylor ever made the "top 200" best-selling albums in any year. Though very little modern jazz of any kind is played on the radio, the situation is especially unfortunate for free jazz. Some major cities never heard more than a few samples of free jazz during the entire decade of the 1960s. In fact there are jazz stations which have never played any of Cecil Taylor's music. The problem is that most listeners find free jazz recordings unswinging, difficult to follow, and chaotic. Yet these musicians do occasionally play to large crowds at concerts. So even if people do not buy many of their records, the avant-garde musicans' names are famous enough to occasionally attract fans to jazz festivals. John Coltrane and Bill Evans were more popular. Coltrane's music was not played on the radio very often during the 1950s or 60s. But his records did sell, and night clubs were almost guaranteed a full house when they booked him. The most avant-garde of Bill Evans' records did not sell well when they were first released. His reception improved over the years that followed, though he was never as widely known as three pianists he influenced—Herbie Hancock, Chick Corea, and Keith Jarrett.

Ornette Coleman's band without Coleman: Don Cherry (pocket trumpet), Charlie Haden (bass), Eddie Blackwell (drums), and Dewey Redman (tenor sax). During the mid-1970s, this personnel went by the name of "Old and New Dreams."

Photo by Bill Smith

CHAPTER SUMMARY

1. Free jazz improvisation doesn't use preset progressions of chords. In some cases it also dispenses with preset melody and steady timekeeping.

2. By comparison with bebop, free jazz uses a wider variation in pitch and tone quality.

3. Some free jazz involves lengthy collective improvisations that are loud and frenzied.

4. Free jazz drummers often generate an ever-changing undercurrent of activity instead of playing standard time-keeping patterns.

5. Prominent free musicians are saxophonist Ornette Coleman and pianist Cecil Taylor.

6. "Modal jazz" is the term applied to long improvisations accompanied only by two-chord, continuously repeating patterns and guided by notes in a scale called a mode, rather than by notes in accompaniment chords.

7. Much modal jazz, especially that of John Coltrane, was as frenzied sounding as free jazz. Many listeners therefore classified it with free jazz despite its preset, un-"free" arrangement.

8. The biggest names in modal jazz were Miles Davis and John Coltrane.

9. Pianist Bill Evans was pivotal in moving the Miles Davis repertory to a modal approach, and his piano style influenced Herbie Hancock, Chick Corea, and Keith Jarrett. He also perfected a rhythmic approach that did not make the beat as obvious as previous jazz piano styles did.

AVANT-GARDE LISTENING

Smithsonian Collection of Classic Jazz contains excerpts from Cecil Taylor's album *Unit Structures* and Ornette Coleman's album *Free Jazz*. It also contains Coleman's "Lonely Woman."

The Jazz Classics Compact Disc for Jazz Styles: History and Analysis, (ISBN 0-13-012693-4; phone 800-947-7700) contains the 1974 Cecil Taylor performance of "Jitney #2," mode-based improvisations on Miles Davis' 1959 "Flamenco Sketches" (with Bill Evans and John Coltrane) and John Coltrane's 1963 "The Promise."

Ornette Coleman — *Free Jazz*, 1960 (Atlantic 1364, CD/LP)

Ornette Coleman — *The Shape of Jazz to Come*, 1959 (Atlantic 1317)

Bill Evans — *Sunday at the Village Vanguard*, 1961 (Fantasy OJC-140)

John Coltrane — *My Favorite Things*, 1960 (Atlantic 1361)

John Coltrane — *A Love Supreme*, 1964 (Impulse/GRP: GRD 155)

John Coltrane — *Intersteller Space*, 1967 (Impulse/GRP: GRD110)

Cecil Taylor — *Silent Tongues*, 1974 (Freedom 41005)

SUPPLEMENTARY READING

Black Music: Four Lives (long interviews with Ornette Coleman and Cecil Taylor) by A.B. Spellman (Shocken, 1966; Limelight, 1985)

As Serious As Your Life (articles on Cecil Taylor, Ornette Coleman, and other avant-garde musicians of the 1960s) by Valerie Wilmer (Original, 1980)

Free Jazz (chapters on Miles Davis, John Coltrane, Ornette Coleman, Cecil Taylor, and other avant-garde musicians of the 1960s) by Ekkard Jost (Da Capo, 1974, 1981)

Chasin' the Trane (biography of Coltrane) by J.C. Thomas (Doubleday, 1975; Da Capo, 1976)

Ornette Coleman: A Life in Harmolodics by John Litweiler (Morrow, 1993)

Avant-Garde Jazz Musicians by David Such (University of Iowa Press, 1993)

John Coltrane: His Life and Music by Lewis Porter (University of Michigan Press, 1997)

The Coltrane Companion: Five Decades of Commentary by Carl Woideck (Schirmer, 1998)

CHAPTER 10

FUSION

Chick Corea and John Pattitucci, 1990   Photo by Dan Morgan

azz-rock fusion is a stream of styles which emerged during the late 1960s. It became the most popular jazz for the next thirty years and the first to have widespread popularity after the swing era.

Jazz, rock, and funk music share similar roots in (1) gospel music, (2) work songs, and (3) the blues. But they represent the products of two different lines of musical evolution. For example, jazz (1) employs aspects of formal European concert music and (2) steers away from vocals. It is primarily instrumental music that is almost as complicated as twentieth-century symphonic music. Rock and funk music, on the other hand, (1) emphasize vocals and (2) stick largely to simple compositional forms such as (a) the four-chord, twelve-bar blues and (b) other brief chord progressions that repeat continuously.

Rock and funk music became a main stream in popular music. Jazz, meanwhile, attracted only a small and specialized audience. While it is true that blues singers from the first part of the twentieth century are routinely cited in jazz history texts, they are usually mentioned in discussions of the origins of jazz rather than the dominant course of jazz itself. The stream of evolving styles that runs from the earliest blues singers through B. B. King to Jimi Hendrix was already essentially separate from jazz by the 1920s.

Prior to the 1950s, blues and gospel music performed by black performers were popular with black audiences. Ranging from Bessie Smith in the 1920s to Louis Jordan in the 40s, these performers made music which marketers called "race records." In 1949, this category acquired a new name: rhythm and blues (R & B). From that time on, it strongly influenced another style of popular music called rock and roll. Besides its R & B roots, much rock also reflects the predominantly white musical streams of country music. Rock is distinctly separate from jazz, further removed than R & B. Note, however, that despite differences in racial and ethnic origins, rock and R & B remain similar because they all use (1) extremely simple melody lines, (2) repeated bass patterns, (3) very steady tempo, and singers as well as instrumentalists who (4) bend the pitches of their notes extensively in a highly stylized manner.

Some R & B in the 1960s contained accompaniment rhythms more complicated than those in rock. During the late 1960s, some black styles which extended R & B became the source for intricately syncopated drum patterns and complementary bass figures. Some of

Bass guitar (also known loosely as "Fender" bass), the key element in jazz-rock rhythm sections.

the rhythm section musicians working for Motown recording artists and for singer James Brown, for example, devised accompaniment patterns which were more complicated than those being used at the time by rock groups. The work of accompanists for Sly Stone during the early 1970s was especially complex, having built upon the Motown and James Brown techniques. (*Demo CD* Track 30) By this time, more people began referring to this music as "funk" and "soul" than calling it R & B. It was this funk-soul category, more than rock, which influenced a number of jazz musicians during the 1970s.

By the mid-1960s, the dominant jazz and rock styles had evolved into uniquely separate idioms with little in common. Then, during the late 1960s, a partial blending of the soul-funk stream and the jazz stream occurred and was labeled "jazz-rock fusion." Some jazz musicians were not affected by funk, and many funk groups were not affected by jazz. But much of the jazz played during the 1970s and 80s was heavily influenced by funk, and some funk groups incorporated more of the improvisation and advanced harmonies found in jazz.

JAZZ vs. ROCK

Jazz of almost any period can be distinguished from rock and funk music in that rock and funk typically have:

1. shorter phrase lengths
2. less frequent chord changes
3. less complexity of melody
4. less complexity of harmony
5. less use of improvisation, especially in accompaniments
6. much more repetition of melodic phrases
7. more repetition of brief chord progressions
8. simpler, more repetitive drumming patterns
9. more pronounced repetition of bass figures
10. More is preset in rock and funk performances than in jazz performances. Jazz ordinarily requires both solos and accompaniments to be improvised fresh each time they occur.
11. Where jazz places emphasis on rhythmic flexibility and relaxation, rock stresses intensity and firmness. Jazz projects a shuffling or loping kind of feeling. Where jazz attempts to project a lilting, bouncy feeling that seems to pull each beat along, rock and funk music seem to sit on each beat. Jazz musicians characterize the time sense of rock and funk musicians as "straight up and down."
12. Jazz musicians tend to choose non-electronic instruments, while their rock and funk counterparts rely heavily on electronic instruments and high amplification of ordinary instruments.

HOW DID JAZZ AND ROCK MERGE?

Jazz-rock fusion mixed jazz improvisation with the instrumentation and rhythms of R & B. This mixture was very popular, both with young musicians coming up and with older established players. Rhythm sections changed instrumentation by replacing piano with electric piano (*Demo CD* Track 98) and synthesizer and by replacing acoustic bass viol ("string bass") with electric bass guitar ("Fender"). Pianists and guitarists often adopted repeating accompanying riffs in place of the spontaneous comping which had been customary since the 1940s. Bassists began collecting the strongly rhythmic, syncopated and staccato bass patterns in the style of James Brown and Motown funk bands of the late 1960s and the back-up groups for Sly Stone of the early 1970s. (*Demo CD* Track 30) Just as some swing era bassists had to switch from brass bass (tuba) to string bass, early fusion bassists often had to switch from string bass ("acoustic") to bass guitar ("electric" or "Fender").

Drummers learned new timekeeping patterns which resembled those of R & B as well as Latin American styles. Jazz-rock drumming style was very full and active. (*Demo CD* Track 8) Following the lead of Tony Williams, the high-hat was snapped shut sharply on every beat instead of every other beat. (*Demo CD* Track 2) There was more emphasis on the bass drum, and less on cymbals for timekeeping. The rhythms were stated insistently and repeatedly, and not in the more

Tony Williams, the drummer who invented a style that set the pace for jazz-rock fusion. He was also a prime force in the innovative band of Miles Davis during the mid-1960s.

Photo by Charles Behnke

subtle, highly varied manner of jazz. The jazz-rock style maintained a high level of tension for long periods. There was considerably less bounce and lilt than in jazz of the 1950s, and timekeeping was more strictly stated than during the exploratory years of jazz in the 1960s.

The more jazz-oriented soloists in jazz-rock fusion tended to draw upon John Coltrane's early-1960s style as a model if they were saxophonists, Freddie Hubbard if they were trumpeters, and Herbie Hancock, McCoy Tyner, and Chick Corea if they were pianists. Bebop melodic rhythms were not compatible with most funk accompaniment patterns, but the lines of Coltrane and Tyner were. The less jazz-oriented pianists in fusion devised their own simpler styles or imitated players who leaned more toward the rock side of the jazz-rock mix. The less jazz-oriented saxophonists in fusion used models from R & B and R & B-oriented jazz such as King Curtis, Junior Walker, Wilton Felder, Hank Crawford, and Grover Washington, Jr. Dave Sanborn and Michael Brecker, who had themselves absorbed the R & B styles, became major influences during the 1980s. Wilton Felder had been a strong influence on Kenny G. Then Kenny G, in turn, became an influence on many saxophonists of the 1990s.

MILES DAVIS AND FUSION

Besides pioneering work in a number of jazz styles, the Miles Davis Quintet of 1964–68 was one of the first established jazz groups to mix rock and funk with jazz. Rhythmic styles other than bouncy, swinging jazz patterns appear on some of their records. But it didn't happen all at once. Little by little Davis' rhythm section players introduced elements that sounded more like rock than jazz. Drummer Tony Williams began playing straight, repeating eighth notes on the ride cymbal, and occasionally stated each beat by sharply snapping closed the high-hat. Bassist Ron Carter sometimes complemented those drumming patterns with simple, repeating bass figures that did not resemble walking bass style. Beginning in 1968, Davis also used electric piano and electric bass guitar. All of this was similar to rock.

Two Davis albums became particularly significant in directing modern jazz of the 1970s. These records were *In a Silent Way* and *Bitches Brew*, both made in 1969. They contained a variety of musical approaches, but their dominant style was a combination of jazz and rock.

Instrumentation

The post-1968 music of Davis differed in several ways from his 1963–68 style. For example, instrumentation was altered as follows:

1. Electric piano and organ replaced conventional piano. Davis often employed two or more electric keyboard instruments at once. (*Demo CD* Track 98)

2. Electric bass guitar replaced acoustic bass viol.

3. Davis used electric guitarists. At one time, he had three in a single band.

4. The Davis saxophonists of this period spent more time playing soprano sax than any other instrument. The high-pitched soprano could make its sound be heard over drums and electric instruments, where a tenor might not cut through. (*Demo CD* Track 70)

5. Davis usually employed two or more drummers. By the early 1970s, he had settled into the pattern of using one player on conventional drum set and another playing auxiliary percussion such as conga drums, shakers, rattles, gongs, whistles, and a large number of instruments from Africa, South America, and India.

Rhythm Section

The rhythm section concept was another way in which Davis' post-1968 groups differed from his 1963-68 groups. The later groups created elaborate colors and textures, and rhythm section members played with a very high level of activity. The beat was easily detectable, but it was surrounded by a mass of constantly changing sounds. Complexity was now concentrated in the accompaniments rather than the melodies. These ranged from delicate to turbulent sounds. Textures often seemed to be created for their own sake rather than what would ordinarily be construed as accompaniments. The "accompaniment" textures on *In a Silent Way* and *Bitches Brew* were as much in the forefront as the written melodies and improvised solo lines. These textures were generated by several electric keyboard instruments (piano and organ), guitar, basses, and several drummers. Bass lines blended rock formulas, a freely improvised non-walking style, and accompaniment figures borrowed from Latin American music. Most post-1968 Davis music centered on a simple idea. This could be a few repeated chords, a repeating bass figure, or a mode.

Performance Format

The ways that soloists improvised in this new style followed techniques that John Coltrane and his pianist McCoy Tyner had developed for improvising on mode-based forms and repeating bass figures. These techniques replaced the bebop concepts of jazz phrasing. None of Charlie Parker's or Dizzy Gillespie's pet phrases were used. In fact, much of the lyricism that had been associated with bebop was not evident in this new style. Improvisers seemed more intent on creating moods than melodies.

In the jazz-rock works of Miles Davis, the mood was usually very outgoing and full of unrelenting tension. The level of musicianship was very high, and the complexity of the music set it apart from rock. Its energy, however, was at the level of many rock bands of the late 1960s and 70s. Davis' music reflected his admiration for such non-jazz musicians as Jimi Hendrix and Billy Preston. The post-1968 Davis recordings displayed a blend of the jazz tradition, 1960s and 70s funk music, and the music of India and South America. It was infused with the spirit of Coltrane, but the tone colors were those of rock.

The mid- and late-1980s recordings of Davis emphasized preset accompaniments that were produced for him. Davis added his trumpet sound over funk vamps, some of which had been prepared for him by computerized synthesizers. His formula for much of the 1980s was to employ a Jimi Hendrix-style player on guitar and a John Coltrane-style player on saxophone. Both could play hot, funky solos on demand. This was placed atop thick layers of sounds from electronic keyboards, all underpinned by a drummer and a bassist playing in the funk style. Davis rarely allowed his keyboardists to solo. His music of this period was highly arranged and not as freewheeling or daring as before. It was energetic, however, and its sound remained distinct from most pop music of the period.

JOHN MCLAUGHLIN

John McLaughlin (b. 1942) is important to jazz history as a fusion guitarist, bandleader, and composer. He was born in England and was active in British rock bands and jazz groups since the late 1950s. He first became known to American musicians during the period 1969–71 when he started recording with Miles Davis and began playing with Lifetime, the fusion band of Davis' drummer Tony Williams.

Despite his status as a jazz musician, McLaughlin uses a tone which is unlike traditional jazz guitar quality. It is hard, not soft; cutting, not smooth; and metallic, not warm. In short, it has the color and texture preferred by rock guitarists, not jazz guitarists. Also, he frequently alters the size and shape of his tone by use of a wah-wah pedal and a phase shifter. (The phase shifter produces a subtle swirling of the sound.) Also, most of his improvisations contain little of the pronounced syncopation and the easy, relaxed swing feeling that had previously typified jazz. The syncopations in McLaughlin's lines are more typical of rock than of jazz. His solos are often composed of long strings of sixteenth notes periodically interrupted by held tones which McLaughlin expressively distorts in waveform and pitch. The inflections he prefers are refinements of those found in rock and blues guitar playing.

McLaughlin's work in Lifetime and in his own Mahavishnu Orchestra conveyed a very high level of energy. This was due to high amplifier settings; rapid-fire, intricate themes; and extremely busy accompaniment. McLaughlin is notable for his phenomenally high level of instrumental proficiency, and he likes to play dazzlingly fast strings of notes with razor sharp precision. There is a quick-paced interaction and intense determination on his Mahavishnu Orchestra albums. Many listeners consider his 1971 *Inner Mounting Flame* and his 1972 *Birds of Fire* recordings to be models of group cohesion and inspired jazz-rock improvisation. Feeling for this music was so high that *Birds of Fire* in 1973 reached the very high position of number 15 on the *Billboard* record sales chart. Most jazz albums never even reach position number 200 on that chart. These two Mahavishnu albums are also distinctive for their use of irregular meters—time signatures which had previously been rare in jazz and rock. Many listeners consider this to have been the greatest of all fusion bands.

Not all of McLaughlin's 1970s output consisted of high-intensity electronic music. He also recorded on acoustic guitar, as on his 1970 album *My Goal's Beyond*. McLaughlin abandoned the non-electric approach for a few years right after this album, but he returned to it when touring and recording with Shakti, a band specializing in Indian music and instruments. During the 1990s he again employed Indian musicians while touring and recording. He innovatively combined rock, classical, and Indian music in many different ways, all the while retaining the attitude of jazz improvisation.

John McLaughlin, virtuoso guitarist and leader of the premier fusion band, The Mahavishnu Orchestra.

Photo by Bill Smith

WEATHER REPORT

In 1971 pianist **Joe Zawinul** joined saxophonist Wayne Shorter and founded a new band called Weather Report. Shorter had composed extensively for the bands of Art Blakey and Miles Davis during the 1960s. Similarly, Zawinul's pieces had been central to the bands of Cannonball Adderley and Miles Davis. In their new group Zawinul and Shorter were joined by a bassist and two drummers, one on conventional drum set and one playing exotic percussion instruments. Though they used a number of different bassists and drummers over the years, Zawinul and Shorter stayed together until 1985. Some people consider them mainly a funk and fusion band, but Weather Report actually created its own idiom and performed a broad range of musical styles.

In the context of Weather Report's first three albums, Zawinul, Shorter, and their colleagues presented a new concept. Though they had the standard instrumentation of saxophone, piano, bass, and drums, Weather Report did not use it in standard ways. For instance, their bassist rarely played walking lines. Their drummer rarely played standard ride rhythms. Zawinul usually did not comp for Shorter. Instead of being played in the usual bebop ways, the instruments in Weather Report were used in a variety of different ways. Spurts of melody might come from any member, not just the saxophone. Rhythmic figures and fills could come from any member, not just a bassist or drummer. For example, **Miroslav Vitous**, Weather Report's first bassist, improvised melodies on bass. (*Demo CD* Track 27) He knew how to engage his bass in musical conversations with other group members. His contributions included fragmented melody statements, bowed sustained tones, and syncopated interjections. He could just as easily bow melody in unison with saxophone as feed rock-style bass figures into the group texture. He could play timekeeping rhythms coordinated with the drummer, or he could coordinate with a rhythm of the pianist. He could quickly go back and forth, too. There was often no distinction between soloist and accompanist. Each member's work contributed to the prevailing mood and color rather than to a solo. Weather Report had exchanged the long solos of conventional jazz for a greater variety of moods and sound textures. With only a few exceptions, they retained this practice thereafter.

An essential aspect of Weather Report's sound after 1972 was the rich combination of orchestral sounds produced by Zawinul's mastery of electronic synthesizers. Among jazz musicians, Zawinul is held in high esteem for his command of electronic instruments, his taste in their use, and his fertile imagination.

An important ingredient in Weather Report's idiom was the sound of **Wayne Shorter's** saxophone playing. It was frequently added to the bubbling layers of colorful sounds made by Zawinul's electronic synthesizers. Sometimes Shorter carried the melody. Sometimes he played brief fragments of a line. Shorter's work was

Wayne Shorter (soprano sax), Miroslav Vitous (bass), and Joe Zawinul (piano), co-founders of the innovative band called Weather Report. They presented collective improvisation in ways that often steered clear of conventional jazz roles for their instruments. Some of their music mixed popular funk styles with jazz improvisation and wide-ranging electronically synthesized sounds with exotic rhythms.

Photo by Bill Smith

soulful at the same time as it was mysterious and otherworldly. Sometimes he held a single tone, as though taking a paint brush and applying one long stroke to a canvas that was busy with other patterns. In this way Shorter's playing functioned in the manner of an orchestral composer instead of an accompanied jazz soloist. Especially significant is that his playing frequently softened the effect of the synthesizer and percussion sounds. Shorter's notes could immediately touch a listener's emotions. And his style was instantly recognizable. It would be hard to mistake for the style of Lester Young, Charlie Parker, or Ornette Coleman.

Weather Report's career had two main phases, their emphasis on collective improvisation of textures and their funk band emphasis. Though they did not entirely abandon collective approaches, much of their work after their 1973 *Sweetnighter* album left collectively improvised approaches in favor of approaches using extensively repeated, written themes and preset rhythm section figures. With *Sweetnighter*, Weather Report began using more repetition. In its new style, compositions were constructed of brief phrases repeated continually and accompanied by a funk rhythm section style. With this new emphasis on repetition and funk, Zawinul sought a larger audience for his band. Their 1977 hit piece "Birdland" culminated that trend.

Weather Report's role was larger in American popular music as a whole than in jazz. Though some jazz groups were touched by their methods, most of the bands that learned from Weather Report played music that was not closely related to swinging jazz. They did not closely follow methods of improvisation used by swing era and bebop models. Some of the styles were closer to new age and funk music. The musicians in Weather Report all had previously achieved considerable reputations in the field of jazz. But their work in Weather Report and their influence on American music was with a group of musical styles that were not necessarily jazz.

Photo by Randy Norfus

Jaco Pastorius, bass guitarist with Weather Report from 1976-1982. His sleek tone and the singing quality of his lines introduced a new style for the bass in jazz-rock fusion.

LISTENING GUIDE

"Birdland" by Weather Report

Composed by Joe Zawinul; recorded in 1977 on piano, Arp 2600 synthesizer, and Oberheim polyphonic synthesizer (Zawinul), tenor and soprano saxophones (Wayne Shorter), bass guitar (Jaco Pastorius), drums (Alex Acuna), and tambourine (Manolo Badrena); originally issued on the album *Heavy Weather* (Columbia 34418; reissued on CD with same number).

"Birdland" is Weather Report's most popular piece. It has been set to lyrics, sung by the vocal group Manhattan Transfer, performed by large jazz groups, marching bands, and lounge acts. It was a hit at discotheques.

Though originally known for freely conceived group improvisations, Weather Report preset everything heard here except Wayne Shorter's tenor sax solo and a few bass guitar and piano remarks. Using set figures is a common practice in rock and funk bands. It has not been as common in jazz, where the emphasis traditionally has been on spontaneity instead. But the swing era and the fusion era attained wide popularity when their music was made of short, repeating riffs of the sort heard on "Birdland." In fact, Zawinul composed his fusion-style "Birdland" as a recollection of hearing the riff-style band of Count Basie play at the New York City night club Birdland.

There are many unusual sounds on this recording. Most prominent among them are tones made by the electronic synthesizers of Zawinul and the electric bass guitar of Jaco Pastorius. The overtones of the bass guitar were used by Pastorius to play high-pitched notes that sound like an entirely different instrument. His very smooth, slurred manner contributes to his unique effect. The second theme of the piece is carried by those unusual sounds, beginning at 19 seconds into the recording. Within the second theme we also hear tambourine playing steady eighth notes (two pulses per beat), and an open high-hat cymbal struck with stick on upbeats and snapped shut on downbeats.

CD Track	Elapsed Time	
89	0' 00"	**First Theme** (2 phrases) played 3 times by bass notes on the Arp 2600 electronic synthesizer
90	0' 20"	**Second Theme** played 4 times by bass guitar overtones, piano harmonizing the melody, accompanied by Arp synthesizer repeating the first theme, tambourine playing steady eighth notes, open high-hat cymbal struck with stick on upbeats and snapped shut on downbeats
91	0' 43"	**Third Theme** played by piano, tenor sax, and Oberheim synthesizer, accompanied by bass guitar playing a different phrase
	0' 56"	**Interlude**
92	1' 03"	**Fourth Theme** played in unison by Oberheim synthesizer and piano 4 times. Arp is sustaining its low note.
	1' 20"	Bass notes on the Arp stretch the opening theme underneath repeats of the fourth theme.

CD Track	Elapsed Time	
93	1' 32"	**Fifth Theme** played by tenor sax in upper register and Oberheim synthesizer, accompanied by sustained tones in bass guitar and piano chords
	1' 46"	Bass guitarist plays by himself.
		brief exchanges between bass guitar playing harmonized remarks and piano playing funk licks
94	2' 00"	**Main Theme**
		First Rendition
		voice, piano, soprano sax
	2' 06"	*Second Rendition*
		voice, piano, soprano sax
	2' 12"	*Third Rendition*
		Oberheim synthesizer joins them.
	2' 18"	*Fourth Rendition*
		same as third rendition
	2' 25"	*Fifth Rendition*
		Oberheim plays harmonized melody with them.
	2' 31"	*Sixth Rendition*
		same as fifth rendition
95		**Interlude**
	2' 38"	Bass guitar, voice, Arp 2600 synthesizer and high-hat cymbals play over a single sustained pedal tone, as though to cool down before more action begins again.
	2' 49"	Synthesizer plays a new theme 3 times in the bass register.
	3' 08"	a sequence of 8 descending chords is played 7 times by piano, bass guitar, and Oberheim synthesizer, answered each time by tenor sax improvisations, piano improvising punctuations that are high pitched and staccato
	3' 29"	a passage occurs here that sounds like the opportunity to cool down before getting hot again
96	3' 36"	**Second Theme**
		Bass guitar overtones sound the piece's second theme while tenor sax talks back.
	3' 48"	Arp begins repeating first theme under bass guitar's melody.
	3' 54"	Synthesizer and tenor sax play second theme in harmony, accompanied by Arp playing first theme.
97	4' 00"	**Third Theme** played loudly, as though a big band
98	4' 13"	**Fourth Theme** played by piano and Oberheim synthesizer
99	4' 24"	**Main Theme** played by sax, piano, and synthesizer, accompanied by bass guitar decorations, hand claps on every other beat, tambourine playing steady eighth notes, high-hat struck on upbeats, snapped shut on downbeats
		Repeats to Fade-out at 5' 54"

Herbie Hancock, composer-pianist-bandleader, surrounded here by the keyboard synthesizers he used so creatively beginning in the 1970s. His hit records *Head Hunters*, *Thrust*, and *Rockit* all featured clever use of electronically synthesized sounds in a funk style.

Photo by Grace Bell

HERBIE HANCOCK

Pianist Herbie Hancock (b. 1940) is best known to the public as a leader of jazz-rock fusion bands. However he is best known to musicians as a tremendously original and versatile jazz pianist and composer. He played with Miles Davis from 1963 to 1969 and became the most sought-after band pianist of the 1960s. Hancock's freshest work is the soloing and accompanying he did with Davis. Hancock comped in a brisk manner and used a gentle, even touch. He managed to sound light and airy, yet muscular and firm, all at the same time.

Though known for his originality, Hancock absorbed several influences while he was developing his style during the late 1950s and early 60s. Some of his playing has funky, bluesy figures and a contagious rhythmic bounce that recall styles within the hard bop idiom. But Bill Evans was the most significant influence on Hancock. Evans' use of harp-like, ringing tones surrounded by silence can be heard in Hancock's playing on slow pieces. And he was also influenced by Evans' harmonies and mode-based thinking. He displayed more bebop than Evans did, however. Hancock also drew from the ideas of twentieth-century classical composers. But he did not merely imitate the music of his models. He extended their methods and added so many original ideas that his style became instantly recognizable.

Another side to Hancock's creativity is his productivity and originality as a composer and arranger. By the early 1970s, he had written every tune on eight of his own albums, and he had written or coauthored many of the tunes on seven more. His "Dolphin Dance" has become a modern classic among jazz compositions. Musicians praise its beauty and the clever progression of chords and pedal points that are intertwined with its delightful melody. His "Maiden Voyage" became a staple for young musicians of the 1960s and 70s, especially because of its modal construction. His funky, bluesy piece "Watermelon Man" also became very popular. Many bands played their own arrangements of it, and it was performed by almost every wedding band in America to satisfy dancers' demands for a funk piece.

Hancock enjoyed immense success for styles that he devised from a type of popular music known as *funk music*. His first big hit came when he imitated the style of Sly Stone's accompanists by creating the *Head Hunters* album, which sold just under a million copies. His follow-up album, *Thrust*, was almost as popular. Most of his funk music since the mid-1970s has featured electronic keyboard instruments instead of conventional ("acoustic") piano. Much of his bandleading and recording has been with groups containing funk style bass guitar playing and funk style drumming.

Between the mid-1970s and the the mid-1980s, his most popular music had less and less jazz improvisation in it, and more and more dance rhythms that were highly syncopated and very repetitive. Melodies were simple and heavily rhythmic. As of this writing, his widest recognition has come from a 1983 work called "Rockit." The recording is a light-hearted construction of novel sound effects in an engaging funk rhythm, all tightly arranged with Hancock's usual sense of balance and completeness. It was included in *Future Shock*, an album that went gold and stayed on the popularity charts for more than a year. As a single, "Rockit" remained in the popularity charts for nine weeks, and as a video it was one of the fifteen most popular of the year. Though much of the public routinely places it in the jazz category, Hancock himself does not consider this music to be jazz. By the 1980s, Hancock's funk music had captured a slice of the market for dance music and youthful party music.

CHICK COREA

Like Herbie Hancock, pianist Chick Corea (b. 1941) is better known to the public as a bandleader in the jazz-rock fusion style than as a jazz pianist. However, Corea followed Herbie Hancock as pianist in the 1968 Miles Davis Quintet and soon became one of the most prominent pianists in jazz. Like Bud Powell and Bill Evans before him, Corea created a harmonic and melodic vocabulary that fostered a new stream of jazz piano styles. (*Jazz Classics CD* Track 88) Yet his approach to piano improvising was only one of several contributions Corea made to jazz history. He also introduced fresh and compelling styles as a composer and bandleader. These styles became almost as widely imitated as his piano playing.

Corea's piano style started with aspects from the approaches of Bud Powell, Horace Silver, Bill Evans, and McCoy Tyner. He also drew from the classical pieces of twentieth-century composers Paul

Hindemith and Bela Bartok. Latin American and Spanish music also inspired Corea's style. His playing often bears the rhythmic feeling and some of the melodic flavor of Latin American music. In addition, his crisp, percussive touch enhances the Latin feeling. This fits with his bright, spirited style of comping.

Corea's work was already important in jazz history prior to his association with jazz-rock fusion. There are several reasons for this. His music was played with a stunning level of musicianship. Its style was not really bebop or hard bop. His manner of choosing notes for his lines was fresh. The way that he related his lines to the accompaniment chords was fresh, too. The rhythms in Corea's compositions and his improvised lines also differ considerably from bebop. They don't have the same patterns of accent that we hear in most bebop style playing. He made his music dance with a snap and lightness that are not conveyed by bebop piano styles. Some of Corea's playing also has the ring of classical music. The sparkling touch of Corea and the bright tone quality he extracts from the piano also remind us of classical music.

Corea led a number of different bands. Each played in a unique style. His group of the early 1970s had considerable impact on jazz-rock fusion styles. For this band, Corea chose to play Fender Rhodes electric piano (*Demo CD* Track 98), an instrument that produces a light, vibraharp-like tone. Stanley Clarke played bass viol and electric bass guitar. Airto Moreira played drums, and Flora Purim sang. The group's music sounded light and happy, full of Latin American rhythms and Spanish themes. The name for the band and its first album was *Return to Forever*. Their second album was titled *Light as a Feather*. (*Classics CD* Track 88) These two albums became favorites among young musicians of that period. Within a few years, the influence of this sound was evident in a number of jazz-rock fusion bands.

A band that Corea carried through the middle 1970s was influenced by rock and funk music. Corea employed rock-influenced electric guitarists—first Bill Connors, then Al Dimeola. Bassist Stanley Clarke remained from the earlier band, now playing electric bass guitar more than acoustic bass viol. Lenny White played drums with the group. White's style was a very full, active approach which combined aspects of modern jazz and funk drumming styles with the techniques of Latin American percussionists. In addition to playing the piano, Corea used a diverse assortment of electronic keyboard synthesizers. In fact he became widely known for his synthesizer playing and continued to master new electronic instruments during the 1990s. Corea's records from this period sold well, and independent recording careers soon resulted for Clarke and Dimeola. White and Dimeola left Corea in 1976, but the Return to Forever group name was retained for a number of Corea's subsequent projects. Thereafter, Corea appeared in a wide assortment of contexts. Al Dimeola, Stanley Clarke, and Lenny White went on to lead jazz-rock fusion bands of their own, occasionally regrouping with Corea for touring and recording.

Chick Corea, pianist-composer-bandleader pictured here in the 1970s playing the electronic keyboard and wearing shirt bearing the name of his first fusion band, Return to Forever. Corea was a major force in acoustic styles and jazz-rock fusion that emerged after hard bop.

Photo by Warren Browne

Corea was widely influential among jazz musicians as a composer in addition to his influence as a pianist. For instance, during the 1970s, his "Windows" and "Crystal Silence" became jazz standards. His "Spain" was so well known among musicians that it became a vocal piece. Singer Al Jarreau's rendition of it became a hit record in the 1980s. Though Corea's acoustic, non-fusion music of the 1960s and 70s appealed to many musicians, it did not gain a particularly large public. On the other hand, his jazz-rock fusion music acquired a mass following. Corea continued to write and perform in that more popular style long after he made his first fusion recordings of the mid-1970s. The Chick Corea Elektric Band of the 1980s and 90s was quite successful.

NEW AGE MUSIC

During the 1980s a new idiom of popular music surfaced. Record stores initially did not have bins for displaying it, so they placed it in the jazz bins because it sounded more like jazz to them than like classical music or rock. Even after this music earned a bin of its own, much of the public continued to call it jazz. Record store clerks sometimes described it as a mixture of jazz and classical music, or "classical jazz." Though the music does employ improvisation as one of its methods, that is about all it has in common with most jazz. It does not swing. In fact its rhythms are purposely designed to avoid creating any of the tension that jazz swing feeling requires.

The methods for creating this music minimize tension in other ways, too. Tone qualities are soft and smooth. Changes in tone color and harmony are made only in the most gradual ways. Often the same chord or mode remains in effect for an entire performance. Loudness levels are usually low and remain that way for long stretches. Changes in loudness are rarely sudden. Models for this music were provided by modern classical composers Lamonte Young, Philip Glass, and Steve Reich. Those composers, in turn, had been influenced by Gregorian chant music from the Middle Ages as well as by the sounds of nature—wind and waves, for example—and continuous machine sounds like an air conditioner's steady hum. Since these composers reduced music to a bare minimum of materials and activity, their musical approach was called "**minimalism**." Some of their music superficially resembled some of the unaccompanied piano improvisations of Keith Jarrett during the 1970s, as well as the solo piano pieces of French impressionist composers Claude Debussy and Maurice Ravel that had inspired some of Jarrett's work. Both products were calm and soothing. Neither projected jazz swing feeling. Much of it explored the sonorities of a single chord or brief chord progression. The Paul Winter Consort and its spin-off group, Oregon, made music like this. Harpist Andreas Vollenweider promoted a similar sound and gained considerable popularity for it during the 1980s. Pianist George Winston imitated Jarrett's long, vamp-based improvisations that meander and seem soothing. Winston's records sold millions of copies, his concerts packed auditoriums, and his style was dubbed "new age."

SMOOTH JAZZ

Many of the radio stations that had broadcast New Age format during the 1980s gradually eased into music in which drumming was more active and louder, bass lines were more intrusive, and saxophones had rougher tone qualities. A few of the bands including some of this funk style in their repertories were The Crusaders, Yellow Jackets, and Spyro Gyra. By the mid-1990s, most New Age radio formats had been replaced by this refined and quieted style of funk music, calling it "smooth jazz" and "cool jazz." (These were unfortunate designations historically because it sounded no smoother than ballads of the swing era, and it had nothing in common with cool jazz of the 1950s.) Often this music was played by jazz musicians capable of more exciting work—Grover Washington, Jr. and Chuck Mangione, for example. But when they played this kind of music, their improvised solos were very stylized rather than adventuresome. Saxophone improvisations recorded by Kenny G fall into this category. You may wish to call this music "light fusion." Many listeners liked to have this music around them because they considered it pleasant and

La Monte Young,
father of minimalism.

Photo by Marian Zazeela

just as easy to ignore as to hear: background music with a beat. Musicians called it "fuzak" because it seemed to be jazz-rock fusion that was as soft and pleasant as the highly processed music that is piped into doctor's offices, marketed by the Muzak company. Most styles of jazz have had their easy-listening variants, and this was fusion's. But unlike its Muzak/background music antecedents, this radio format programmed selections which usually contained improvised solos. *The extent of improvisation was one element which qualified smooth jazz as jazz, rather than merely a continuation of the instrumental pop tradition of background music.*

Smooth jazz became quite popular. By the late 1990s it was the fastest growing radio format. Among the most prominent saxophonists who specialized in this style were Grover Washington, Jr., Kenny G, and Najee. Each of these men also had a number of imitators. Between 1986 and 1995, sales of some Kenny G albums ran into the millions of copies. This means, for example, that sales of just one of his albums (as many as four to seven million copies) would exceed all the recordings ever sold by Charlie Parker and John Coltrane combined. *Though perceived by many musicians as more decorative than substantial, the music of Kenny G and smooth jazz defined jazz for a very large segment of American listeners during the 1980s and 90s.* Unlike other modern jazz, this sound was not relegated to small night clubs and limited-range radio stations, but heard frequently in airports and banks, auditoriums and arenas.

ACID JAZZ

The term "acid jazz" was coined during the late 1980s by English disc jockeys Gilles Peterson and Chris Bangs at a weekend-long party in England where each room provided a different kind of music. One was a type of dance music originating in Detroit and Chicago called "house music." Some of it was intended to accompany the effects of taking the drugs called "ecstasy" and LSD, nicknamed "acid." So it became known as "acid house music." Announcing the availability of jazz in one of the rooms, Peterson reportedly remarked to the partiers, "Now that you've had your fill of 'acid house,' we're going to give you acid jazz." Though originally offered as a joke, the term was soon applied whenever disc jockeys combined current pop dance music with excerpts from old jazz albums. Gilles Peterson and other British disc jockeys particularly liked funky hard bop recordings of the 1960s from the Blue Note and Prestige firms, sometimes by Art Blakey, Horace Silver, Lou Donaldson, Herbie Hancock, and Grant Green. Gilles Peterson's firm, in turn, founded a subsidiary called Acid Jazz, and some of the groups they hired thereby defined the genre. Like the swing style of the 1930s and 40s, acid style functioned primarily as dance music.

At the same time, rap groups were beginning to borrow jazz sounds. They had at least two reasons. First, they needed a new way to get accompaniments cheaply. So they were excerpting the introductions, during which the pace and feeling of the original selections were established. At first they borrowed accompaniment riffs from the funkiest of jazz records because it helped provide a continuous pattern of repeating rhythms to play under their rap. Second, some rappers believed that their performance would gain a jazz flavor if any element associated with jazz were incorporated. This might consist of a very brief part of a trumpet or saxophone improvisation, a few piano chords that typified jazz of the 1960s or 70s, a walking bass pattern, or a jazz drummer's ride rhythm. Some rappers felt that just naming famous jazz musicians within the rap itself would make their product more hip.

Within some acid jazz selections, even those without rap, jazz horn work is overdubbed in a way that merely decorates whatever else is happening. It is not the main focus of attention. For example, in some selections, horn sounds provided only minor coloration, while the drum beat remained the most prominent aspect of the sound. This reversed the roles traditionally occupied in most jazz. Drums were background, while horns were foreground. *Though using jazz solos as decoration reversed the trend for jazz, it continued a long tradition in popular music.* "Hot solos," as they were called, had been added to otherwise nonjazz pieces as early as the 1920s. They were commonly included in performances by rhythm and blues singers of the 1940s and 50s. Early rock bands frequently carried a saxophonist for this purpose. Soul bands of the 1960s and 70s had occasionally used brief jazz improvisations, too.

Sampling
Much of acid jazz depends upon electronically excerpting portions of old albums. This procedure is called "sampling." Among producers, the term is used in two slightly different ways. The older meaning refers to recording samples of a given instrument's tone from each pitch range. The result remains stored in a computer to be altered according to the programmer's wishes. Entire melodies and accompaniments can be pasted together by electronically changing the pitch and rhythms of that tone. The synthesizers can even determine the ways that tones begin and end. The programmer can thereby give them the character of a live hornman or human voice, for instance. This had been common in pop music products since at least the early 1980s.

The newer meaning for "sampling" is the one that applies more to acid jazz. Entire phrases from an old album are recorded into a computer. Then they are re-synthesized into another recording apparatus if a new album is being created. Or they are re-synthesized into playback facilities if a disc jockey is using them spontaneously at a dance party. In some of the earliest acid jazz mixtures, disc jockeys sampled more than just accompaniment phrases. They excerpted a few moments of intact music from an old jazz album. The particular way the phrases were mixed was determined by the creativity of the disc jockey. Performing these procedures became a career for disc jockeys who termed themselves "**mixers**." When devised during a dance party, the resulting mixtures were not usually saved. When devised in the studio, however, the mixtures often became part of CDs that the disc jockey copyrighted and marketed as new material.

Looping
In many acid jazz selections, the instrumental phrase that was sampled came from the accompaniment portion of an old recording. It was then repeated continuously by a process called "looping." This produced an accompaniment groove. On top of this was placed an assortment of additional sounds from samples or electronically synthesized sources. Often the additions included a loud snare drum sound on every other beat. This is known as a "back beat" if it happens on the second and fourth of every group of four beats. Sometimes the addition was a closed high-hat cymbal struck twice for each beat, thereby providing a continuous pulse. A strong bass drum rhythm was also added in some mixes. Usually all these elements were added. Then a collection of new raps and jazz improvisations were placed on top of that foundation. In other words, acid jazz was not invented by musicians. It was invented by disc jockeys and rap artists.

Overdubbing
The methods for creating acid jazz were not entirely new. For instance, overdubbing had been used already for several decades in pop music. But among most jazz musicians and purist fans, it was considered cheating. Though it was uncommon in jazz until the 1970s, guitarist Wes Montgomery's popular recordings of the 1960s had expanded the practice. By the 1980s, most of Miles Davis' albums used at least some overdubbing. Also for more than a decade, disc jockeys had been devising original mixtures by adding sound

effects to recordings and by taking sounds from one recording and adding them to another.

Sampling was not new, either. For example, *by the mid-1980s, composer-arrangers owned electronic samples of most musical instrument sounds.* This conveniently allowed composers to excerpt and reprocess sounds to create complete performances without hiring musicians. **Producers had assumed the role of performers several years before the emergence of acid jazz.**

What was new with acid jazz was the extent to which disc jockeys became involved in making the music themselves, instead of only playing the work of others. Musicians were hired by disc jockeys to record fresh improvisations on top of accompaniments prepared by synthesizer, drum machine, and loops. Occasionally a disc jockey actually toured, as though a bandleader. He would plug in his playback equipment and allow one or two musicians to perform live music over the recorded sounds.

The converse of this situation had been presented by jazz musician Herbie Hancock when he added a disc jockey to his touring band to contribute his own original sounds. Some were made by scratching records with the stylus while the system was connected to loudspeakers. Some were achieved by mixing various sounds electronically. Hancock's hit recording "Rockit" had incorporated such sounds.

From selection to selection, the amount of improvised jazz that could be found in "acid jazz" varied widely. The term eventually became applied to hip hop music that was only slightly jazzy and usually did not have fresh jazz improvisation. In the mid-1990s, "Acid Jazz" appeared on the labels of some recordings that contained only rap music.

Categories of Acid Jazz

In summary, acid jazz can be divided into three categories. (1) **Fusions devised by disc jockeys of jazz elements with various pop dance music styles** current from the mid-1980s into the 1990s, such as hip hop, techno, trip hop, and rap. Medleys were devised spontaneously by disc jockeys during parties in England. Some medleys and mixtures were prepared in studios and issued for sale. Some of their mixture incorporated excerpts from the funkiest hard bop albums of the 1960s and 70s, particularly the selections that maintained a groove and had tempos similar enough to loop into the continuous medleys. Selections featuring organ and guitar were particularly welcome. Though most music in this category is described above, a slice of their programming somewhat overlapped the format that American radio stations of that period called "smooth jazz." This music contained improvisation but rarely swung in the jazz manner. Rhythmic feeling in some smooth jazz was less stiff than in most acid jazz, however. It was more elastic because a group of musicians, as live performers in smooth jazz, do not keep absolutely perfect time, whereas machine-made rhythms that typify acid jazz are perfectly constant. Though many listeners don't realize when they are hearing a drum machine, real drumming has an organic quality not conveyed by electronic imitations. A drum machine supplies neither the richness and depth of tone qualities nor the spontaneous variations in rhythms. The most important part missing is the subtle ebb and flow of tensions. Of course, smooth jazz recordings that used drum machines resembled acid jazz in rhythmic feeling. (2) **Fresh music** made specifically for this audience by bands based in cities all over the world, not just England and America. Their music exhibited a wide range of styles.

(3) **Renamed music from earlier recordings.** A commercial enterprise in America and England during the mid-1990s applied the "acid jazz" designation to their old recordings and resold them. This succeeded as long as the selections were sufficiently funky and sustained a groove. Record companies reclassified several of their previous recording artists, for example Ahmad Jamal, Roy Ayers, Houston Person, and Don Patterson, as "legends of acid jazz." Some companies used the term "roots of acid jazz" to designate their old music by Wes Montgomery and Jimmy Smith. They sold it in different combinations of selections, with new album covers and new commentary. In other words, "acid jazz" served more as a marketing term than a musical style. But it was so loosely applied in music stores that a customer might have to seek the "rap music" bins to locate it.

Dominant Aspects of Acid Jazz

Despite the diversity of sounds that have been called "acid jazz," at least three aspects of acid jazz make all but category #3 something more than a mere marketing term. (1) The most dominant aspect is the accompaniment rhythm and the way it feels. This is termed "the groove." It is very important because the music serves to stimulate dancing. (2) Another distinguishing aspect is that few chord changes occur. Often an entire selection revolves around two chords that continuously alternate with each other. Much of it borrows the introduction from some other funky recording, for instance, soul music, disco, or boogaloo. Then the selection repeats that introduction continuously, with occasional variations. Based almost entirely upon an introduction, the harmonic content of most acid jazz selections is understandably limited because the function of an introduction is to set the pace, not offer harmonic development. (3) Melodic development is less elaborate than in any other style of jazz. In fact, many acid jazz selections have no melody at all.

In these three respects, acid jazz is more African than any other kind of jazz because much African folk music is focused primarily on rhythm and tone quality, not melodic or harmonic development. It is no coincidence that one category of pop music from the mid-1990s that was being incorporated into British acid jazz around 1996 was called "jungle music."

Herbie Hancock's first fusion band. Notice the Fender Rhodes electric piano Hancock is playing and the electric bass guitar Buster Williams is playing. Bennie Maupin is playing bass clarinet and Eddie Henderson is on fluegelhorn.

Photo courtesy of Cleveland Press Collection/Cleveland State University Archives

BUT IS IT JAZZ?

After fusion had arrived, many musicians and jazz fans did not consider it to be a form of jazz. Most of them eventually softened in their view, but some still consider fusion styles to be separate from the descendants of dixieland, swing, and bop. Keep in mind, however, that before fusion, many reacted to the avant-garde of Ornette Coleman and Cecil Taylor by saying that it was not jazz, either. But despite the views of some musicians and purist jazz fans, both the avant-garde of Coleman and Taylor and the fusion of Miles Davis, Weather Report, and Kenny G continue to be found in the jazz bins of music stores, not in the classical or rock bins. This indicates that—at least to the outsider—these styles sound more like jazz than like anything else. Were the outsiders missing the distinctions? Or were the insiders missing the commonalities? Incidentally, big band swing had been classified as nonjazz by many dixieland fans during the 1930s and 40s. They felt that it was not true jazz, partly because it represented a dilution of jazz traits. Collective improvisation did not occupy as much of each performance as it did in early jazz, for instance. Swing big bands emphasized refinement more than spontaneity.

Different people use different criteria for deciding whether a given performance is jazz. For those whose definition requires both improvisation and jazz swing feeling, much music by Weather Report fails to qualify because its rhythmic properties do not resemble the swing era or bop grooves, though they do achieve their own infectious groove. The piano music of New Age stylist George Winston would not qualify because it fails to swing. Music stores, on the other hand, use much looser criteria and display both Weather Report and George Winston in their jazz bins.

Jazzy Pop

Rap

Jazzness in Acid Jazz

Watered- Down Jazz

Let us examine three other labelling dilemmas. (1) For those who find jazzness in music whenever it uses saxophones and a particular accompaniment style, music by Kenny G qualifies as jazz, even though it would not qualify by a strict definition that requires swing era or bop rhythmic properties. Musicians might be more specific, though, and call music of Kenny G "jazzy pop." (2) Classification procedures are so loose that jazz journalists once contemplated including rap in the jazz category. Perhaps this was suggested by the African American origins they share. However, (a) most rap does not have melody. It is poetry recited atop a repeating funk rhythm. Though rhythmically compelling, (b) most rap does not swing in the jazz sense, and (c) not much of it is freshly improvised for each performance. (3) If a personal perception of jazzness increases with the number and obviousness of aspects that remind a person of jazz, then acid jazz performances would qualify to the extent that they featured instruments and harmonies associated with jazz, even without improvisation or swing feeling. If any passages conveyed swing feeling, for instance, they would bear more jazzness.

There is another motive for saying something is not jazz despite its roots in the jazz tradition: rejection of pop jazz. To say a style is not jazz is merely another way that some jazz fans recognize that (1) improvisation does not occupy as much of each performance as in more serious jazz and/or that (2) improvisations in it are not as elaborate or (3) as well-crafted or (4) as rhythmically compelling as in other styles. Or it is a way these fans say (5) they do not like it and are refusing to give it their stamp of approval by calling it "jazz." Some dislike it because of reasons 1 - 4. Some dislike it for other reasons. *There has long been a reluctance among musicians and purist fans to include within the jazz category any watered-down variants of a style that derives from the jazz tradition.* This was why distinctions were made between swing bands and sweet bands during the 1940s. Count Basie fit the former category, and Glenn Miller fit the latter, for instance. During the 1990s, the same distinctions could be made between saxophonists Michael Brecker and Kenny G. So you see that to be fair in classifying styles, we need to consider the actual characteristics of the music, not just the reactions of listeners. When one listener dislikes a style, this does not necessarily mean that another listener will also consider it bad music. We have also learned that if one listener does not consider a musical style to be jazz, this does not necessarily mean the style will not qualify as jazz for another listener.

THE APPEAL OF FUSION

By 2000, rock had maintained a high level of popularity three times as long as swing's popularity. Jazz-rock fusion itself had been popular for three decades. It became the first jazz style since the swing era to gain anywhere near as much popularity.

By incorporating elements of R & B and rock into their music, several established jazz figures achieved popular success as great as that of any jazz player since the end of the swing era. Though jazz instrumentals ordinarily sold fewer than 10,000 to 20,000 copies, jazz-rock albums of the 1970s and 80s frequently sold more than 100,000 copies. This music was so popular that it also came to be referred to as "**crossover**" music because sales of the records crossed over from the jazz market into the popular music market.

This new success for jazz musicians did not depend so much on their music's jazz character as on its *jazz-rock* character. As with swing era big band recordings, those pieces with the least improvisation tended to receive the most popular acclaim. And, as with the hits of the swing era, jazz-rock hits were identifiable by simple, repeating riffs syncopated in a catchy way. Much of what went by the jazz-rock label consisted of little more than funky rhythm vamps, simple chord progressions, and an improvised solo riding on top.

There are several possible explanations for the new popularity of jazz and jazz-rock in particular. (1) Rock had already been popular for more than fifteen years by the time that Herbie Hancock's *Head Hunters* was released. So perhaps when jazz adopted the electric instruments and the accompaniment rhythms associated with rock, listeners found it more familiar and therefore easier to listen to. (2) The increased prominence of drums was more inviting to dancers. (3) The relative simplicity of chord progressions found in jazz-rock. The new music was more complex than rock had been before, but it was harmonically less complex than other jazz styles. (4) The extensive use of repetition for a single accompaniment pattern. Technically this is known as *ostinato*, which means that a particular rhythm or brief melodic figure is repeated continuously. It was basic to most of the jazz-rock hits of the 1970s. Many of the largest-selling recordings in every category of music, not just jazz, are simple, rhythmically striking, and very repetitive. This combination of features could also account for much of jazz-rock's commercial success.

The electric jazz-funk band that ended a five-year retirement for trumpeter Miles Davis in 1981: (left to right) soprano saxophonist Bill Evans (his tenor sax is sitting to his right), bass guitarist Marcus Miller, Miles Davis (wearing hat, holding trumpet), Mino Cinelu (playing conga drum), Al Foster (playing full drum set). Guitarist Mike Stern, a regular member of this group, is not shown.

Photo by Mark Vinci

CHAPTER SUMMARY

1. Jazz and rock represent different streams in African American music, but they have occasionally overlapped.

2. Jazz differs from rock in its (a) smaller amount of repetition, (b) larger amount of improvisation, (c) greater complexity, and (d) higher level of musicianship.

3. Guitarist John McLaughlin led several innovative bands containing musicians who were themselves important jazz-rock bandleaders.

4. Herbie Hancock and Chick Corea were important jazz pianists during the 1960s who became better known as composers and bandleaders during the 1970s and 80s because of the fusion styles they created.

5. Joe Zawinul's compositions and arrangements formed the basis for the important 1969 Miles Davis jazz-rock albums *Bitches Brew* and *In a Silent Way* and for Weather Report, an innovative fusion band which lasted from 1971 until 1985 with saxophonist Wayne Shorter.

6. Weather Report originally began with much collective improvisation but eventually adopted approaches employing extensive preset repetition and the feeling of soul music. This culminated in Zawinul's riff-based hit "Birdland."

7. The post-1968 work of Miles Davis displayed a blend of the jazz tradition, funk music, and the music of India and South America.

8. New Age music and "smooth jazz" became the easy listening variants of jazz-rock fusion. George Winston and Kenny G were the best known practitioners.

9. Acid jazz emerged during the late 1980s as a blend of hip hop and rap music with jazz improvisations added as decoration.

10. Acid jazz was devised by disc jockeys mixing excerpts from old recordings with the sounds of drum machines and repeating loops of accompaniment sounds.

JAZZ-ROCK FUSION LISTENING

Miles Davis—*Bitches Brew*, 1969 (CBS G2K 40577)

Miles Davis—*Filles de Kilimanjaro*, 1968 (CBS CK 46116)

Weather Report—*Weather Report*, 1971 (CBS 48824)

Weather Report—*Heavy Weather*, 1977 (has "Birdland") (CBS 65108)

Weather Report — *I Sing The Body Electric*, 1971–72 (has "Surucucu")
(CBS 46107)

Tony Williams/John McLaughlin/Larry Young — *Emergency!*, 1969
(Verve 314 537 075-2)

Mahavishnu Orchestra (John McLaughlin, 1971) —
The Inner Mounting Flame (CBS CK 31067)

Mahavishnu Orchestra — *Birds of Fire*, 1972 (CBS 31996)

Return to Forever (Chick Corea) — *Light as a Feather*, 1972
(Polydor 827148-2)

Return to Forever — *Return to Forever*, 1972 (ECM 78118-21022-2)

Return to Forever — *Hymn of the Seventh Galaxy*, 1973
(Polydor 825 336-2)

Herbie Hancock — *Future Shock*, 1983 (has "Rockit") (CBS 38814)

Herbie Hancock — *Head Hunters*, 1974 (Columbia CK 65123)

Herbie Hancock — *Maiden Voyage*, 1964 (has "Dolphin Dance")
(Blue Note 46339)

US3 — *Hand on the Torch*, 1993 (Blue Note 0777 8088325)
(has Acid Jazz)

Miles Davis — *doo-Bop*, 1991 (Warner Bros. 926938) (has Acid Jazz)

Note: The *Jazz Classics Compact Disc for Jazz Styles, History and Analysis* (ISBN 0-13-012693-4; phone 800-947-7700) has "Surucucu" from 1972 by Weather Report, Herbie Hancock playing piano with Miles Davis on the 1967 recording of "Masqualero," and Chick Corea playing "Steps" in an acoustic trio format from 1968.

SUPPLEMENTARY READING

Jazz-Rock Fusion by Julie Coryell and Laura Friedman (Dell, 1978)

The Rolling Stone Illustrated History of Rock and Roll by Anthony DeCurtis, et al., Eds. (Random House, 1992)

Milestones 2 (discusses the Miles Davis fusion period) by Jack Chambers (University of Toronto Press, 1985; also distributed by Birch and Morrow)

Miles: The Autobiography by Miles Davis (Simon and Schuster, 1989)

Jazz-Rock by Stuart Nicholson (Schirmer, 1998)

ELEMENTS OF MUSIC

n describing the nature of jazz and the characteristics of different styles, several basic musical terms are quite helpful. This chapter is devoted to defining some of these terms, and I urge all readers, including those who are musically knowledgeable, to examine them carefully.

When people think of jazz, they usually think of rhythm first. But because the word rhythm is often used to describe a large variety of musical characteristics, some uses convey inaccurate or contradictory meanings. Much of the confusion can be avoided by first understanding three related terms for which rhythm is often mistaken: beat, tempo, and meter.

Beat

Music is often said to have a pulse. The unit of pulse is called a beat. When you tap your foot to music, you are usually tapping with the beat. Here is a visualization of the pulse sequences we call beats.

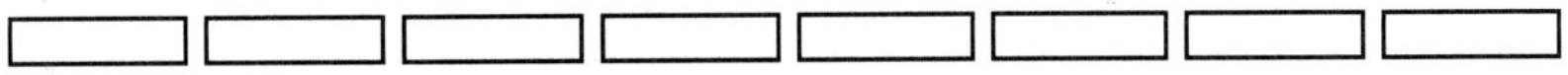

Tempo

Tempo refers to the speed or rate at which the beats pass. If you describe a piece of music as fast, you probably mean it has a rapid tempo, not that it occupies a short time span. When the beats continue at a regular rate, we say the tempo is constant. A clock's ticking is a good example of constant tempo. If the passage of beats is rapid, the speed is called "up tempo."

Meter

The beats in music are rarely undifferentiated. They are usually heard as being grouped. Meter describes the type of grouping. Our perception of grouping results when sequences of beats are set off from each other. This occurs in several ways. Every third or fourth beat may be louder or longer than the others. It may be distinctive because it has a different pitch or tone quality. Those differences are perceived as emphasis or accent. If we hear a sequence of beats grouped in fours, it may be due to a pattern of accents which creates this effect: **ONE** two three four **ONE** two three four. That pattern represents a meter which musicians simply call "four."

If the beats fall into the pattern, **ONE** two three, **ONE** two three, **ONE** two three, musicians say that the music "is in three" or in "waltz time."

Meters of four and three are quite common, but there are also meters of five, six, seven, and others. A meter of five might sound like **ONE** two three four five, **ONE** two three four five, **ONE** two three four five, with a large accent on the first beat and no other accents. Or there may be a strong accent on the first beat and a smaller accent on the fourth: **ONE** two three FOUR five, **ONE** two three FOUR five, **ONE** two three FOUR five; or a smaller accent on the third beat: **ONE** two THREE four five, **ONE** two THREE four five, **ONE** two THREE four five. A meter of six usually feels like **ONE** two three FOUR five six, **ONE** two three FOUR five six.

Each group of beats is called *a measure*. When the meter is three, there are three beats in a measure; when the meter is four, there are four beats in a measure.

Rhythm

In the broadest sense, rhythm simply refers to the arrangement of sounds in time, and therefore encompasses beat, tempo, and meter. But rhythm has come to mean something more specific than these features. In fact, beat, tempo, and meter furnish the framework in which rhythm is described.

Imagine a continuous sequence of beats occurring at a constant tempo, with four beats to a measure. The steady beat which in musical notation is represented by a string of quarter notes can also be visualized as a series of boxes, representing equal amounts of time. Our meter would be called "four." Each beat is called a quarter note, and each unit of four beats constitutes a measure.

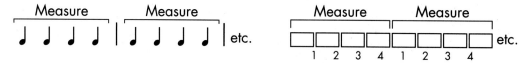

The sound within a measure can be distributed in an infinite number of ways, one of which includes "filling" the measure with silence. Rhythm is the description of how that measure or a sequence of measures is filled with sound.

Let us take a few examples, numbering the four parts of the measure one, two, three, and four, respectively. We shall create rhythms by using a single sound mixed with silence. First, divide a measure into four equal parts, filling only the first and third with sound.

We have a rhythm. It is not complex, but it does what a rhythm is supposed to do: it describes the distribution of sound over time. In fact, this is the bass drum part in numerous marches, and it is the string bass part in many slow dance pieces.

Now, instead of taking just one measure, take two measures as a unit of repetition. In other words, the rhythm is two measures long.

Finally, repeat a one-measure rhythm to fill two measures' worth of time. This might be heard as a two-measure rhythm or as two one-measure rhythms.

Rhythm is the distribution of sound over time, but rhythm also refers to the way sounds are accented. Usually, the first beat of a measure is accented. An example would be the typical OOM pah pah accompaniment for a waltz. In a measure of four, the first and third beats are often accented, as in the BOOM chick BOOM chick drum pattern used in much popular music.

Syncopation

Examining our use of accents can lend understanding to a rhythmic element called *syncopation*, a crucial aspect of jazz feeling. For example, if we expect to hear a sound on every beat but only hear it in a few odd places, the upset we feel is the result of syncopation. This upset can be very stimulating and contribute a prime component of jazz feeling. (Listen to Track 20 on the *Demo CD*.)

Examine this manner of filling two measures.

Note that the sounds which occur, bordered by silence, in positions other than on the first and third beats seem to stand out. They seem to be self accenting. If we additionally stress these odd positions by making the sounds in those positions louder than the sounds in other positions, syncopation is enhanced: one TWO three four ONE two three FOUR.

The concept of syncopation partly depends on a listener's expectations. For example, if we are expecting to hear *ONE* two THREE four, but we actually hear one *TWO* three FOUR, we are experiencing syncopation. Jazz drummers often keep time by playing boom CHICK boom CHICK (one TWO three FOUR) instead of BOOM chick BOOM chick. This syncopation is part of what makes a performance sound like jazz. Another frequently used syncopation occurs when we hear one two three FOUR when we are expecting to hear ONE two three four. So you see that rhythm involves the arrangement of stresses in addition to just describing the arrangement of sound over time. We have also seen that a phenomenon called syncopation results when the sounds are arranged or stressed in unexpected ways. Of course, what is expected depends on what the listener is accustomed to hearing. Therefore the statement that syncopation consists of unexpected accent is inadequate. Perhaps a more useful definition involves the accent of beats other than the first and, in measures of four beats, also the third beat. Silence can also be syncopating. For example, if we encounter silence at a time when we are expecting to hear ONE, the feeling of syncopation results.

Eighth Notes

To understand more complex syncopations and another essential element of jazz feeling, the swing eighth note, requires an acquaintance with ways in which beats are divided into smaller units. Here is a measure in four, with four quarter notes to the measure. We can divide each quarter note in half to produce eighth notes.

There are two eighth notes for every quarter note. If we place accents on the eighth notes according to the way we previously accented the measure of quarter notes, we have *ONE* two three four *FIVE* six seven eight. The time span for a measure of eight eighth notes is identical to that in a measure of four quarter notes, but keeping track of eight eighth notes is cumbersome. So we express the eighth notes in terms of subdivided quarter notes, saying "and" for the second half of each quarter note (every other eighth note): one and two and three and four and. Each word, whether it is the name of a number or the word "and," represents an eighth note.

Syncopation occurs when any of the "and's" receives more emphasis than the numbered units. Accenting the "and's" is essential to rhythms frequently employed in jazz. The final two beats in a measure are often divided into eighth notes with the last one accented the most: three and four AND. Many notes which appear in written form on the first beat of a measure are played on the *and* of the fourth beat in the preceding measure when given a jazz interpretation. The practice of playing a note slightly before or slightly after it is supposed to be played is a syncopating device which jazz musicians apply to pop tunes in order to lend jazz feeling to a performance.

Triplets

The quarter note can also be divided into three equal parts to produce what are called eighth-note triplets.

Sixteenth Notes

Here, each quarter note is divided into four equal parts, called sixteenth notes.

Dotted Eighth-Sixteenth Note Pattern

So far we have examined equal divisions of the quarter note. But it is also possible to divide it into notes of unequal value, for instance, a long note and a short note. One such pattern consists of a dotted eighth note followed by a sixteenth note. A dot after a note means that the note receives one and a half times its usual value; therefore the dotted eighth note has the combined value of an eighth note and a sixteenth note.

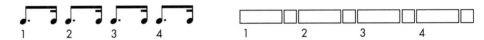

Tied Triplet Figure

Another long-short pattern is based on the triplet division of the quarter note. The pattern is called a tied triplet figure. Here, the first note has the value of two-thirds of a quarter note, and the second has the value of one-third.

Jazz has one rhythmic quality which, to my knowledge, is not found in any other kind of music: jazz swing feeling. A discussion of it appears in the "What Is Jazz?" chapter, but that discussion hinges on the *swing eighth note,* which is examined next.

Having heard the term "swing eighth note," you might wonder how, if an eighth note is simply half the duration of a quarter note, we can have different types of eighth notes, swing eighth note being one of them. Strictly speaking, you cannot have different types. An eighth note is an eighth note. Our descriptive language is loose enough, however, that we can use the term to label notes of slightly more or less duration than the eighth note is understood to receive.

Legato and Staccato

Listen to examples in *Demo CD* Track 44–45.

This looseness in applying the term "eighth note" is not exclusive to jazz musicians. Non-jazz musicians often use terms such as **legato**, which means long or slurred together or connected. They use the term **staccato**, which means short, abruptly separated. A legato eighth note equals a full-value eighth note. A staccato eighth note, on the other hand, has variable duration. Its length depends on the style of performance, and its value may actually be less than half that of a legato eighth note. It can be called an eighth note only because it is immediately followed by silence which fills up the remaining time that a full-value eighth note requires. Perhaps a staccato eighth note should be called a sixteenth note, or it should bear some designation that is more precise than the label of "staccato eighth note."

Quarter notes

Eighth notes

Eighth note triplets

Tied eighth note triplet figures

Dotted eighth-sixteenth note figures

Swing Eighth-Note Pattern

A wide assortment of eighth note durations and stresses are found in jazz styles. There are no jazz musicians who divide the beat in only one way. But there is a pattern that is more common than any other. It is a long-short sequence which is close, but not identical, to the pattern of durations found in the tied-triplet figures. The tied-triplet figure, you may remember, consists first of a long sound, then a shorter sound which is half the duration of the first sound. The two sounds together fit the duration of a single beat in the manner of a quarter-note triplet. Researcher Mark C. Ellis has found the average ratio of durations for first member to second member of swing eighth-note pairs to be 1.7 to 1. In other words, the first member of the pair is shorter than the first member of a tied-triplet pattern, and the second member is somewhat longer than a triplet eighth note. But neither member's duration is truly equal to an even eighth note, what musicians call "a straight eighth."

 Listen to examples in *Demo CD* Track 43.

The stress patterns for swing eighth-note patterns are distributed differently from player to player. Sometimes within the work of a given player, the stresses are distributed differently from performance to performance, sometimes from passage to passage. Basically, however, the first in a group of such swing eighth notes is louder than subsequent notes which occur on upbeats.

There is considerable confusion about notation of swing eighth notes. Such lack of uniformity exists in this regard that about the only accurate statement is that, when reading eighth notes, the desired choice of duration patterns usually depends upon the particular band and the style of arrangement being played. A little history might make this point a bit clearer. In countless written arrangements of jazz-oriented pieces which were published before the 1960s, dotted-eighth sixteenth figures appeared whenever the arranger wanted a swing eighth sound. (The arranger did not want true dotted-eighth sixteenth note patterns in which long-short meant the long member sounded three times the duration of the short one.) The notation appeared as even eighths thereafter in most arrangements, but the intention was for those notes to also be played as swing eighths. (If an arranger of this period wanted *truly even* durations, a written message appeared above the notes: "even 8ths." The musician's assumption was to otherwise play all the written eighth notes in a swing rhythm.)

Polyrhythm

To appreciate the rhythms which typify jazz, we should keep in mind the fact that several rhythms are usually played simultaneously. *Polyrhythm* (meaning *many rhythms*) is very important to jazz. When you listen carefully to a modern jazz performance, you should be able to hear several different rhythms at the same time. These include the rhythm in the melodic line, that of the bassist, the rhythm played by each of the drummer's four limbs, and each of the pianist's two hands.

Polyrhythms are often created by patterns which pit a feeling of four against a feeling of three. In other words, two measures can be played at the same time, with one being divided by multiples of two and the other being divided by multiples of three. In addition to that, the onset of one pattern is often staggered in a way which results in something less than perfect superimposition atop another pattern. Pitting three against four and staggering the placement of rhythms can project the feeling that the rhythms are tugging at each other. The resulting combination of stresses can be extremely provocative, and it can produce new syncopations in addition to those already contained in the separate patterns.

You can now understand why to say that jazz is quite rhythmic is to make an almost meaningless statement. All music has rhythm, and most music has syncopated rhythms. What sets jazz apart from many other types of music is the preponderance of syncopated rhythms, the swing eighth-note sequences, and the frequent presence of polyrhythm.

Scales, Keys, Tonality, and Modality

Understanding scales is basic to appreciating chord progressions, and an acquaintance with scales and chord progressions aids our knowledge of the rules which guide jazz improvisation. Everyone is familiar with musical scales. No one has been able to live very long without hearing a friend, neighbor, or family member practice "his scales."

Scales comprise the rudiments of beginning practice routines for singers and instrumentalists alike. Even people who cannot read music are familiar with the sequence *do* (pronounced "dough"), *re* (pronounced "ray"), *mi* (pronounced "mee"), *fa, sol, la, ti* (pronounced "tee"), *do.* Those eight syllables do not represent exact pitches as C, D,

E, F, G, A, B, C; they are only the names of acoustic relationships. (Do not let that term, "acoustic relationships," scare you. It is one of the simplest concepts in music. It means only that no matter what frequency of so many vibrations per second is assigned to *do*, the remaining seven pitches are determined by set multiples of it, for example twice the frequency, 1½ the frequency, and so forth.)

"*Do re mi fa sol la ti do*" numbers eight elements, the eighth element carrying the same name as the first, *do*. Its relationship to the first is exactly double the frequency of the first. For example, if the first *do* were 440 vibrations per second, the next higher *do* would be 880. It is no more complicated than that. That last *do* ends one sequence and begins another. The relationship between the bottom *do* and the top *do*, the first and eighth steps of the scale, is called an *octave*. The sound of two notes an octave apart is so similar that if they are played simultaneously, you can easily mistake the pair for a single tone. Most naturally produced tones contain an octave as one component of all the frequencies that combine to give a tone its own characteristic color or quality. The octave is called a harmonic or an overtone of the tone's fundamental pitch. That is the reason two tones an octave apart sound like one when they are played at the same time.

Since the interval of an eighth, from *do* to *do*, represents a doubling of frequency, you have probably guessed that those intervals between the first and the eighth must be fractions. You guessed correctly. The ratio of the fifth step (*sol*) to the first step (*do*) is ³⁄₂; that of the third (*mi*) to the first (*do*) is ⁵⁄₄, etc.

The seven-note scale has many labeling systems. We have already used three of them: a) do, re, mi, fa, sol, la, ti, do; b) first, second, third, fourth, fifth, sixth, seventh; and c) the frequency ratios: re/do = ⁹⁄₈; mi/do = ⁵⁄₄; fa/do = ⁴⁄₃; sol/do = ³⁄₂; la/do = ⁵⁄₃; ti/do = ¹⁵⁄₈. Next is the system which uses alphabet letters A, B, C, D, E, F, and G.

Look at the diagram of the piano keyboard printed here.

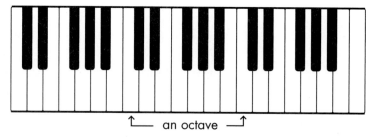

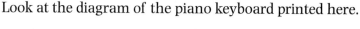
an octave

It is constructed so that the pattern of eight white keys and five black keys recurs again and again. The distance, or interval, between the beginning of one pattern and the beginning of the next is called an "octave." The scale which beginners usually learn first is the C scale; the C scale is obtained by playing eight of the white keys in succession, starting with the one labeled C. That scale, C, D, E, F, G, A, B, C, contains the same note relationships which we know as do, re, mi, fa, sol, la, ti, do. Play the notes of the C major scale in the order in which they are numbered in the diagram.

Look again at the piano keyboard.

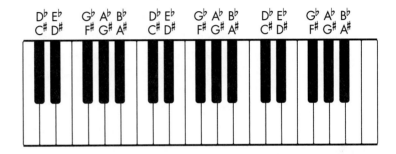

The black keys are known as sharps and flats. Sharp is symbolized # (like the number sign on a typewriter) and flat is symbolized b (like the lower case b on the typewriter). The black keys derive their names from the white keys which are next to them. The black key to the right of A is called "A-sharp" because it is slightly higher than A. But it is also referred to as "B-flat" because it is slightly lower than B. If we want only a C scale, going up an octave from C to C, we use none of the black keys. But if we want scales which begin on any note other than C, we have to employ at least one (and sometimes all) of the black keys. For instance, to play a major scale on D, it is necessary to make use of two sharps, F-sharp and C-sharp.

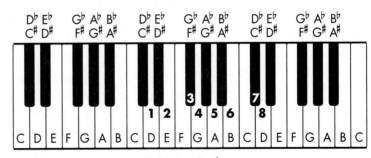

D Major Scale

A scale may be played starting from any black or white key. Altogether there are twelve such scales. Going up (moving left to right) from C, they are the scales of C, C-sharp, D, D-sharp, E, F, F-sharp, G, G-sharp, A, A-sharp, and B. Or, naming them in descending order, C, B, B-flat, A, A-flat, G, G-flat, F, E, E-flat, D, and D-flat.

When musicians say that a tune is in a certain key, for instance, the key of C, they mean that the song is played with the notes of the major scale beginning on C.

The relationship of the notes of the major scale gives a song a particular kind of sound and structure which is called **tonality**. Although tonality is a complicated idea, it can be understood as the feeling that a song must end on a particular note or chord. A key defines a scale which, in turn, defines that key. If a piece of music has the feeling of reaching for the same note, the key note, or it seems loyal to some note more than to any other, the overall harmonic character of the piece is called **tonal**.

There is another term like the term "scale" that is not inter-changeable with "key." The term is **mode**. Like a scale, a mode describes a sequence of acoustic relationships. Some modes even have the same number of elements as the scales we just explored. In fact, the C scale has a mode name: Ionian. But if we use the notes in the C scale and start the sequence on D, we produce another mode, Dorian. In other words, if we go from D to D in the key of C, we have constructed the Dorian mode.

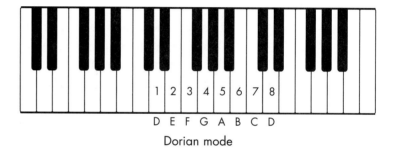

Dorian mode

For each of the seven scale steps in a key, there is a corresponding mode. The major scale itself has a mode name: Ionian; beginning on the second step produces the Dorian mode; the third step, the Phrygian mode; fourth, the Lydian mode; fifth, the Mixolydian mode; sixth, the Aeolian mode; and seventh, the Locrian mode. Each has a different sound because each has a different sequence of acoustic relationships which results from starting on different steps of the scale. I urge you to find a keyboard and play these modes. The concepts outlined here mean little without the sounds they describe.

We have seen that there are twelve keys, C, C# (or Db), D, and so forth. We also know that for each key there is a corresponding seven-note scale starting on the note which bears the name of the key (C D E F G A B for the C scale). Within each key there are modes, one mode beginning on each of the seven steps. The mode constitutes an octave of its own. Scales (modes) of fewer than seven notes and greater than seven notes also exist. The most common scale constructed of more than seven notes is the chromatic, simply that sequence of all the piano keys in an octave, white ones and black ones. Scale is a poor name because **the chromatic scale is actually just another way of dividing an octave into twelve equal parts.** It does not indicate a key as the C scale and the Bb scale do. *The chromatic scale is only a sequence of very small intervals called half steps.*

The chromatic scale has twelve steps: C, C#, D, D#, E, F, F#, G, G#, A, A#, and B. Unlike the modes, which have to be started on certain scale steps to guarantee their unique qualities, the chromatic scale can be started on any note, proceed through an octave and create the same identifiable chromatic quality no matter what note is chosen for its starting position. That means the C chromatic scale is identical to the C# chromatic scale (and all others). Perhaps it should be called "chromatic scale starting on C" or "chromatic scale starting on C#," specifying exactly what tone is to be the reference note.

The chromatic scale is very important because it expands the number of acoustic relations possible. Given twelve different tones in place of only seven, we have the option of raising and lowering (sharping and flatting) virtually any note we wish. Most Western European music of the past two centuries uses the chromatic scale instead of limiting itself exclusively to notes within one key at a time or, what is even more restrictive, only one mode at a time. Music was produced during the twentieth century which used all twelve tones equally and discarded the feeling of particular keys. Tonal music, you remember, is simply music which seems to be loyal to a certain note, always reaching for that note. Music without tone center is called *atonal*.

Most music has key feeling even when employing all twelve tones in the chromatic scale. This is just another way of saying that most music has tonality. During improvised music, tone centers might shift, but they usually remain long enough for their effect to be perceived. Most jazz employs tone center. It is extremely difficult to improvise without at least implying temporary tone centers and key feelings. The twelve tones are usually employed to enrich the conventional do re mi tonal orientation instead of providing a harmonic orientation all their own, one of atonality. Keep in mind that some music employs more than one key at once, but this type of music is not generally termed atonal. It is called *polytonal*, which means many keys.

If you play within the do re mi scale and enrich your melody with chromatic tones, the character of your playing can be partly described by how often you employ certain chromatic tones. Many people consider *bluesy quality* essential to jazz. A central component of bluesy quality is the frequent use of chromatics, three chromatics in particular: the *flat third, flat fifth,* and *flat seventh* notes of the scale. In other words, chromatic scale tones are employed to enrich the seven tones already available.

In the key of C, the blue notes are E-flat, G-flat, and B-flat. Remember the C scale consists of C, D, E, F, G, A, and B; there are no sharps or flats (none of the piano's black keys). To create a blue note we lower the third step of the scale. In the key of C this means changing E (a white key) to E-flat (a black key). We use both E *and* E-flat in constructing jazz lines, but the E-flat stands out because it is not one of the notes in the C major scale.

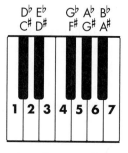

C scale without any blue notes

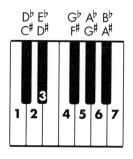

C scale with the flat third blue note

Listen to examples in *Demo CD* Track 55.

The second most common blue note is achieved by lowering the seventh step of the scale. In the key of C, this means changing B (a white key) to B-flat (a black key). Again we use both B *and* B-flat for our lines, but the B-flat is more distinctive because it is not in the key of C.

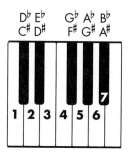

C scale with the flat seventh blue note (B-flat)

Note that the concepts of regular third step and blue third step are like the concepts of major chord and minor chord (the sounds of which you can demonstrate for yourself, using the following keyboard diagram as a guide to positioning your first, third, and fifth fingers).

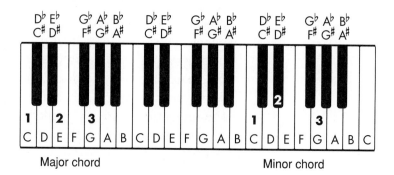

Major chord   Minor chord

The third most used blue note is the lowered fifth. Its use was not frequent until modern jazz began in the 1940s, but thereafter it became a standard device to convey a bluesy feeling, much as the lowered third and seventh had been in early jazz. In the key of C, a flat fifth is achieved by lowering G (a white key) to G-flat (a black key).

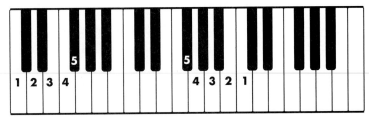

Going up to the flat fifth (G-flat)   Coming down to the flat fifth (G-flat)

Blue Notes

The term "blue note" does not have a single, universally accepted use. Some writers use it to designate the flat third and flat seventh that were discussed above. These sounds might best be termed "chromatically lowered" pitches because they are lowered by one step of the chromatic scale, the interval known as a "half step," a "chromatic semitone." Some writers use the term "blue note" to designate any pitch that is not completely a half step below another. This makes its classification "indeterminate" because, instead of being a clearly identifiable pitch of the chromatic scale, it is a pitch we might obtain only if we could play a note from the region within the cracks between the piano keys, so to speak. Musicologists variously call such pitches "neutral thirds," "heptatonically equidistant," or "indeterminate pitches." (For a closer examination, see "Blue Notes and Blue Tonality" by William Tallmadge, *The Black Perspective in Music,* 1984, Volume 12, Number 2, pages 155-165.) These pitches cannot be produced on the piano, but that does not mean that pianists have not wanted to produce them. The recent proliferation of synthesizers in the hands of jazz-rock pianists saw the molding of numerous solos employing this second kind of blue note, apparently because synthesizers are capable of generating pitches that represent fine gradations between those found on the piano. Playing with pitches is termed "pitch bending." (Listen to the *Demo CD* track 58 for examples.)

The attraction that jazz musicians have for out-of-tune thirds and sevenths might be the result of differences between European and African preferences for tuning. One origin is suggested here. The European seven-tone scale (do, re, mi, fa, sol, la, ti, do) is not based on equal divisions of the octave. It is a sequence of whole steps and half steps (the "diatonic" system) in which each half step represents about one twelfth of an octave. (The interval between C and D is a whole step, as is that between E flat and F. The interval between B and C is a half step, as is that between E flat and E.) A mix might have resulted between the European seven-tone approach and a West African seven tone (heptatonic) approach in which the interval separating each successive scale tone is equal, not the unequal pattern we find in whole steps and half steps. This African "equidistant heptatonic" scale has pitches that coincide fairly closely to those in the European diatonic scale. However, the third and the seventh steps are flat in relation to their counterparts in the European scale. This means that if an African sang his own pitch in a European piece, the third and seventh steps would sound "blue" or not perfectly in-tune to the ears of a listener who was accustomed to the European scale. If African American singers and musicians retained their taste for this particular kind of tuning, and seasoned European music to suit their tastes, then they performed European-style music in the "blue" manner we today associate with jazz.

Chords and Chord Progressions

Familiarity with the concept of scales allows us to explore the concept of chords and chord progressions, which, in turn, is essential to appreciating the harmony that jazz improvisers follow. These concepts are quite simple, but they have far-reaching applications, not only in jazz, but in all music which uses harmony.

A chord is obtained by sounding three or more notes simultaneously. Try these:

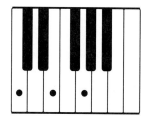
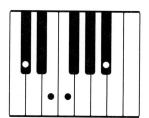

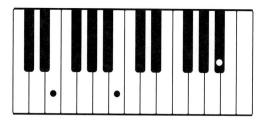
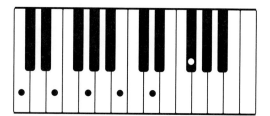

Although chords can be constructed from any tones, they are usually described in terms of scale notes and given Roman numeral names. The most common chord, one alternately described as a tonic chord, a major triad, the key chord, or a I (Roman numeral for 1) chord, employs the first, third, and fifth notes of the scale: *do, mi,* and *sol.* In other words, this chord is produced by simultaneously sounding do, mi, and sol in any key, any register, with any loudness or tone color.

Chords are named for the scale step on which they are based. A I chord is based on the first step of the scale, do; a II chord is based on the second step, re; a III chord on the third step, mi; a IV chord on fa; a V chord on sol; a VI chord on la; and a VII chord on ti. This system of naming is very handy for describing chord progressions.

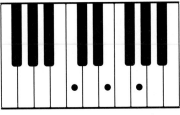

I chord in key of C

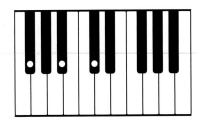

I chord in key of F-sharp

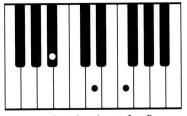

I chord in key of B-flat

A chord change is simply what it says, changing a chord. If we move from one chord to another, we have executed a **chord change**. We have moved forward, progressed, from one chord to another. In other words, a **chord progression** has been made. If the chords involved are those based on the first and second steps of the scale, respectively, we could describe the chord change as a I-II progression. If we move from a chord based on the first step to a chord based on the fourth, we create a I-IV progression. The reverse of that is a IV-I. If we move from the I chord to the V chord, and then back to the I chord, we create a I-V-I progresssion. (Listen to *Demo CD* Tracks 16, 17, and 18.)

To hear the sound of a very common chord progression, the I-IV-I-V-I blues progression, find a piano, an organ, an accordion, or any other keyboard instrument and strike all the keys simultaneously, the number of counts (1234, 2234, etc.) indicated in the diagram on the next page. You need not worry about what fingers to place on what keys. In fact, go ahead and use fingers from both hands if necessary. Try to keep a steady rate for striking the keys. If you can keep a steady rate, you may find that you are sounding like you have heard pianists and guitarists in rhythm and blues bands sound. (Listen to *Demo CD* Track 19.)

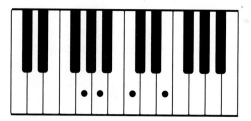

1234 2234 3234 4234 (**I** chord for 4 measures)

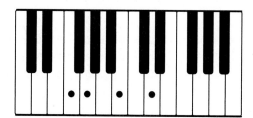

1234 2234 (**IV** chord for 2 measures)

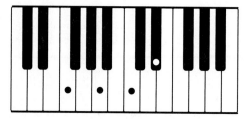

1234 2234 (**I** chord for 2 measures)

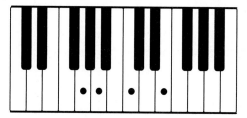

1234 2234 (**V** chord for 2 measures)

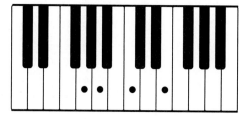

1234 2234 (**I** chord for 2 measures)

Chord Voicing

Most music uses chords that have been **voiced**. The concept of voicing is easy to understand. Merely use the keyboard to imagine a succession of repeating octaves.

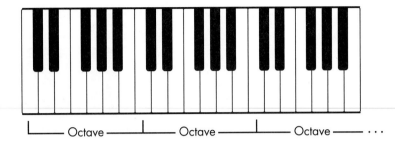

With the resulting repetition of notes available, we can pull each chord note away from the position it holds within a single octave and spread the chord over a wider range. We can also include additional notes and/or omit some of the original notes. All these manipulations fall under the heading of "voicing."

The same chord (three notes) arranged in different positions across the keyboard:

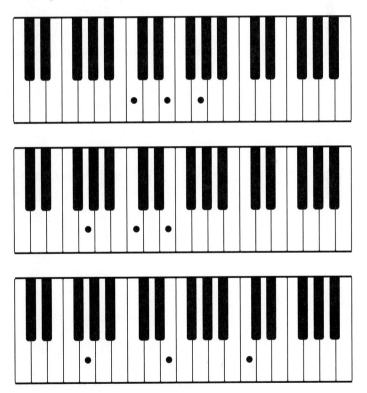

Jazz pianists can often be identified by the way they voice chords, and characteristic preferences in piano voicing are important components of the style in almost every period of jazz. In recent jazz, for example in the work of pianists McCoy Tyner and Chick Corea, **voicing in fourths** is quite common. Voicing in fourths means that chords are made up of notes four steps away from each other. In other words, a chord voiced in fourths might contain do, fa, and ti instead of do, mi, and sol. (The interval between do and fa is called a perfect fourth. To create a perfect fourth between fa and ti, the ti must be flatted. In building a chord composed of perfect fourths, each successive note is considered do of a new scale and the fourth note, fa, in that scale is used.) You can hear the sound of a chord voiced in fourths by playing this:

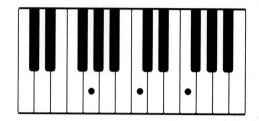

The term "voicing" also refers to how the notes of a chord are assigned to instruments in an orchestra or band. The ranges of the instruments as well as their tone colors are taken into consideration in voicing chords. Characteristic voicings serve to identify the work of different arrangers. Duke Ellington, for instance, voices chords in a manner distinguishable from Stan Kenton. Both Ellington's chords and his choice of instruments differ.

Voicing is also a term used to identify the instruments playing a melody. For example, we might say Duke Ellington "voiced the lead (the melody) for clarinet, trumpet, and tenor sax," meaning that those instruments played a unison passage in a particular Ellington arrangement.

The Blues

The term "the blues" has several meanings. It can describe

1. a sad feeling, or music which projects a sad feeling
2. a rhymed poetic form
3. a slow, funky, earthy type of music
4. a type of chord progression, usually contained in twelve measures, which has certain predictable chord movements in the fifth, seventh, ninth, and eleventh measures
5. any combination of the above

Blues poetry is so common in popular music that a technical description of the positions of accent and rhyme is not necessary in order for you to recognize the form. A single, very characteristic example can serve to illustrate the structure of blues poetry:

My man don't love me, treats me awful mean.   (pause)

My man don't love me, treats me awful mean.   (pause)

He is the lowest man I've ever seen.   (pause)

The I, IV, and V chords are basic elements of harmony used in the blues. In the twelve-bar blues, which is the most common blues form, these chords are distributed over twelve measures in a particular way. Although many variations are possible, the basic form is always the same. The chords and their respective durations are shown in the following chart. Each slash (/) indicates one beat. Perhaps it is helpful for you to think of a chord played on each beat by a rhythm guitarist. Note that the principal chord changes occur in the fifth, seventh, ninth, and eleventh measures.

I				IV		I		V	I	
////	////	////	////	////	////	////	////	////	////	//// ////

Although the chord relationships of the fifth, seventh, ninth, and eleventh measures usually hold, the remaining measures are the scene of countless alterations. Modern jazz blues progressions often employ more than one chord in a single measure and at least one change every measure. It is not unusual to have ten to twenty chord changes in the space of twelve measures. Sometimes the principal chords of the fifth, seventh, ninth, and eleventh measures are also altered. When the blues is sung, the words are often distributed in a standard way over the twelve-bar progression. (Study the lyrics and chords to "Fine and Mellow" which follow.)

A blues can be fast or slow, happy or sad. It may have lyrics, or it may be a purely instrumental piece, and its chord progressions may be simple or complex. For a piece to be a blues, the only requirement is that the I-IV-I-V-I chord progression or a variant of it be presented in a twelve-measure form.

The Thirty-Two Bar A-A-B-A Tune

Another form on which jazz musicians often improvise is the thirty-two-bar A-A-B-A tune. The thirty-two bar tune is made up of four eight-measure sections. The opening eight measures, called the A section, is repeated in the second section. The third part is the B section, sometimes referred to as the bridge, release, inside, or channel. The last eight bars bring back the material of the first eight. So the tune falls into what is called A-A-B-A form. Thousands of pop tunes composed during the 1920s, 30s, 40s, and 50s were thirty-two bars long in A-A-B-A form.

Listening for the Twelve-Bar Blues and Thirty-Two-Bar Forms

To gain a practical familiarity with chord progressions, glance at the list of tunes on page 209. These are categorized as twelve-bar blues or thirty-two-bar tunes in A-A-B-A form. Go to a record collection, and find performances of tunes from the list. Then choose one of them. Listen to approximately the first thirty seconds to determine whether this rendition has an introduction or begins immediately with the tune itself. Also determine how fast the beats are passing. A clue can often be found in the bass playing. If the bass is walking, there is a bass note for every beat, four beats to the measure. Listening to that sound, you should be able to hear the pulse as though the bassist were a metronome. The sound of the drummer's ride cymbal may also be a good indication of where the beats lie.

Having listened long enough to determine the tempo, you will also have discovered whether there is an introduction, and the point at which it ends and the tune begins. If you are not sure whether the beginning of the piece is an introduction or part of the tune itself, wait a while and listen for it to recur. If it does not recur, it is probably an introduction. In A-A-B-A form, the first part, A, is immediately repeated, A-A, before a new section, B, occurs. The routine for most twelve-bar blues tunes consists of repeating the entire twelve bars before beginning improvisation. Musicians occasionally use the same music for an ending that they used for the introduction. So if you hear something familiar at the end which does not seem to fit exactly in twelve or thirty-two bars, it may be the introduction attached for use as an ending.

By now you should know both the tempo at which to count beats and the moment to begin counting. Start when the tune itself starts (right after the introduction, in most cases). For a twelve-bar blues count: "1234, 2234, 3234, 4234, **5**234, 6234, **7**234, 8234, **9**234, 10 234, **11** 234, 12 234." Listen and count until you can detect the chord changes in measures five, seven, nine, and eleven:

```
I                        IV        I        V        I
//// //// //// //// //// //// //// //// //// //// //// ////
```

Listen to examples in
Demo CD Track 33.

If your counting is accurate, you will eventually be able to anticipate these important chord changes. That should provide some insight into harmonies that the jazz musician uses in his improvisation.

Count like this for a thirty-two-bar A-A-B-A tune:

"1234, 2234, 3234, 4234, 5234, 6234, 7234, 8234,
repeat   234, 2234, 3234, 4234, 5234, 6234, 7234, 8234,
bridge   234, 2234, 3234, 4234, 5234, 6234, 7234, 8234,
back to A 234, 2234, 3234, 4234, 5234, 6234, 7234, 8234."

Listen and count over and over until you can not only hear the bridge and the repeated sections, A-A, when they occur, but anticipate them. Do not become discouraged if you find it necessary to start and stop many times. Counting beats and measures requires practice. It is very important because it may be your only clue to the tune's form once a soloist has begun improvising. Learning to count accurately may take a few minutes, a few hours, or even a few days, but it is essential to an understanding of jazz improvisation. It will be well worth the effort. You might get especially good at anticipating the B section. If you know the tune, or can learn it by listening a few times, try humming it while listening to the soloists improvise on its chord changes. This will help clarify the relationship between the improvisation and the original tune. It will also help you keep your place.

Blues poetic form in relation to the 12-bar blues chord progression. The lyrics shown are from Billie Holiday's "Fine and Mellow." Available on *The Sound of Jazz*; Columbia: 45234, CD/AC, 1957.

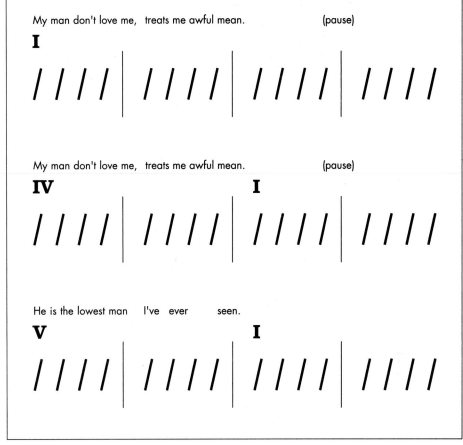

COMPOSITIONS WITH THIRTY-TWO BAR A-A-B-A CONSTRUCTION

"Ain't Misbehavin"
"Angel Eyes"
"Anthropology"
"Birth of the Blues"
"Blue Moon"
"Body and Soul"
"Budo" ("Hallucinations")
"Darn That Dream"
"Don't Blame Me"
"Don't Get Around Much Anymore"
"Easy Living"
"52nd Street Theme"
"Flamingo"
"Four Brothers"
"Good Bait"

"Have You Met Miss Jones?"
"I Can't Get Started"
"I Cover the Waterfront"
"I Love You"
"I'm Beginning to See the Light"
"It's Only a Paper Moon"
"I Want to Talk About You"
"Jordu"
"Lady Be Good"
"Lover Man"
"Lullaby of Birdland"
"Makin' Whoopee"
"The Man I Love"
"Midnight Sun"
"Misty"

"Moten Swing"
"Move"
"Oleo"
"Over the Rainbow"
"Perdido"
"Robin's Nest"
"Rosetta"
"Round Midnight"
"Ruby, My Dear"
"Satin Doll"
"September Song"
"Take the 'A' Train"
"Well, You Needn't"
"What's New?"
"What Is This Thing Called Love?"

TWELVE-BAR BLUES COMPOSITIONS

"Bags' Groove"
"Barbados"
"Billie's Bounce"
"Bloomdido"
"Bluesology"
"Blue Monk"
"Blues in the Closet"
"Blue 'n' Boogie"

"Blue Trane"
"Cheryl"
"Cool Blues"
"Cousin Mary"
"Footprints"
"Freddie the Freeloader"
"Goodbye Porkpie Hat"
"Jumpin' with Symphony Sid"

"Mr. P. C."
"Now's the Time"
"One O'Clock Jump"
"Sid's Ahead"
"Soft Winds"
"Straight, No Chaser"
"Walkin"
"Woodchopper's Ball"

Detecting Other Forms

Not all tunes fit into the twelve-bar blues form or the thirty-two-bar A-A-B-A form. "I'll Remember April" is a forty-eight-bar A-B-C-D-A-B form. "I've Got You Under My Skin" is a fifty-six-bar A-B-A-C-D-E-F form. Together, the twelve-bar blues form and the thirty-two-bar A-A-B-A form probably describe more tunes than any other single form, but they actually describe less than forty percent of all tunes written between 1910 and 1960. Let us examine a few other forms.

The twelve-bar blues is a particular set of chord progressions (I-IV-I-V-I) in a twelve-measure package. There are twelve-bar forms which are not blues simply because they do not follow the I-IV-I-V-I progression or any variation of it. For example, Richard Rodgers' "Little Girl Blue" is an A-A-B form in which each section is twelve bars long, but it is not a blues. It is also not uncommon in pop tunes to find a twelve-bar section which is actually an eight-bar progression with an extra four-bar progression connected to it.

The word "blues" in a song title does not necessarily signify the twelve-bar blues form. Both musicians and nonmusicians use the term "blues" to describe any slow, sad tune regardless of its chord progression. "Birth of the Blues" is a thirty-two bar A-A-B-A tune and "Sugar Blues" is an eighteen-bar tune. The "St. Louis Blues" is actually a twelve-bar blues plus an eight-bar bridge and an additional twelve-bar blues. Performers sometimes choose to repeat, delete, and reorder sections of "St. Louis Blues" when they play it.

Some people use the terms "eight-bar blues" and "sixteen-bar blues." Usually the tune they are describing has the I-IV movement in the first five bars and deviates from the twelve-bar I-IV-I-V-I progression thereafter. Some tunes of lengths other than twelve bars sound very much like twelve-bar blues simply because they contain the I-IV-I-V-I progression, but the durations of a few chords may be changed, and certain sections may be repeated. Herbie Hancock's "Watermelon Man," for example, has been called a "sixteen-bar blues."

Unlike the twelve-bar blues, the thirty-two bar A-A-B-A form is not always based on the same basic chord progression. Many different chord progressions have been used in the A-A-B-A form. Fats Waller's "Honeysuckle Rose" and Erroll Garner's "Misty" are both thirty-two-bar A-A-B-A tunes, yet they have almost completely different chord progressions.

The form A-A-B-A does not always contain thirty-two bars nor does each section necessarily have the same number of measures. In "Girl from Ipanema," which is A-A-B-A, the A section has eight bars while the bridge has sixteen. In "Secret Love," another A-A-B-A tune, the A section has sixteen bars while the bridge has only eight.

There are also elongated versions of the basic twelve-bar blues and thirty-two-bar A-A-B-A forms. Lee Morgan's "Sidewinder" is a twenty-four-bar blues: each chord lasts twice as long as it would in a twelve-bar blues. Another example is the sixty-four-bar A-A-B-A form in which each section is sixteen bars long instead of eight. Ray Noble's "Cherokee" and Lerner and Loewe's "On the Street Where You Live" are both sixty-four bar A-A-B-A tunes. Charlie Parker's

"Ko-Ko" is based on the chord changes of "Cherokee"; consequently it is also a sixty-four-bar A-A-B-A tune. There are shortened versions of the thirty-two-bar A-A-B-A, too. Sonny Rollins' "Doxy" is a sixteen-bar A-A-B-A tune; each section is only four bars long.

A-A-B-A is not the only common thirty-two bar form for pop tunes. Numerous tunes fit an A-B-A-C form (both the C section and the B section differ from the A section). "My Romance," "On Green Dolphin Street," "Indiana," "Sweet Georgia Brown," and "Out of Nowhere" all fall into a thirty-two bar A-B-A-C form. In addition to the thirty-two bar A-A-B-A and A-B-A-C, there is also the thirty-two bar A-B-A-B. "How High the Moon" is an example. There are shortened versions of these, also. "Summertime" is a sixteen-bar A-B-A-C tune.

Hundreds of tunes fit into sixteen measures. "Peg o' My Heart" is a sixteen-bar pop tune. Horace Silver based his "The Preacher" on the sixteen-bar pop tune "Show Me the Way to Go Home." Wayne Shorter has written many sixteen-bar tunes, including "E.S.P.," "Nefertiti," "Prince of Darkness," etc. Some chord progressions are used in sixteen-bar tunes almost as often as the I-IV-I-V-I progression appears in the twelve-bar blues. Certain sixteen-bar progressions have become standard.

Verse and Chorus.   It is important to note that the forms we have been examining refer only to chorus length. A large number of tunes consist of two major parts, a verse followed by a chorus. The verse traditionally differs from the chorus in tempo, mood, and harmony:

1. The chorus might be played at a faster tempo than the verse.
2. Verses are often performed freely, with accelerations and decelerations of tempo.
3. The verse might feel as though it is leading up to something, whereas the chorus usually has the stamp of finality to it.
4. There may be little similarity between chord progressions used in the verse and those in the chorus.
5. The key of the verse is sometimes different from that of the chorus.
6. Choruses are repeated, but once a verse is played, it is usually over for the entire performance.
7. The chorus is the section of the tune jazz musicians usually choose as basis for improvisation.

Breaking into Multiples of Two.   When you are listening to performances and trying to detect forms, be aware that arrangements of thirty-two-bar A-A-B-A, A-B-A-C, and A-B-A-B tunes sometimes depart from strict repetition of those thirty-two bars. Arrangements sometimes contain four-, eight-, and sixteen-bar sections, formed by omitting or adding to portions of the original thirty-two-bar tune. Note also that many tunes, especially pre-1930s Dixieland tunes, have long, elaborate forms similar to those of marches and of nineteenth-century European dance music (such as the quadrille). Forms for many tunes in pre-1920s jazz were derived from march music. A piece might have a series of sections consisting of multiples of eight bars. Designating each section by a letter of the alphabet, a piece might conceivably follow a pattern like this:

$$A - A - B - B - C - D - E - F - C - D - E - F$$
$$16 - 16 - 16 - 16 - 16 - 16 - 24 - 32 - 16 - 16 - 24 - 32$$

When listening for form, keep in mind that even in the most intricate pieces, forms can usually be broken down into two-bar segments. So if you are unable to divide a piece neatly into either four-bar or eight-bar sections, try using a few two-bar sections. "Sugar Blues" can be heard as 18 or as 8+10 or as 8+8+2. That form poses problems for the improviser because it tends to break the flow of ideas conceived in four- and eight-bar melodic units. It is like being forced to walk left, right, left, right, left, left, right. The form of the original "I Got Rhythm" is:

$$A — A — B — A + \text{tag}$$
$$8 — 8 — 8 — 8 + 2 \text{ or}$$
$$8 — 8 — 8 — 10$$

When jazz musicians improvise on its chord progression, they omit the two-bar tag. If included, the tag would interrupt the flow of the improvisations and again be like having to take two steps with your left foot before going back to an alternation of right with left. Another popular tune that has an unusual structure is "Moonlight in Vermont." It follows the form:

$$A — A — B — A + \text{tag}$$
$$6 — 6 — 8 — 6 + 2$$

Modal Forms

During the late 1950s and especially during the 60s and 70s, modal forms practically eliminated the "change" part of "chord change." In modal music, improvisations are based on the extended repetition of one or two chords. Those chords contain so many notes that they either include or are compatible with all the notes in a scale. The term "mode" is synonymous with scale, hence the term "modal music." Although this is not the definition of modal employed by classical composers and in textbooks on classical music, it is what jazz musicians and jazz journalists have come to mean by "modal." In most instances, jazz musicians also employ notes which are not contained in the mode or in the repeated chords. Some of John Coltrane's work, for example, is not strictly modal, but has the flavor of music which is.

In modal music, the entire improvised portion of the performance is often based on a single chord and scale. Usually the chord and its scale are minor, Indian, Middle Eastern, or in some way more exotic-sounding than the chords used in most pop tune progressions.

Because it is based on a single scale, the music has no real chord changes, just a drone.

Sometimes a melody containing chord changes of its own precedes the improvised section of a modal performance. John Coltrane's recordings of the Rodgers and Hammerstein tune "My Favorite Things" are good examples. Coltrane played the original melody while his rhythm section played the appropriate chord changes. Then the entire group improvised only on the primary chord of the tune (and the scale compatible with that chord). Near the end of their improvisations, they switched to another chord, which lent the piece a slightly different character. Coltrane could have retained the chord progressions of the tune and used them as the basis for improvisation, but he chose not to.

Some modal music does have chord changes, or "mode changes." One rich chord (or scale, depending on how one cares to conceive it) is the basis for four, eight, or perhaps sixteen measures. Then a different chord is in effect for another similar duration. The Miles Davis tune "Milestones" is based on one mode for the first sixteen bars, a different mode for the second sixteen bars, and a return to the original mode for the final eight bars. The melody has the form A-A-B-B-A, and each section is eight bars long. Herbie Hancock's "Maiden Voyage" has a thirty-two-bar A-A-B-A construction; here each mode lasts for four bars. The A section is based on two different modes, each lasting only four bars. The B section makes use of another two modes also lasting four bars each. If each mode were labeled by letter name, "Maiden Voyage" could be described as X-Y-X-Y-Z-W-X-Y. "So What" (on the Miles Davis album *Kind of Blue*) has a melody in thirty-two-bar A-A-B-A form, and the use of modes corresponds to that form: there are sixteen bars of one mode, eight of another, and a return to the original mode for the last eight bars. John Coltrane's "Impressions" not only takes the same form as "So What" but also uses exactly the same modes.

Much jazz of the 1960s and 70s was based on infrequent chord changes (another way of saying modal) instead of the frequent chord changes found in most twelve-bar blues and thirty-two-bar forms. Many groups abandoned both the blues form and the thirty-two-bar forms. Some groups used complex melodies and intricate rhythm section figures, yet their improvisations were based almost exclusively on one or a small number of chords ("Freedom Jazz Dance," for example).

The Effects of Form on Improvisation

Song forms of four- and eight-bar sections tend to break improvisations into small segments of similar length. Divisions of form, in other words, can influence the flow of improvised lines. This is not necessarily a disadvantage, however. The divisions in form can frame well-chosen melodic figures, and they can provide a means of transition from one figure to another. This creates more continuity than a solo might contain without chord progressions. Forms based on single modes sounding indefinitely tend to free the improviser, enabling him to create lines that are as long or short, tense or relaxed as he desires. No preset tension-relaxation devices in the form of chord progressions are there to suggest construction patterns for his improvised lines.

Bridges.   The B section of an A-A-B-A tune is called the bridge. It bridges the gap between repetition of the A sections, and it usually provides a contrast to the material in the A sections. The bridge can break up or lift the mood established by repeated A sections. Many bridges are placed a few keys higher than the A section. A key change can be a boost in any situation, but is especially effective after the repeated A sections.

The bridge is important to improvisers because a good improviser can capitalize on the bridge's natural capacity to provide contrast. Some of the greatest solo segments in jazz are those improvised over the chord progressions of a tune's bridge. The rhythm section also takes advantage of the bridge and is often especially active just before the bridge is entered and just before it is exited. Heightened rhythmic activity can announce the arrival or departure of the bridge.

Combos often use the bridge as a container for solo spots. Sometimes a tune's melody will be played for the final time in the performance, and when the bridge occurs, everyone stops playing except the drummer. It becomes his feature. Then the entire band returns precisely on the first beat of the final A section.

In some jazz tunes the bridge consists only of chord changes. Such pieces require improvisation during the bridge but return to the written melody when the final A section is reached. Sonny Rollins' tune "Oleo" is an example. Many groups also use that approach on "The Theme," a popular up-tempo number for jazz combos of the late 1950s and early 60s.

Turnarounds.   Another important part in the construction of standard tunes is the turnaround (also known as the turnabout or turnback). In many, perhaps in most songs, the seventh and eighth measures of each section are occupied by a single sustained tone or two long tones. That part of the tune might be considered dead space due to the lack of melodic movement, but the jazz musician uses that space. He fills it with chord changes which lead directly to the beginning of the next section. Jazz musicians are expected to know a variety of chord progressions common to turnarounds. The manner in which they fill that space with chord changes and improvised lines is the art of the turnaround.

The whole combo digs in when a turnaround comes up. Drummers tend to kick more and, thus, tie together the musical statements of one section and bring in the next. Those bassists who almost invariably walk are more likely to vary this pattern in a turnaround. Tension can be built during a turnaround and resolved by the onset of the next section of the piece.

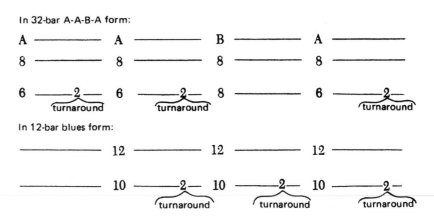

Phrasing in Relation to Form

Jazz musicians prior to the mid-1940s tended to improvise phrases which coincided with the tune structure. Most progressions consist of two- and four-bar units, and improvised solos often proceeded in phrases of similar length. Furthermore, soloists tended to make larger silences at or near the end of an A section or B section. They rarely connected tune sections by continuing phrases through the turnarounds. They stopped at or before the turnarounds, and then started anew at the beginning of the next section. They treated the eighth bar line as a barrier. Twelve-bar blues solos often contained phrases which started at the beginning of each chorus regardless of what happened at the end of a previous chorus, thus treating the twelfth bar line as a barrier.

One characteristic of modern jazz (beginning in the 1940s) and the music of the players who most influenced it was the use of phrases which began somewhere within an eight-bar section and continued into the next section without a pause. There was no lull during the turnaround.

A characteristic of some modern jazz during the 1960s and 70s was the absence of preset chord progressions. That free approach significantly loosened the tendencies of jazz phrasing. Although players retained patterns common to preceding jazz eras, they were free to phrase with greater variety due to the lack of underlying chord movements. Some jazz of this type projects a feeling of expansiveness quite unlike the crowded feeling often projected by modern jazz of the 1940s and 50s.

Some tunes which appeared during the 1960s, especially those of Wayne Shorter, were sixteen or more bars without any repeated sections. The A section was not repeated, there was no bridge, no turnaround. These tunes were "all A." That form enabled improvisers to play with great continuity yet without the crowded, segmented feeling which sometimes characterizes improvisations based on standard A-A-B-A and A-B-A-C forms with the usual turnarounds and bridges. Sometimes a free, floating feeling could be projected by improvisers using these "all A" forms. This kind of form was employed by composers who were departing from the tradition of pop tunes.

Tone Color

An important element of music, usually the first to be perceived, is tone quality or tone color. This element is also known as timbre (pronounced tamm´ burr).

How can you tell the difference between the sound of a flute and the sound of a trumpet if they each play only one note, and it is the same note? The difference is tone color, the spectrum of frequencies generated by each instrument in its own unique way.

This definition is an oversimplification of a complex situation in which many factors come into play.

The spectrum of frequencies produced by an instrument is not fixed. The spectrum varies depending on the pitch and the forcefulness with which it is played. The ways in which a player starts and stops a note, the attack and release, also are important in determining tone color. The attack and release are accompanied by temporary changes in a tone's frequency spectrum.

Another complication arises from our tendency to associate an instrument's tone color with the aggregate effects of all the notes being played on it rather than the spectrum of frequencies present in a single note.

Finally, when sounds come to our ears, they are modified by room acoustics and by recording and playback techniques. The way our ears deal with that variability is quite involved.

Tone color varies greatly from one instrument to another, and there are also especially discernible differences in tone color among jazz musicians playing the same instrument. For example, to speak of the tenor sax tone color of John Coltrane or Stan Getz is to describe sounds so unique that some inexperienced listeners could differentiate them as easily as they could distinguish flute from trumpet. The evolution of jazz tenor saxophone playing reflects not only changes in the phrasing and rhythms, but also changes in tone color.

Tone color is a very personal characteristic of a player's style. Jazz musicians place great emphasis on creating the particular tone colors they want. A jazz musician's attention to tone color is comparable to an actor's concern for costume, make-up, and voice quality combined. Tone color is so important to saxophonists that many spend lifetimes searching for the perfect mouthpiece. They also experiment with different methods of blowing and different ways of altering the vibrating surface of the cane reeds that are attached to their mouthpieces.

Because the tenor saxophone is capable of producing an exceptionally wide variety of tone colors, it is easier to differentiate jazz tenor saxophonists by tone color alone than it is to recognize a particular trumpeter or pianist. That is not to say that differences are absent from trumpeter to trumpeter or from pianist to pianist. The differences are just more subtle.

Two pianists can play the same piece on the same piano and produce quite different sounds. No two pianos have the same tone color, and one piano can produce distinctly different tone colors, depending on how hard the keys are struck. The use of the pedals and a pianist's timing in releasing one key and striking the next are crucial to the sound. A key may be released before, after, or at the same time as the next is struck. When a note is short and ends well before the next note begins, we call it a staccato note. If one key is released after the next is struck, the two sounds overlap in time. Notes played smoothly one after the other are said to be legato. The amount of overlap influences the clarity of attack and the dimension of legato-staccato. Our ears hear sounds in combined form rather than as single tones. Whatever is left in the air from a preceding sound mixes and colors the subsequent sound. The relationship between consecutive sounds, ranging from complete separation to extreme overlapping, are resources which contribute to the personal character of a pianist's style. Count Basie's touch and tone color differ remarkably from Duke Ellington's. Perhaps you will perceive Basie's touch as lighter than Ellington's. No matter how you describe the sound, you will notice a difference if you listen carefully.

Guitarists' interest in tone color is manifested by their search for different types of picks, guitar strings, and amplifiers. Guitar amplifier dial settings are essential to the control of tone color. Bass players are also concerned with many of the same factors.

Trumpeters and trombonists explore available tone colors by experimenting with mouthpiece changes, methods of blowing, mutes, and instruments which represent different manufacturers and models.

Intonation is also an important aspect of tone. Intonation refers to playing in tune, playing sharp or flat. Playing sharp means playing at a pitch level somewhat higher than the average pitch of the ensemble. Playing flat refers to playing a pitch somewhat lower than that of the ensemble. Do not confuse the terms sharp and flat with words describing actual note names such as C-sharp and B-flat. These notes are raised (sharped) and lowered (flatted) by a larger amount than is usually the case in out-of-tune playing. That is, the interval between C and C-sharp is greater than the interval between C and that of a performer playing C a bit sharper than his fellow ensemble members. Small deviations of pitch occur all the time even in the best ensembles, but larger deviations lead listeners to comment "someone is playing out of tune."

Why is intonation described in this section on tone color? Intonation affects the tone color of both the soloist and the ensemble as a whole. If a group of musicians played the same piece twice, once without listening or adjusting to each other's pitch (perhaps by pretuning their instruments and then wearing ear plugs for the performance), and then a second time, listening carefully to each other's pitch and continuously adjusting accordingly, you would hear two performances, each having distinctly different tone colors. Ensembles which lack precision tuning have a thicker, rougher sound than precisely tuned ensembles. One element of a slick ensemble sound is careful and consistent tuning.

Mutes. (Listen to examples on *Demonstration CD* Track 68.)

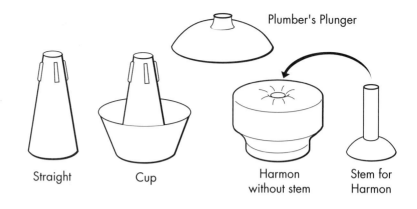

Straight   Cup   Harmon without stem   Stem for Harmon

Plumber's Plunger

Trombonist Quentin Jackson playing into plunger mute.

Photo courtesy of John Richmond

Miles Davis playing into cup mute.

Courtesy of Frank Driggs

Trombonist Dicky Wells
playing into straight
mute.

Photo by William Gottlieb

Trumpet with Harmon
mute inserted.

Photo by Dan Morgan

For tone color reasons, some soloists systematically play a little "high," meaning a bit sharp. Intonation is a musical resource for them. This is common in most types of music, including symphonic, but it is especially true for jazz soloists. A tone cuts through an ensemble if it is a bit sharper than the average pitch of that ensemble. Some jazz soloists seem to play at the average pitch. Others tend to different degrees of sharpness. That is another component of tone color which helps us identify a particular player's work.

Album Buying Strategies

Minimizing Risk in Selecting Albums

One key to being a happy jazz fan is finding the right albums. This section of the book provides guidelines and short cuts to help you.

1. **Beware of endorsements in newspapers and magazines.** They represent knowledge and understanding no greater than that of one individual. The reviewer might not be knowledgeable or perceptive. Moreover, his tastes might differ from yours. For instance, staples in the record collections of musicians are sometimes unknown by many critics, and some of these masterpieces were given only lukewarm reviews by the critics who did notice them. Albums that win Grammy awards are not necessarily outstanding, either. They are merely among the albums that a small committee of journalists has heard and voted upon within the preceding twelve months. (Over a thousand albums are issued each year in the U.S. alone.) A parallel might be helpful. You probably remember a few Academy Award winning movies you did not find enjoyable. Conversely, you might have also found yourself liking a few movies that received bad reviews. You may have been impressed by a few movies that no one was talking about, too. Similarly, *albums receiving the most press and airplay are not necessarily the highest quality.* Extent of press and airplay is determined largely by the record company's promotional budget, luck, and persistence, plus the tastes of disc jockeys and journalists. Some of the best albums never get publicized.

2. **Listen to the music before you buy it.** Try to avoid album buying as an impulse purchase. Unless you want a record for purely academic reasons or historical perspective, you might realize too late that you spent your money on something you don't enjoy. This is worth keeping in mind

unless you can afford to experiment expensively. Friends, libraries, jazz courses, and radio programs can often expose you to new albums. If there is a jazz radio station near you, don't hesitate to phone and ask them to play a particular album. (College radio stations not only broadcast more jazz than commercial stations, but they are also more likely to be interested in your requests.) And when you hear something you like, you could also phone the station and ask for its album title and record company name.

3. **Use a broad sampling of recordings before forming your opinion of a particular player.** One good reason is that *few jazz improvisers are extremely consistent in producing inspired recordings.* Some of even the greatest jazz musicians have had whole strings of unexciting albums. This means that, if the only recording you hear is from an off day for that player, you derive a nonrepresentative view of his talent. You are not fair to him.

Another reason for using a broad sampling is that, *if the player had more than one style period in his career, you cheat yourself if you draw a conclusion from sampling only one of them.* For instance, Sonny Rollins had a creative peak in the middle 1950s, and another in the 1990s with a different style. This means that, if you heard a few recent Rollins records and did not like them, you might not seek any mid-1950s Rollins material, even though you might have liked it. The converse would also be true.

4. **Don't accept substitutions.** The quality and character of improvised music can vary drastically from album to album, even if made by the same band during the same period as the music you seek. So once you decide which albums you really want, don't get others first, merely because they are available and look similar.

5. **Don't wait for your desired albums to appear in stores.** They probably won't appear. Quality of music and availability often seem inversely related. Try mail-order sources, and stick to what you really want. See listing for mail-order firms at the end of this section.

Confusing Album Titles

Be suspicious of titles for compilations. Let's examine reasons for caution with two categories of compilations: (a) *Greatest Hits* and (b) *The Best of, The Indispensable,* and *The Essential.* **Problems for both categories often occur when the compilation comes from only one company's recordings,** and that particular company did not record the artist during his creative peak (invalidating *The Best of* designation) or during his height of popularity (invalidating the *Greatest Hits* designation). Another company did. For example, a Verve album of 1950s recordings called *The Essential Lester Young* is probably "essential" only to those Lester Young collectors who already have much of Young's creative peak represented in his 1930s Count Basie recordings, reissued by Columbia/SONY and Decca/MCA/GRP.

A second set of problems arises **when musicians have had several different styles during their careers** and a creative peak for each. They may have been recording for a different company during each important period. For example, John Coltrane made important recordings as a bandleader for three different companies (Prestige, Atlantic, and Impulse). Each company documented a stylistically different stage in his career. (And some of his best work was recorded with Miles Davis's bands for Columbia, a *fourth* record company.) This means, for example, that an Atlantic album called *The Best of John Coltrane* cannot contain Coltrane's best work from all three periods—although it could sample some of his best Atlantic sessions if the compiler knew what he was doing.

A third set of problems results **when musicians made their best recordings as sidemen in the bands of others**, not as bandleaders, yet the compilation draws only from recording sessions where they were bandleaders. For instance, Lester Young's best work was done as a sideman with the 1936–41 combos and big bands associated with Count Basie. The music on his combo recordings as leader does not sound like his music on the Basie recordings. This means that an Emarcy album called *Pres at His Very Best,* containing music from 1943–44 in which Young was bandleader, is probably not his "very" best recorded improvisations, though it might represent the best playing he recorded as a bandleader. The Emarcy album title is misleading.

Here are some other examples of the confusion arising from album titles not coordinated with varied careers. In the 1960s, pianist Herbie Hancock and saxophonist Wayne Shorter both recorded for Blue Note as bandleaders. During much of that time they were also recording for Columbia as sidemen in the Miles Davis Quintet. Most of their playing on the Davis recordings is superior to that on their own records. But since they were bandleaders for Blue Note, the Blue Note recordings, not the Columbia recordings, provide the pool for albums titled *The Best of Herbie Hancock* and *The Best of Wayne Shorter.* Hancock's and Shorter's work on Blue Note is excellent music, and it also features the outstanding composing for which Hancock and Shorter are distinguished. But when heard strictly as piano and saxophone improvising, their work on Blue Note may not be the absolute best of either man's career, as claimed by an album title. Incidentally, a Columbia album called *The Best of Herbie Hancock* (JC 36309) contains neither his innovative playing with the 1963–69 Miles Davis groups nor his distinguished composing within the Blue Note work. The album samples a third facet: Hancock's jazz-rock material of the 1970s.

A fourth reason for approaching compilation titles with caution is that **sometimes compilers are not qualified for their task.** This means that, even if an artist recorded solely for one company during his creative peak, a *Best of* album might omit his *best* work because the person in charge of preparing the compilation was not familiar enough with all the artist's work for that firm. The compiler might not have had sufficiently developed taste, either, or he did not realize how much he needed to call upon the taste and knowledge of consultants. This may explain why a number of single-company compilations of several jazz giants, which emerged on compact disc during the 1990s, had knowledgeable consumers wondering why so many unremarkable selections had been included while outstanding performances remained untapped in the company's vaults. It might also explain why even a few multi-company compilations have had jazz fans puzzled about odd choices.

Greatest Hits can be misleading as an album title because, in addition to all the previously mentioned problems, a player's best-selling material might not even appear on it. For example, the largest-selling Miles Davis recording for Columbia was his 1969 *Bitches Brew* (GP 26). Yet it is not represented on the Columbia album *Miles Davis' Greatest Hits* (PC 9808). The 1964 recording of "Girl From Ipanema" for the Verve company was the highest selling recording of Stan Getz's career. Yet there is an album titled *Stan Getz's Greatest Hits* (Prestige 7337) drawn from 1949 and 1950 sessions made for the Prestige company. The Prestige material is excellent, perhaps better than the Verve material, yet it does not include his largest-selling hits as the album title deceptively implies.

To avoid being misled by compilation titles, first learn about the musician's career. Then check details on the album wrapper or box insert to confirm that recording dates, titles, and personnel match what you seek. It is also wise to consult authorities to determine what companies were recording the artist during critical portions of his career and what selections are deemed outstanding.

By seeking prescreened items such as the types of anthologies discussed above, rather than making impulse purchases, you lessen risks in finding music you will want to keep. Ultimately you need to remember, however, that the main reason for buying compilations and samplers is to become familiar with a wide range of music for a small price. But also bear in mind that just because selections on the samplers are critically acclaimed or generally popular does not guarantee you will like them.

While you are pursuing this strategy, you will rarely see a desired album in the stores. Jazz fans have become accustomed to the fact that *most current jazz albums must be special-ordered, and all out-of-print albums must be obtained through special sources.* So-called out-of-print material frequently becomes available in repackaged formats, discussed below as reissues. Sources are listed at the end of this section.

Locating Albums

Many people think certain albums are available only in big city stores. But no matter where you live, **most records can be obtained by mail.** In fact, many of them will never surface in big city stores. It might be more practical to get records by mail even if you live in or near a big city that has many music stores, such as New York or Los Angeles, for instance. The cost of getting there could exceed the price of an album.

When you arrive at the store, the clerk may end up ordering your request by mail anyway. The main point is that *most of the jazz records mentioned in this book will not be found in average stores.* If they are available to a store, they will probably require a special order. You therefore ought to phone ahead to determine whether traveling an inconvenient distance will be worthwhile. Some stores accept special orders over the phone. You then need only call the store periodically, and find out whether your order has arrived. Some will mail them to you, also. Keep in mind, however, that most stores are not interested in your special order business. It is an unprofitable hassle for them, though they will often fail to admit this to you. They will take forever to fill your order or never bother to notify you when they give up trying to find a particular item. Perhaps the most expedient path is to forget the stores, and go mail order. A few reliable sources are listed at the end of this section. Incidentally, out-of-print records can be obtained by getting your name on the mailing lists for jazz record auctions. You merely scan their fliers, then bid by mail on what you want. The addresses for jazz magazines and specialty record stores on page 229 can be used to begin this process. Note that auctioneers advertise in jazz magazines.

About Reissues

When seeking out-of-print recordings, there are several things to keep in mind. Many jazz recordings which have disappeared from catalog listings return later in altered form. This includes the category known as *reissues, re-releases,* and *repackages.* Before we discuss them, here is some relevant history. Prior to the widespread use of twelve-inch, 33⅓ rpm (revolutions per minute) LP (long play) records, most jazz was issued on ten-inch, 78 rpm records. Twelve-inch 33s were not common until the 1950s, so many bop- and cool-style bands—in addition to Dixieland and swing bands—were initially presented on 78s. Due to the size of the record and the speed of rotation, most 78s could accommodate only about three minutes of music per side. An *album* consisted of several records packaged much like a photo album. Each record had its own pocket or sleeve. The set was bound in cloth or leather. Then when the LP arrived, many of the three-minute selections originally on 78 were issued again (reissued) as compilations within 33⅓ rpm albums. This time, the word *album* meant one disc containing many selections. All the recordings in this book's premodern section and a few modern items are to be found in this kind of "reissue." Later on, LPs themselves began to be reissued, re-released, and repackaged as "new" LPs. Then when compact disc technology emerged, the contents of old LPs began appearing in CD format. Sometimes additional selections were included when the album was reissued on CD because the CD could accommodate up to about 77 minutes of music instead of the 50-minute limit that was common for LPs. Sometimes two LPs were represented on one CD. This is the altered form in which you can often find music originally available on records which have "disappeared" from the catalog.

Many albums that are no longer marketed by U.S. firms are available in foreign countries under the same titles they carried before they went out of print in the U.S. For instance, Japanese and European distributors have been repackaging out-of-print American albums, sometimes selling them with the original album jacket art and liner notes intact. Because of this, a list of importers and their addresses appears at the end of this section. More can be found advertised in jazz magazines. Relying on imports is not always dependable. So first match tune titles, personnel, and recording dates to determine whether a foreign release is the same as the American original you seek.

There is something else to consider when searching for a reissue of a particular recording. *It is common for jazz groups to record several versions of the same tunes, and some players record the same tunes with different groups.* Since you are a jazz fan, you are seeking recordings of particular improvisations, not merely the tunes they are based on. So you must find the actual performances you want. A musician's improvisations on other versions of the tune might not even resemble what you want.

When you are trying to locate music from a recording that has gone out of print, you will be looking for it in new compilations of old material. For these new packages, album titles are sometimes changed, and material from the original album is scattered over several different compilations. Another common problem is that the recordings may have belonged originally to companies which later sold their material. The original company's name helps you identify reissued material. For instance, one group of important Charlie Parker recordings was originally made for the Dial company, and its reissued form is called *The Dial Masters.* However, when record companies are bought and sold, sometimes the music is reissued intact, causing you no headaches. For example, Impulse was bought by ABC, then by MCA, then GRP, but many of the important albums John Coltrane made for Impulse during the 1960s continued to be distributed intact, though with GRP catalog numbers.

Another key to locating material in reissued form is that it is often identified by where it was recorded. For example, the pivotal Bill Evans-Scott LaFaro music originally made at New York City's Village Vanguard night club for Riverside record company, originally issued on albums titled *Sunday at the Village Vanguard* and *Waltz for Debby,* has been reissued by Fantasy-Prestige-Milestone as *The Village Vanguard Sessions.* Recordings from an outstanding 1953 concert by Charles Mingus, Charlie Parker, Dizzy Gillespie, Bud Powell, and Max Roach are frequently identified only by recording site: Toronto's Massey Hall (*The Massey Hall Concert*).

When seeking music that you think is out-of-print, you need a complete listing of the musicians, the pieces, the recording dates, the original album title, and the name of the record company. It also sometimes helps to have the original catalog numbers. Personnel listings can be especially useful because material is sometimes reissued under the name of a musician who was a sideman on the original recording session but has now become more significant than the leader. It is packaged as though he were leader at that original session. For example, a 1956 Tadd Dameron album called *Mating Call* was reissued under John Coltrane's name and called *On a Misty Night*. Coltrane was a sideman on it but is now in much demand in his own right. Several reissues of Joe Oliver's Creole Jazz Band have come out under Louis Armstrong's name, even though Armstrong was a sideman, not the leader, on Oliver's recordings. Much pre-1940 Lester Young material is available in reissues under Young's name, though it was originally recorded under Count Basie's leadership.

There are several ways you can keep up with what is being reissued. Reading jazz magazines is the most efficient. This will allow you to keep up with material that won't be broadcast on radio. As this book went to press, the magazines that attempted to announce most new albums and reissues were *Jazz Times* (8737 Colesville Road, Silver Spring, MD 20910-3921) and *Cadence* (Redwood, NY 13679). You can also phone or visit music stores to track listings in their *Phonolog, Spectrum,* or *Muse.* Several mail-order services give information and take orders by phone. If you do not want to wait for a given album to be reissued (and some never are), watch for it in the bins of cut-outs and used albums at music stores, garage sales, house sales, and flea markets. *Or contact rare record dealers and auctioneers, advertised in the back pages of jazz magazines.*

Many Versions of the Same Tune

The problem of a single tune recorded many times by the same artist increased substantially during the past forty years. This was due to increases in: (1) legitimate reissue programs by major firms, (2) illegitimate releases (called bootleg or pirate records) by numerous small firms, and (3) the discovery, or rediscovery, of a seemingly endless variety of broadcast performances, called *air shots* or *air checks.* (Music of the 1930s and 1940s, unlike that of the 1950s and 1960s, is well documented by air checks because most jazz groups made live radio broadcasts in those days.)

Beginning in the 1960s, record companies began massive distribution of repackaged material. Hundreds of albums with new titles were introduced. Many contained music originally on 78s. Other albums had music originally available on LPs. Some of the albums featured alternate, but originally rejected, versions of tunes. These are called *alternate takes.* (Some are labeled as alternate takes, but for others, you have to hear both versions to know whether they differ. They sometimes have improvisation equal or superior to the versions originally issued.)

Albums flooded the market from companies, both American and foreign, which operated without the consent of the recorded artists (or of their estates, in the case of deceased artists). Those albums constitute the illegitimate releases mentioned earlier as *bootlegs.* The companies were small and disappeared quickly. Some of their material had appeared previously on other records, but much of it had never been available before. A lot of it came from homemade recordings of night club appearances and radio broadcasts. Many albums have incorrect tune titles. Few contain complete personnel listings and recording dates. Many display poor sound fidelity. But if you can tolerate all those weaknesses, you might be well rewarded by the music itself. It is also worthwhile to be aware of bootleg recordings because the appearance and distribution of them is very common and likely to continue.

With the bootleg material added to the legitimate releases and reissues, it became possible to own, for instance, more than eighty albums of Charlie Parker, or more than one hundred of Duke Ellington. The record collector might be confronted with five to ten Parker versions of "Confirmation" and "Ornithology" and just as many Ellington versions of "Mood Indigo" and "Sophisticated Lady." Keeping track of recording dates and personnel became essential to discussing particular performances of these frequently recorded tunes.

A few Charlie Parker classics illustrate the usefulness of having personnel, tune titles, recording dates, and original record company name before you begin seeking a particular recording. The much praised music that Parker originally made in the form of 78s for Dial Record Company has been sold in numerous forms, some of them offered by tiny, obscure record companies that worked without the consent of Parker's estate. Take "Embraceable You," for example. Parker recorded many different versions of it. But if you want his famous Dial recording of it, remember that he made two different versions at the same session in 1947 with pianist Duke Jordan, bassist Tommy Potter, and drummer Max Roach. Any deviation from that particular combination of identifiers will indicate that you are holding another version of the tune instead of the famous version. It is also essential to note the record company name and recording date if you want to locate Parker's famous 1945 "Now's the Time," which was made for Savoy record company with the Miles Davis trumpet solo that was later adapted and recorded by pianist Red Garland on the Miles Davis *Milestones* album. It is especially easy to become confused in this instance because another version of the same tune was also recorded by Parker without Davis in 1953 and released on a Verve album called *Now's the Time.* There are instances in which historic figures recorded only one version of a given tune, but the more you study jazz, the more you will find it beneficial to **keep track of details to ensure you're buying what you originally set out to buy.**

One final example is offered to illustrate the usefulness of having complete information about an improvisation you seek. If you have a transcription of a Miles Davis trumpet solo from a performance of "Joshua," and you want to hear the original or play along with it, you cannot just run out and buy the correct album, even if you already have the personnel listing and the year of recording. Miles Davis recorded "Joshua" at least three times with saxophonist George Coleman, pianist Herbie Hancock, bassist Ron Carter, and drummer

Tony Williams. Two out of the three times were in the same year, 1963. One version was released on *Seven Steps to Heaven,* an album which was issued with two different catalog numbers: Columbia CS 8851 and CL 2051. Another version was released on *Miles Davis in Europe* (Columbia CL 2183 and CS 8983). Then Davis recorded another version in 1964 that was released in *"Four" and More* (Columbia 9253 and CL 2453) that was reissued on CD under a new title and new catalog number in 1992.

Rare Record Dealers, Importers, and Auctioneers

Worlds Records
P.O. Box 1992
Novato, CA 94948
(800) 742-6663

Cadence Record Sales
Cadence Building
Redwood, NY 13679
(315) 287-2852

Roots and Rhythms
P.O. Box 837
El Cerrito, CA 94530
(510) 525-1494

International Association of
Jazz Record Collectors
P.O. Box 855
Tenafly, NJ 07670
(Write for a membership listing, then determine who specializes in the style you seek, and write that member.)

Memory Lane Out-of-Print Records
1940 East University Drive
Tempe, AZ 85281
(800) 326-5343

Jazz Record Mart
444 North Wabash Avenue
Chicago, IL 60611
(800) 684-3480

Mosaic Records runs a broad-ranging program of reissuing hard-to-find items. Their reissue packages are prepared in a very intelligent and conscientious manner with excellent annotation. As this book went to press, Mosaic was still carrying material by Stan Kenton, Duke Ellington, Louis Armstrong, Maynard Ferguson, George Shearing, Miles Davis, Nat Cole, Don Cherry, Charlie Parker, and others. Mosaic also was running a subsidiary, called True Blue, which distributed Blue Note recordings, a source for pivotal music from the 1950s and 60s that has become difficult to locate. Request a catalog from Mosaic Records, 35 Melrose Place, Stamford CT 06902-7533; phone (203) 327-7111.

A Small Basic Collection of Jazz Videos

Listening to Jazz by Steve Gryb (Prentice-Hall) 60 minutes; demonstrations of instruments and their combo roles, corresponding to the audio illustrations in the *Jazz Styles Demonstration Cassette/CD* for the *Jazz Styles: History and Analysis* textbook by Gridley; ISBN 0-13-532862-4; phone (800) 947-7700.

The Sound of Jazz (Vintage Jazz Classics) 58 minutes; an unedited copy of the 1957 kinescope of the CBS broadcast with performances by Count Basie, Lester Young, Coleman Hawkins, Ben Webster, Billie Holiday, Roy Eldridge, Thelonious Monk, Jimmy Giuffre, and others.

Trumpet Kings (VAI) 60 minutes; hosted by Wynton Marsalis; includes Louis Armstrong, Bunny Berigan, Roy Eldridge, Red Allen, Dizzy Gillespie, Miles Davis, Freddie Hubbard, and others.

Piano Legends (VAI) 63 minutes; hosted by Chick Corea; includes Earl Hines, Fats Waller, Art Tatum, Thelonious Monk, Bill Evans, Cecil Taylor, and others.

Reed Royalty (VAI 69072) 58 minutes; hosted by Branford Marsalis; includes Johnny Hodges, Charlie Parker, Gerry Mulligan, Eric Dolphy, Lee Konitz, Sidney Bechet, Ornette Coleman, Benny Goodman, Sonny Stitt, and others.

Tenor Titans (VAI 69073) 60 minutes; assorted tenor saxophonists: Coleman Hawkins, Lester Young, Stan Getz, John Coltrane, Wayne Shorter, Sonny Rollins, Dexter Gordon, and others.

Jazz Masters Vintage Collection, Vol. 2: 1960-61 (A-Vision 50-239-3) 45 minutes; Ben Webster, Ahmad Jamal, Miles Davis Quintet with John Coltrane, Miles Davis with Gil Evans Orchestra.

One Night With Blue Note, Vol. 1 (SVS) 55 minutes; Bobby Hutcherson, Herbie Hancock, Ron Carter, Freddie Hubbard, Joe Henderson, Tony Williams, Stanley Jordan, Art Blakey, Curtis Fuller, Johnny Griffin, Walter Davis, and Reggie Workman.

One Night With Blue Note, Vol. 2 (SVS) 60 minutes; Kenny Burrell, Grover Washington, Grady Tate, Reggie Workman, McCoy Tyner, Jackie McLean, Woody Shaw, Cecil McBee, Jack DeJohnette, Charles Lloyd, Michel Petrucciani, Lou Donaldson, Jimmy Smith, and Cecil Taylor.

Sun Ra: A Joyful Noise (RHAP) 60 minutes; documentary and much live music.

Satchmo (CBS) 86 minutes; documentary on the career of Louis Armstrong.

Duke Ellington and His Orchestra (JCVC-101) film clips of the Ellington band, 1929-52.

After Hours (RHAP) 27 minutes; 1961; featuring Coleman Hawkins, Roy Eldridge, and Cozy Cole.

Thelonious Monk: Straight, No Chaser (Warner Bros.) 89 min.; performances and recording session, some dialog.

Bill Evans: The Universal Mind (RHAP) 45 minutes; Evans talks and plays.

The Coltrane Legacy (VAI) 61 minutes; John Coltrane, Eric Dolphy, Elvin Jones, McCoy Tyner, Reggie Workman, Jimmy Garrison; performances; interviews with Jimmy Cobb, Elvin Jones, Roy Haynes, Reggie Workman.

Note: These videocassettes can sometimes be found in video stores, libraries, and music stores. To keep up with new and reissued videocassettes, watch for reviews and advertisements in jazz magazines. At the time we went to press, some of the above videocassettes and several others were available by mail from these distributors:

Rhapsody Films (RHAP)
46-2 Becket Hill Road
Lyme, CT 06371
(860) 434-3610

Spectrum Music Videos
P.O. Box 1128
Norristown, PA 19404
(800) 846-8742

Jamey Aebersold
P.O. Box 1244
New Albany, IN 47151
(800) 456-1388

Cadence Record Sales
Cadence Bldg.
Redwood, NY 13679
(315) 287-2852

Jazzland
Box 366
Dayton, Ohio 45401
(800) 876-4467

GLOSSARY

Acid Jazz usually the creation of a disc jockey who takes funky accompaniments that have been synthesized electronically and/or sampled from jazz recordings, then repeats them continuously with raps and/or jazz improvisations superimposed atop them.

Antiphonal an adjective describing a common pattern of interaction between improvisers or between sections of a band, taking the form of a question and answer or a call and response.

Arco the technique of playing a stringed instrument with a bow.

Atonal the character and organization possessed by music that has no key (see page 199 for further explanations and illustrations).

Attack the very beginning of a sound (opposite of release).

Back beat strong accent on the second and fourth beats of every four-beat measure; a term usually applied to the work of a band's drummer.

Ballad a slow piece.

Big band an ensemble of ten or more players.

Blue note
1. a pitch somewhere between a major third and minor third or between a major seventh and minor seventh step of the scale (see pages 199–202).
2. minor third or seventh scale step (see page 200).

Blues
1. a simple, funky style of black music separate from but coexistent with jazz; beginning at least as early as the turn of the century, probably much earlier; exemplified by such performers as Blind Lemon Jefferson, Leadbelly, Lightnin' Hopkins, Muddy Waters, T-Bone Walker, and Robert Johnson. It has been and continues to be an influence on jazz and rock. The majority of blues compositions employ the I-IV-I-V-I chord progression or a variation of it.
2. a piece characterized by any one or any combination of the following—
   a. the I-IV-I-V-I chord progression or some variation of it in a twelve-measure package
   b. a sad feeling
   c. a slow pace
   d. poetry in the form of paired couplets in iambic pentameter
   e. many lowered third, fifth, or seventh intervals (see page 200 for further explanation).

Bomb a pronounced accent played by the drummer.

Boogie woogie a premodern jazz piano style associated with Meade Lux Lewis and Albert Ammons. It is characterized by a repetitive left-hand bass figure that states almost every beat by dividing it into dotted-eighth sixteenth-note patterns.

Bop (bebop) the style associated with Charlie Parker, Dizzy Gillespie, Thelonious Monk, Bud Powell, Dexter Gordon, and Sonny Stitt (see pages 87–110).

Break
1. the portion of a piece in which all band members stop playing except the one who improvises a solo. The tempo and chord progressions are maintained by the soloist, but, because the band has stopped, it is called a stop-time. Rarely do such breaks last longer than two or four measures (see *Demo CD Track 34*).
2. the solo itself.

Bridge the B part of an A-A-B-A composition; also known as the channel, the release, or the inside (see page 207 for further information).

Broken time
1. a style of rhythm section playing in which explicit statement of every beat is replaced by broken patterns which only imply the underlying tempo, exemplified by the 1961 Bill Evans trio with Scott LaFaro and Paul Motian.
2. the manner of playing bass or drums in which strict repetition of timekeeping patterns is not maintained, but constant tempo is; exemplified by the 1960s and 70s playing of Elvin Jones.

Chart the jazz musician's term for what is written as musical arrangement. This is distinguished from the classical musician's "score" because not all the notes are present. Many spaces in the chart are filled only by symbols indicating the chord progression that guides improvisation. Often the drum "parts" are almost blank.

231

Chops   instrumental facility

Chord progression

1. when one chord changes or "progresses" to another chord.

2. a set of harmonies in a particular order with specified durations; for example, the twelve measure I-IV-I-V-I blues progression (see pages 206–207 and 236).

3. the sequence of accompaniment chords intended for a song but used instead as the basis of a jazz improvisation.

Chorus

1. a single playing through of the structure being used to organize the music in an improvisation.

2. a jazz solo, regardless of its length.

3. the part of a pop tune performed in constant tempo and repeated several times after the verse has been played, usually the only portion of a tune's original form used by the jazz musician (see page 211 for further explanation).

Collective improvisation   simultaneous improvisation by all members of a group together.

Comping   syncopated chording which provides improvised accompaniment for simultaneously improvised solos, flexibly complementing the rhythms and implied harmonies of the solo line (see *Demo CD* Track 20 for further explanation).

Cool

1. an adjective often applied to describe the subdued feeling projected by the music of Bix Beiderbecke, Lester Young, Claude Thornhill, Gil Evans, Miles Davis, The Modern Jazz Quartet, Gerry Mulligan, Lee Konitz, and Jimmy Giuffre (see pages 111–122).

2. sometimes used as a synonym for West Coast style.

3. sometimes used to denote modern jazz after bop.

Counterpoint   two or more lines of approximately equal importance sounding together.

Creole

1. French- or Spanish-speaking individual born in the New World.

2. a person who has mixed French and African ancestry and was born in the New World (also known as "Creole of Color," as opposed to the white-skinned Creole defined above).

Decay   the very end of a sound; also known as a release. Opposite of attack (see *Demo CD* Tracks 46–53 for discussion).

Dixieland style

1. Chicago combo style that was prominent during the 1920s.

2. a synonym for all preswing-era combo jazz.

Double stop   sounding two bass strings at the same time.

Double-time   the feeling that a piece of music or a player is going twice as fast as the tempo, although the chord progressions continue at the original rate.

Fender bass   electric bass guitar, used to play bass lines instead of chords; common in jazz rhythm sections after 1970.

Fill   in general, anything a drummer plays in addition to basic timekeeping patterns; in particular, a rhythmic figure played by a drummer to—

1. fill a silence

2. underscore a rhythm played by other instruments

3. announce the entrance or punctuate the exit of a soloist or other section of the music

4. stimulate the other players and make a performance more interesting.

Free jazz   an approach associated with Ornette Coleman and Cecil Taylor, in which the music contains improvised solos which are free of preset chord progressions, and sometimes also free of preset meter (see pages 146–150).

Front line   musicians appearing directly in front of the audience, not blocked from view by another row of musicians. This designation is sometimes used to separate hornmen (because they stand in the front of a combo) from accompanists (who usually appear to the rear of the hornmen).

Funky

1. earthy or dirty

2. mean, "low down," evil, or sexy

3. bluesy

4. gospel-flavored

5. containing a predominance of lowered third, fifth, and seventh steps of the scale.

(Note: During the 1970s this adjective was applied to describe rhythms as well as melody, harmony, and tone color characteristics.)

Fusion   a synonym for jazz-rock style (see pages 161–165).

Fuzak   music that blends the characteristics of jazz-rock fusion styles with the characteristics of Muzak. It tends to stress electric instruments, steady funk rhythms, smooth textures, without many surprises. Used as background music during the 1980s and 90s by listeners who liked the softer variants of fusion and funk. Often applied to music of Kenny G, Grover Washington, Jr., Earl Klugh, and Najee.

Growl style   a method used by some trumpeters and trombonists in which by unorthodox use of mutes, lips, mouth and blowing techniques a sound is produced that resembles the growl of an animal. Despite the odd assortment of sounds that the growl includes, recognizable melodic figures can be played with this alteration of tone quality. (See Bubber Miley, Cootie Williams, and Joe "Tricky Sam" Nanton.)

Hard bop   the jazz style associated with Horace Silver, Art Blakey, and Cannonball Adderley (see page 123–126 for further explanation).

Head   the melody or prewritten theme for a piece.

Head arrangement   a band arrangement that was created extemporaneously by the musicians and is not written down.

High-hat (sock cymbal) an instrument in the drum set which brings two cymbals together by means of a foot pedal (see page 15 for illustration and *Demo CD* Track 2).

Horn general label for any wind instrument; sometimes includes stringed and percussion instruments as well (the most general term for all instruments is ax).

Jam session a musical get-together where improvisation is stressed and prewritten music is rare (jam means to improvise); may refer to a performance which is formally organized or casual, public or private, for profit or just for fun.

Jazz-rock a variety of styles beginning in the late 1960s that use electric instruments, funk rhythm accompaniments and jazz improvisation; also known as fusion music; often applied to the post-1968 music of Miles Davis, Spyro Gyra, Weather Report, the Crusaders, John McLaughlin, the electric music of Herbie Hancock and Chick Corea (see pages 161–165.)

Laid back an adjective used to describe a feeling of relaxation, laziness, or slowness; often describes the feeling that a performer is playing his rhythms a little later than they are expected, almost after the beat or "behind" the beat.

Lay out to stop playing while other players continue.

Legato a style of playing in which the notes are smoothly connected with no silences between them (opposite of staccato).

Lick a phrase or melodic fragment.

Locked-hands style a style of piano playing in which a separate chord parallels each note of the melody because both hands are used as though they are locked together, all fingers striking the keyboard together; also known as block chording, playing the chord notes as a block instead of one at a time. (Listen to Milt Buckner, Lennie Tristano, George Shearing, Ahmad Jamal, Red Garland, and Bill Evans.)

Modal music in which the melody and/or harmony is based on an arrangement of modes. In jazz, the term can mean music based on the extensive repetition of one or two chords or music based on modes instead of chord progressions (see pages 213 and 239–240 for further explanation).

Mode
1. the manner of organizing a sequence of tones, usually an ascending sequence of an octave.
2. the arrangement of whole steps and half steps common to scales.

(See pages 212–213 and 236–238 for further explanation.)

Mute an attachment which reduces an instrument's loudness and alters its tone color (see pages 218–219 for illustrations).

New Age music that is soft and soothing, lacks variety in rhythm, loudness, and chords. Often applied to the work of George Winston, selected works of Pat Metheny and others who recorded for Windham Hill, Narada, and ECM record companies. It tends to combine characteristics of

1. the minimalist style associated with nonjazz composers Philip Glass, LaMonte Young, and Steve Reich.
2. the style that Keith Jarrett developed for his unaccompanied solo piano improvisations of the 1970s and 80s.
3. music of classical musicians, including members of the Paul Winter Consort and Oregon, who improvised soft, smooth sound textures that did not swing.

Pedal point low-pitched, repeated, and/or sustained tone. It usually retains its pitch despite changes in chords and improvisations occurring around it; common in the 1960s work of John Coltrane and McCoy Tyner.

Pitch bending purposeful raising or lowering of a tone's pitch; usually done for coloration or expressive purposes (see *Demo CD* Tracks 46–53 for illustrations and explanation).

Pizzicato the method of playing a stringed instrument by plucking instead of bowing.

Polyrhythm several different rhythms sounding at the same time (see page 195).

Progressive jazz music associated with Stan Kenton (see pages 118–120).

Ragtime
1. a popular turn-of-the-century style of written piano music involving pronounced syncopation.
2. a label often applied to much pre-1920 jazz and pop music, unaccompanied solo piano styles as well as band styles, improvised as well as written music.
3. the style of music associated with composers Scott Joplin and Tom Turpin.

Release
1. the manner in which a sound ends or decays (opposite of attack).
2. the bridge of a tune.

Rhythm section the group of players whose band function is accompanying. This role is particularly common for pianists, bassists, and drummers, but it is not exclusive to them (see pages 12–15 for explanations and *Demo CD* Tracks 1–8, 20, 23–26, 29–30).

Ride cymbal the cymbal suspended over a drum set, usually to the player's right, struck by a stick held the drummer's right hand; used for playing timekeeping patterns called ride rhythms (see page 15 for illustration).

Ride rhythm the pattern a drummer plays on the ride cymbal to keep time, the most common being ding-dick-a-ding-dick-a (see *Demo CD* Track 3).

Riff
1. phrase
2. melodic fragment
3. theme

Rim shot the drum stick striking the rim of the snare drum at the same time as it strikes the drum head.

Rip an onset ornament in the form of a quick rise in pitch directly preceding a tone. (Listen to Bix Beiderbecke or Louis Armstrong.)

Rubato free of strict adherence to constant tempo.

Scat singing jazz improvisation using the human voice as an instrument, with nonsense syllables (dwee, ool, ya, bop, bam, etc.) instead of words.

Sideman a designation for each musician in a band except the leader.

Smooth Jazz a designation for the styles of music played on radio stations subscribing to "The Wave" format of the 1980s and 90s: a blend of Kenny G, Grover Washington, Jr., Earl Klugh, Lee Ritenour, Larry Carlton, George Benson, Bob James, and their disciples.

Sock cymbal see high-hat

Staccato brief and separated (opposite of legato).

Stride
1. left-hand style used by early jazz pianists. It usually employs a bass note on the first and third beats of each measure and a chord on the second and fourth.
2. the piano style of James P. Johnson and Willie "The Lion" Smith.

Swing
1. a word denoting approval—"It swings" can mean it pleases me; "to swing" can mean to enjoy oneself; "he's a swinging guy" can mean he is an enjoyable person.
2. the noun indicating the feeling projected by an uplifting performance of any kind of music, especially that which employs constant tempo (see page 4 for further explanation).
3. the feeling projected by a jazz performance which successfully combines constant tempo, syncopation, swing eighth notes, rhythmic lilt, liveliness and rhythmically cohesive group playing (see page 6 for further explanation).
4. the jazz style associated with Count Basie, Duke Ellington, Jimmie Lunceford, Benny Goodman, Art Tatum, Roy Eldridge, and Coleman Hawkins, as in the "swing era" (see page 55).

Syncopation
1. stress on any portion of the measure other than the first part of the first beat (and, in meter of four, other than the first part of the third beat), i.e., the second half of the first beat, the second half of the second beat, the fourth beat, the second half of the fourth beat, the second beat, etc.
2. stress on a portion of the measure least expected to receive stress (see page 191 and *Demo CD* Track 20 for further explanation).

Synthesizer any one of a general category of electronic devices (Moog and Arp, for example) which produces sounds or alters the sounds created by other instruments.

Third Stream a style which combines jazz improvisation with the instrumentation and compositional forms of classical music.

Tonal inflection alteration of a tone's pitch or quality, done purposefully at the beginning, middle, or end of a sound (see pitch bending, and see *Demo CD* Tracks 46–53).

Tone color (timbre, tone quality) the characteristic of sound which enables the listener to differentiate one instrument from another, and, in many cases, one player from another.

Tremolo
1. fluctuation in the loudness of a sound, usually an even alternation of loud and soft.
2. a manner of playing a chord by rapidly sounding its different notes in alternation so that the chord retains its character, but also sustains and trembles (*Demo CD* Track 42).
3. the means of sustaining the sound of a vibraharp (see *Demo CD* Track 47).
4. an expressive technique for use by instruments in which vibrato is very difficult (flute, for example) or in which the variation of pitch necessary for vibrato may not be wanted (some styles of oboe playing, for example).
5. the rapid reiteration of the same note.

Turnaround (turnback, turnabout) a short progression within a chord progression that occurs just prior to the point at which the player must "turn around" to begin another repetition of the larger progression (see pages 214–215 for further explanation).

Two-beat style a rhythm section style which emphasizes the first and third beats of each four-beat measure, often leaving the second and fourth beats silent in the bass; sometimes called boom-chick style.

Vamp a short chord progression (usually only one, two, or four measures long) which is repeated many times in sequence. Often used for introductions and endings. Much jazz and pop music of the 1960s and 70s used vamps instead of more involved chord progressions as accompaniment for melody and improvisation.

Vibrato the slight fluctuation of a tone's pitch, alternating above and below its basic pitch; used as an expressive device, varied in speed and amplitude by the performer to fit the style and feeling of the music (see *Demo CD* Tracks 46–49).

Voicing
1. the manner of organizing, doubling, omitting, or adding to the notes of a chord (see page 205).
2. the assignment of notes to each instrument (see page 206 for further explanation).

Walking bass a style of bass line in which each beat of each measure receives a separate tone, thus creating a moving sequence of quarter notes in the bass range.

West Coast style the jazz style associated with Gerry Mulligan and Chet Baker during the 1950s (see **cool** and page 116 for further explanation).

FOR MUSICIANS

You have now entered the technical part of the appendix. This section is designed to give musically literate readers a chance to experience some of the musical elements discussed in the main body of the text. Keep in mind that it is possible to learn more by playing the examples at the piano than by merely reading the attached explanations. Once you have played these demonstrations yourself, the principles will be more obvious to you when they occur in jazz recordings.

Chords and Chord Progressions

One way to understand how chords can be constructed is to imagine them as being built from tones in the major scales. For instance in the key of Bb, tones for the chords can be drawn from the notes in the Bb major scale (Bb C D Eb F G A Bb). In the key of C, they can be drawn from the notes in the C scale (C D E F G A B C). Beginning with a single tone, the chord is made by adding every other tone in the scale. In other words, the first, third, and fifth tones are used when the beginning tone is the key note (first tone of the major scale). The second, fourth, and sixth tones are used when the chord is based on the second step of the scale. The third, fifth, and seventh tones are used when the chord begins on the third step of the scale.

If a chord is based on the first tone of the major scale, it is called the "one chord," symbolized by the Roman numeral for one, I. The chord based on the second step of the major scale is a II chord. The labeling system continues through the VII chord.

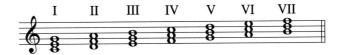

The system is more involved that what we have discussed. Before you can apply chord knowledge to studying improvisation, you must become acquainted with construction of many type of chords: dominant sevenths and major sevenths; major, minor, diminished, and augmented chords; chords with added ninths, elevenths, and thirteenths; chords with added fourths and sixths, flat fifths, raised ninths, etc. You will also need to confront a collection of different chord labeling systems.

Twelve-Bar Blues Progressions

Though basically a I-IV-I-V-I progression, the twelve-bar blues may contain a huge assortment of chord progressions. Here are three possibilities for a blues in the key of C.

Modes

Though used for centuries in classical music, modes just recently became popular harmonic bases for jazz improvisation. To get a rough idea of what is meant by the term "modes," we can use the tones of the major scale to produce different modes if we play ascending sequences, starting on different steps of the scale. Each mode's unique sound is the result of its particular arrangement of whole steps and half steps. For example, in the Ionian mode (also known as the major scale), half steps occur only between the third and fourth steps and the seventh and eighth steps. (The eighth step is an octave up from the first step.)

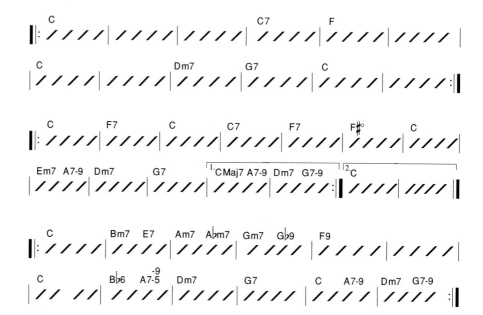

The Dorian mode is constructed from the same tones as the Ionian, but it begins on the second tone of the major scale. The Dorian mode has half steps between its second and third and its sixth and seventh tones.

There is a mode for each step of the major scale. Each mode has a distinct musical personality because its half steps fall in different places.

Examine the following modes. Play them, and listen carefully while you play them. Find the positions of the half steps in each mode. Once you know a mode's pattern of whole and half steps, you should be able to begin it on other notes. Remember that the interval between Bb and C is defined as a whole step, as is that between E and F#. Remember also that the interval between B and C is a half step, as is that between E and F.

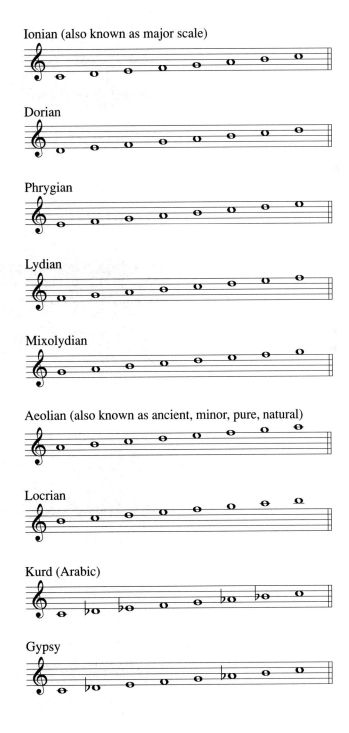

Ionian (also known as major scale)

Dorian

Phrygian

Lydian

Mixolydian

Aeolian (also known as ancient, minor, pure, natural)

Locrian

Kurd (Arabic)

Gypsy

Hungarian

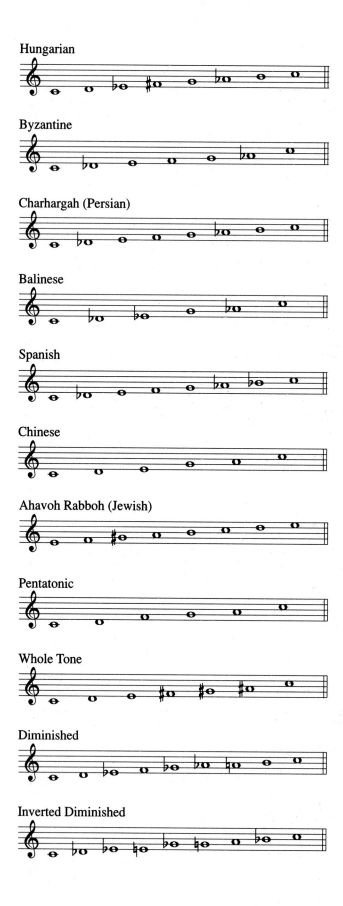

Byzantine

Charhargah (Persian)

Balinese

Spanish

Chinese

Ahavoh Rabboh (Jewish)

Pentatonic

Whole Tone

Diminished

Inverted Diminished

Modal Construction of "Maiden Voyage"

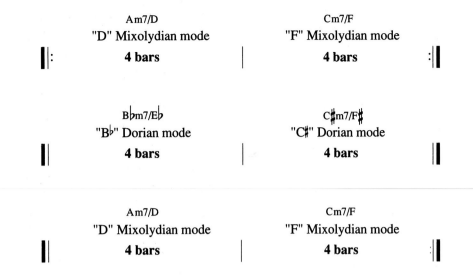

Am7/D
"D" Mixolydian mode
4 bars

Cm7/F
"F" Mixolydian mode
4 bars

B♭m7/E♭
"B♭" Dorian mode
4 bars

C♯m7/F♯
"C♯" Dorian mode
4 bars

Am7/D
"D" Mixolydian mode
4 bars

Cm7/F
"F" Mixolydian mode
4 bars

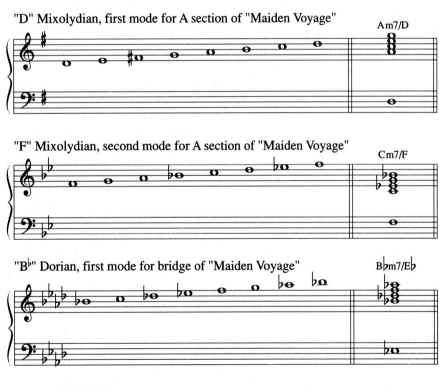

"D" Mixolydian, first mode for A section of "Maiden Voyage"

Am7/D

"F" Mixolydian, second mode for A section of "Maiden Voyage"

Cm7/F

"B♭" Dorian, first mode for bridge of "Maiden Voyage"

B♭m7/E♭

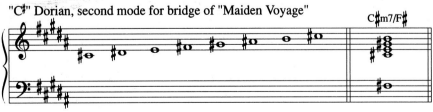

"C♯" Dorian, second mode for bridge of "Maiden Voyage"

C♯m7/F♯

Modal Construction for "So What" and "Impressions"

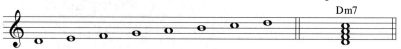

"D" Dorian mode for first sixteen bars of "So What" and "Impressions"

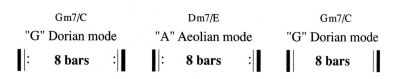

"E♭" Dorian mode for bridge of "So What" and "Impressions"

Modal Construction of "Milestones"

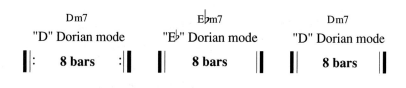

"G" Dorian mode for first sixteen bars of "Milestones"

"A" Aeolian mode for bridge of "Milestones"

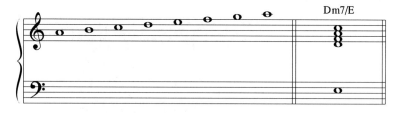

Walking Bass Lines

Walking is meant to provide timekeeping in the form of tones chosen for their compatibility with the harmonies of the piece and style of the performance. Ideally, the walking bass complements the solo line.

Three choruses of walking bass are shown here. They display three increasing levels of complexity for walking bass lines for the 12-bar blues in the key of C (conceived and notated by Willis Lyman).

Comping

Here are two examples of piano accompaniments, or comping, for a jazz twelve-bar blues solo. Comping is accompaniment that is simultaneously composed and performed to fit the style of a piece and the directions in harmony, rhythm, and melody that are taken by the soloist. Comping usually contains pronounced syncopation.

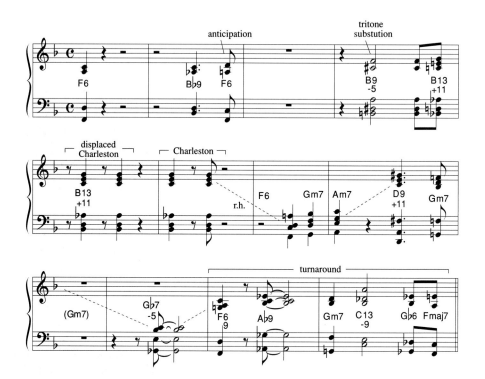

Bebop-Style Comping (notated by David Berger)

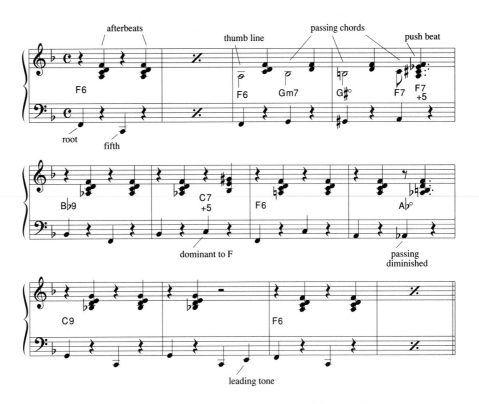

"Boston" or Two-Handed Stride-Style Comping (notated by David Berger)

Comping Figures for "Rhythm Changes"

This is a typical example of piano comping for improvisations that follow the chord changes used by George Gershwin to accompany his melody "I Got Rhythm." This would also fit "Cottontail," "Shaw Nuff," "Lester Leaps In," and "(Meet the) Flintstones." Other comping examples for Flintstones can be heard on the *Demo Cassette/CD*, with and without the Flintstones melody. (Comping composed and notated by Jerry Sheer.)

INDEX